Praise for *Surviving Dirty John*

"Debra Newell's journey, her tale of survival and her openness in sharing her story, is awe inspiring. By helping the world better understand the twisted manipulative power of coercive control, she is helping us all to identify it. By sharing her story, she has created a pathway for communication in a corridor that has for too long been dimly lit."

—Eric Bana

"Debra is a true survivor. You may think you know her story, but you don't—and you should. This really could happen to anyone. Coercive control has many guises and faces and is much more common than you think. This book may just save your life."

—Laura Richards, criminal behavioral analyst, coercive control and stalking expert, formerly with New Scotland Yard

"God bless Debbie Newell, my fellow warrior in the fight against the silent and shame-fueled epidemic of intimate partner violence/domestic violence. God bless you, Debbie, for writing *Surviving Dirty John* and not being shamed into silence by half-truths and mischaracterizations of your hellish journey with the monster, John Meehan. God bless you for having the strength to survive and become more than a victim, more than a survivor. By having the courage to share your *real story* in *Surviving Dirty John,* you are saving many lives and stopping much suffering. I am so proud to call you friend! Well done, Debbie and M. William Phelps!"

—Robin McGraw, author and founder of When Georgia Smiled Foundation

"Debra's book is a must-read for anyone who has experienced trauma in their life, has loved someone who has experienced trauma, or is in the helping professions working to heal trauma with clients. Her honest and gripping account of her experiences and her inspiring story of recovery will help empower and educate all people about the impact of coercive control and impart important lessons about how to overcome extreme adversities."

—Dr. Judy Ho, clinical and forensic neuropsychologist, tenured professor, and author of *Stop Self-Sabotage*

"In her book *Surviving Dirty John,* Debra Newell has bared her soul to the world, providing intimate details to help other women learn from her experiences and avoid the horror of being manipulated and abused by a partner. Debra has shown us that searching for love can be a dangerous game and we need to always have our eyes wide open and trust our instincts. I have seen the dangers and pitfalls that are out there myself and have written about them as well. This book is both eye-opening and empowering and is a must-read for all women in the dating scene."

—Tonia DeCosimo, president and editor in chief of P.O.W.E.R and *P.O.W.E.R. Magazine*, and author of *Single and Not Settling: A Journey of Surviving the Dating World*

SURVIVING
DIRTY JOHN

MY TRUE STORY OF LOVE, LIES, AND MURDER

DEBRA NEWELL
with M. WILLIAM PHELPS

BenBella Books, Inc.
Dallas, TX

The events, locations, and conversations in this book, while true, are re-created from the author's memory. However, the essence of the story, and the feelings and emotions evoked, are intended to be accurate representations. In certain instances, names of persons, organizations, and places, and other identifying details, have been changed to protect the privacy interests of individuals.

BenBella Books, Inc.
10440 N. Central Expressway
Suite 800
Dallas, TX 75231
benbellabooks.com

Send feedback to feedback@benbellabooks.com

BenBella is a federally registered trademark.

Printed in the United States of America
10 9 8 7 6 5 4 3 2 1

Library of Congress Control Number: 2021006207
ISBN 9781953295507 (paperback)
SBN 9781953295842 (ebook)

Editing by Joe Rhatigan and Robb Pearlman
Copyediting by Jennifer Brett Greenstein
Proofreading by Michael Fedison and Douglas Johnson
Text design PerfecType, Nashville, TN
Cover design by Kara Klontz
Cover photo courtesy of the author; additional cover images © Shutterstock/DFLC Prints (torn paper), Shutterstock/nirut jindawong (burnt paper), and iStock/Pinkybird (pills)
Printed by Lake Book Manufacturing

For all the female victims' voices silenced and unheard;
my beautiful, supportive children;
and my sister, Cindi Ambrose Vickers, who was
taken away from us far too soon

Sometimes—just sometimes—cupid's dart,
departing from the romantically assigned rôle of the poet's gentle image,
is metamorphosed into an arrow, a barbed and lethal thing.

—"The Rattenbury Tragedy," *Chronicles of Murder,*
William Roughead

CONTENTS

Acknowledgments *xi*

Introduction *1*

1 **Our Time** *5*
2 **Be Water** *14*
3 **Doctor's Orders** *24*
4 **Careless Whisper** *29*
5 **Approachable Dreams** *34*
6 **Second Chances** *43*
7 **Tragic Endings** *47*
8 **Love Is in the Eye of the Beholder** *52*
9 **Evil Seems to Always Survive** *59*
10 **Balboa Island** *63*
11 **A Growing Divide** *71*
12 **The Bully Pulpit** *82*
13 **The Break-In** *87*
14 **I Just Died in Your Arms Tonight** *92*
15 **Hurt People Hurt People** *99*
16 **Silent Night, Holy Hell** *105*
17 **Imposter** *109*
18 **Discrepancies** *115*
19 **He Has a Knife** *120*

20 **Private Eyes Are Watching You** *129*
21 **Murder by Mail** *134*
22 **Killing Is Easy** *140*
23 **"I Could Take Liz Out . . ."** *149*
24 **Duped** *155*
25 **Elevator Ride** *164*
26 **"John Is Very Dangerous, Debbie"** *173*
27 **Filthy, Dirty, Nasty John** *183*
28 **The Tormentor** *189*
29 **Rap Sheet** *194*
30 **Lies and More Lies** *197*
31 **Game Change** *202*
32 **"I Know You Are Going to Leave Me"** *209*
33 **Happy Anniversary—I Hate You!** *214*
34 **Money—The Root of John's Evil** *217*
35 **A Shark and His Prey** *223*
36 **I Am the Victim** *232*
37 **"You Will Lose"** *239*
38 **Where There's Smoke . . .** *244*
39 **Laura** *249*
40 **Locked and Loaded** *253*
41 **Dirty John Makes His Move** *259*
42 **Fearless Hero** *267*
43 **Tortured** *271*
44 **No One Dies Alone** *277*
45 **Life Goes On** *281*

Epilogue: Updates and Important Contact Information for Victims *282*
About the Authors *287*

ACKNOWLEDGMENTS

This book would not be in your hands right now without a host of people making it possible.

I would like to thank my beautiful children for always being there, through the good times and the bad. Each of you has filled my heart with so much joy throughout the years, and I cherish you deeply. I am extremely blessed to have your love and support, and I am forever grateful to all of you! I would like to honor my mother, Arlane, for loving and guiding me constantly and teaching me the gift of forgiveness. No matter what challenges I have faced in my life, I have always relied on seeking the strength from within that you taught me at such an early age. I am able to keep moving forward in faith because of you. I also thank my girlfriends Suzi Brownfield and Nancy Earle for supporting and loving me through life's challenges. Thank you for lifting me up and being there for me through thick and thin. Thanks are due, too, to Laura Richards for standing up for me and helping me empower other women who have battled coercive control. Laura is a support not only to me but also to millions of other women enduring similar situations.

Thank you to Jason Verona for creating such a beautiful opportunity to share my story. Thank you to Danielle Reimann for helping me to make this dream of mine a reality. Working with such a beautiful soul made this journey incredible. Thank you to M. William Phelps, who has gone through the journey with me and allowed me to open up my heart and speak my truth. We have all gone through this battlefield together, and I am extremely grateful to all of you for believing in me and standing up for me no matter what. It is because of the three of you that I am able to share my story and use my voice to inspire and empower others, and I am truly honored to be given this opportunity.

I desire nothing more than for anyone reading this book to know you are not alone. I believe in you and I will fight for your voice and your freedom until my last breath. My wish is that my story will help shed light on the traumatic effects of coercive control and lead others to safety. Thank you to all my loving family and friends and my incredible support system, who have allowed me to move past this trauma and do everything I can to stop the abuse of coercive control.

—Debra Newell
March 2021

I want to thank Debra Newell for trusting me with her story. From the day we started talking about writing this book, I was honored and humbled by the strength Debra and her daughter Terra Newell displayed after what they had gone through. To be given the opportunity to be Debra's storyteller is an honor. She took a tremendous risk trusting me.

My goal from day one was to tell the *entire* story, not the diluted version most have seen on television or, with all due respect to the *Los Angeles Times* and reporter/podcast host Christopher Goffard, heard on the *Dirty John* podcast or read in Goffard's story. The narrative that unfolded as Debra and I talked is far removed from the Dirty John story line out there in the public as we go to press on this book. First, the domestic violence issue that should be at the forefront of this story, which I would come to understand as coercive control, puts the victim in a position where she is being controlled without even realizing it. Second, as I looked into the social media coverage of Debra's story, I found the thought of anyone blaming Debra for what happened outrageous and disgusting, but not at all shocking in the shame-and-blame culture in which we live today.

Debra is a victim. Period. There is nothing else to be said about that.

I'm extremely grateful, as well, to Mark Gottlieb, my literary agent at Trident Media Group Literary Agency, who thought of me when this story crossed his desk. Mark is a top-notch agent and an incredible human being who has been an inspiration and guide for me, a rare publishing person who knows this business inside and out. I am grateful and lucky to be a part of the Trident team.

Additional thanks to Danielle Reimann, Debra's diligent and hard-working public relations director, who was instrumental in managing the flow of emails, documents, information, and research between Debra and me. Danielle kept this thing moving along without delay. I'll speak for Debra and myself in saying that the book would not have gotten done *without* Danielle.

Of course, I need to thank the usual suspects. You know who you are.

One last thing: As I hand this book in, my daughter enters her senior year of college, studying to become a physician assistant. I have watched this young woman, over the past three years, study her ass off, working day and night. Her love and support for me—during what was a difficult time in my life—was what made the difference. She is my rock and inspiration. She has shown me every day what unconditional love is.

—M. William Phelps
March 2021

INTRODUCTION

It should be no surprise to anyone—although I bet it will be—that domestic violence is the leading cause of injury to women, surpassing muggings, rapes, and car accidents *combined*. Meeting and falling in love with "Dirty" John Meehan was not my introduction to domestic violence, though John brought it to another level and, in turn, changed my life forever. I think this goes without saying to anyone who knows even a few scant details about my story.

Logging on to an online dating site one night and receiving a message from John, I could never have imagined I would be, years later, writing this book and dedicating part of my life to helping victims of domestic violence. We think we are immune to the horrific stories of bloodshed and extreme violence we see on television. We think evil visits only the person next door. We think that simply meeting another human being for a casual coffee date, or a dinner we hope could evolve into a relationship and maybe even love, is never going to turn around and serve as a catalyst for violence.

And yet it happens every single day in this country.

I am not suggesting we should be fearful of every person we encounter, online or otherwise. Or that there are evil people around every corner. What I am saying is, read this book, take what happened to me, and use it as an example of what *can* happen to any woman venturing out into the dating world—especially online. Complacency and denial are your enemies within the dating world today. You are not doing anything wrong by checking the background of a person you are meeting. This *could* be as easy as a reverse phone lookup—in which you find out the man has a record or is lying about his last name, his age, where he lives, or all of the above. One lie should be enough to question everything about the person and should certainly be a red flag telling you to move on. I do not say this self-righteously; I say this from experience. I wish someone had said it to me.

Rapists, sexual predators, and criminals in general use online dating sites to search for future victims. Some reports claim the numbers are in the 25 percent range. Imagine—one in four guys you encounter online is a potential predator. Furthermore, the Pew Research Center found in a recent poll that "57% of female online dating users ages 18 to 34 [reported] someone ha[d] sent them a sexually explicit message or image they did not ask for."

More than half!

What is more, it is much easier and far more inconspicuous to stalk a person online than it is in person.

Every nine seconds a woman is assaulted or beaten in the United States.

We are facing a serious (and neglected) epidemic in this country.

As time would tell, Dirty John proved himself to be the most manipulative, controlling, and violent person I have ever known. I am a peacemaker, a people pleaser. John understood and knew this about me almost right away and zeroed in on my vulnerabilities, working hard at convincing me of his lies. John understood that once I believed something, I was all in. He knew that loving him made me the perfect victim.

People will judge. I cannot stop that. The most common judgment being: *How could you have allowed this to happen and stay with him as long as you did?* On November 25, 2018, the Bravo television network aired *Dirty John*, a dramatized limited series based on my story. Connie Britton played me; Eric Bana played John. The series was later released on Netflix. According to Bravo's description, the series captured "how a romance with the charismatic John Meehan spiraled into secrets, denial, manipulation, and ultimately, survival—with horrific consequences for an entire family."

Bravo's description is partially accurate. The way I was portrayed in the series, however, as a woman who kept making the wrong choices because of weakness and vanity, was horribly unfair and inaccurate, in my opinion. So much of my character was overdramatized and invented. I was depicted as a naïve woman, ignorant of red flags, who sought out one man after another while setting aside her morals and values for love. Victim shaming was rampant after the Bravo drama series aired. Many viewers believed that the fictionalized version of my story portrayed in the series was gospel truth. The shaming ramped up after the series aired and grew in intensity after a larger audience tuned in on Netflix. I was blamed all over again. I was suddenly the one responsible for becoming John's next victim.

Unfairly, the focus was on me, not John.

What you are about to read is my true story, bumps, bruises, character defects, and all. I am unafraid of the truth. *Surviving Dirty John* was not written with my coauthor to turn me into any sort of hero or to explain myself. I have laid bare my faults and mistakes during this incredible ordeal. Still, for the first time I have decided to tell *my* side of the story. Not just for me and my family, but for every woman who has gone through or continues to live in a situation like the one I was fortunate enough to walk away from with my life.

1

OUR TIME

He seemed kind, smart, and sincere. He was good-looking. There was a mutual attraction. After several long phone conversations, we met for dinner at a steak house close to the penthouse I was renting and living in with *Liz*,* one of my adult daughters.

We sat and talked, hitting all those rather redundant first-date topics: kids, career, romantic history, religion, shared interests. After a few hours, we hugged and said good night.

I felt nothing. Zero chemistry.

"Just wanted to make sure you got home okay," he said, calling an hour after dinner. "I really like you, Debbie. Did you feel that spark between us?"

"I enjoyed myself. Very sweet of you to call." I hesitated. I didn't want to hurt his feelings but decided he needed to hear the truth. "I . . . I, look, you're a great guy. I like you. But I do not think we would be anything more than friends."

It pained me to tell him this. He was successful and kindhearted. I had not picked up any weird vibes or negative energy. But the thing is, I never wanted to give someone the wrong idea or lead a man on. I need to feel something. If it's not there, I move on.

---

* *A name appearing in italics the first time is a pseudonym; the person has requested to remain anonymous.*

The latter part of 2014 was the height of the online dating boom. Tinder, which I had never used, was the fastest-growing app. The never-been-married crowd made up 30 percent of dating profiles. Nearly one-third of American adults used a dating app. It was a world, I learned quickly, that was treacherous to navigate, full of surprises, liars, con men, and dudes looking to get laid, with the occasional sweet guy mixed in. In my experience, half of what men told me during those app dates was fabricated; the half they didn't share, of course, often reflected the very worst of who they really were.

In early October 2014, I was fifty-nine years old and single. I was in the process of moving beyond a painful breakup from a man who had emotionally abused and duped me. I had just sold my house in Irvine, California. A high-rise penthouse, Marquee Park Place, on the border of Irvine and Newport Beach, which I'd had my eye on for some time, was now my home. Newport Beach is a sophisticated yet casual seaside community with a pristine, postcard coastline. A short walk and you're standing in front of any store you can imagine, alongside upscale strip malls and trendy boutiques. The homes are expensive.

My business, Ambrosia Interior Design, a company I had spent thirty years nurturing, was enjoying a long run of success I could not have predicted under the best economic circumstances, and certainly could not have predicted after the 2008 housing bubble burst.

All four of my kids were grown. Brandon, my oldest, was born in 1977. He lived in Orange County with his wife and three children. Next was thirty-five-year-old Nicole. Married to a wonderful, caring man in his mid-forties, she worked with me at Ambrosia. Their two children, *Thomas* and *Kylie*, were the joys of my life. My middle daughter, Liz, had turned twenty-six earlier that year and was living in the penthouse with me because she was in between leaving one place and finding a new one. My youngest, Terra, was twenty-three and living in Nevada with her boyfriend.

Autumn is one of my favorite seasons. In this area of Southern California, October tends to be around eighty to ninety degrees, with robin's egg–blue skies providing a flawless canvas for harmless, puffy white clouds. Pure bliss.

I could feel optimism in the marrow of my bones: this was *my* time.

The zero-chemistry guy was one of eighty-four men who had responded to a profile I'd placed on OurTime, a dating site for the over-fifty crowd. After receiving those "hearts," I logged into my profile to see if anyone interested me. With the majority of the intense pain from my recent breakup gone, I was dating again.

"Liz, come over here, hurry up," I said, sitting at the keyboard. It had been another twelve-hour day at work. I was home unwinding, scrolling through profiles.

"What, what, what?" Liz said. She had a friend over. They both stood over my shoulder, staring at the monitor.

"Look at this," I said, pointing.

"Eighty-four," I said as Liz and her friend looked at the computer screen.

"What are we looking at, Mom?"

"Eighty-four men responded to my profile. Can you believe it?"

We laughed at how many of them were not my type at all. I mean, I enjoyed outgoing, energetic men—not men heading into retirement.

"Let's narrow it down," Liz suggested. "Make a shortlist."

"Yes, good idea," I responded. I could tell by the look on her face that Liz was thinking about the myriad hardships I'd endured over the course of my romantic life. The pain and abuse I had suffered at the hands of men. She had seen and lived some of it. With so many disastrous relationships behind me, it was easy to blame myself. To believe *I* was the problem. Many times I'd sit and think, *It has to be me.*

Or I could have told Liz that I had just about given up on love. The idea of romantic love had become a mirage, an image that disappeared every time I ran toward it. In my experience, romantic love had become a power I had given to another human being to hold over me, which, in turn, had been used to try to destroy me. I had trusted—over and over—and lost. I had repeatedly opened my heart only to have it shattered to pieces.

In fact, if you'd have asked me about love at the beginning of 2014, I would have said I had completely given up on finding an honest, decent man I felt a connection with, which further fed into my self-image as a person who was too old for love. The time had passed for me to ever experience it again. With failed marriages behind me, the feeling of being truly in love seemed, contradictorily, not only like a fairy tale but something I would never find again.

Being truly in love. You know the feeling. When you meet *that* person and nothing else in your world exists but him. Time becomes meaningless. You're feeling alive; there's a bounce in your step. You agree to do things you would never have considered before meeting him. You're ricocheting glowingly off the inside walls of a euphoric bubble, where everything is about him. Your thoughts. Your body. Your soul. You wake up; he's on your mind. You go to bed thinking about him. You fantasize about a future together. You cannot wait to see him. The mere sight of him curbs any anxiety or trouble you've had that day.

Was that actually real? Could that still be out there for me?

To make matters worse, the guy I had broken up with earlier in the year had made me feel less-than and inadequate. "You're putting on weight," he had said near the end. Just one of the many insults. I left the relationship broken, with a body-image complex on my back like a sack of sand. He had shamed me. The perfect man *was* a mirage; he existed only in fairy tales and dreams.

But instead, Liz, her friend, and I whittled the list to five men who were more my type, and I replied to them as if I were going to hire them—and really, isn't that what dating is? Meeting people in coffee shops and restaurants and interviewing them for a position in your life? We have this set narrative of our lives we lay out to them, and they, in turn, add to and subtract from their history for us. It's a game we all play: set the hook, cast the line, and then, once we've caught each other, allow the slime to ooze out from between our scales.

One of my top-five choices was an evangelist/private detective. Really.

"He seems nice," I said.

"Maybe," Liz said, my cautious little girl coaching me.

When I first logged into OurTime, I was sold on its pitch instantly: "At last! A dating site that not only understands what it is to be over 50, but also celebrates this exciting chapter of our lives." OurTime honored freedom and wisdom, the site continued. Its research proved your fifties and sixties "can be among the happiest and most fulfilling" times of your life. I recall the caption near the smiling blonde with white teeth, pictured next to a handsome black-haired man of some woman's dreams, on OurTime's "About Us" page: "At this stage of your life, you're proud of your achievements."

I was, indeed, proud of the woman I had become. I felt like I had a lot to offer.

After thirty years of building a multimillion-dollar company with an office in Irvine, I bit hard on the achievement angle OurTime sold. My success *was* something to be proud of. What's more, I had worked hard to put together an A+ team of the best designers and a terrific marketing director. One of my greatest accomplishments was hiring many single women and mothers. That feeling of being alone, with children, wondering how you were going to provide health care and raise your kids to be loving, caring human beings, was a part of my life I could never forget. I related to being a pregnant mother, without a spouse, without a steady income, because I had lived it. Getting by day to day meant walking on a constant tightrope. One setback—a problem with your car, a sick child—and you were contemplating moving in with family or being homeless. And here I was, offering opportunity to people who now didn't have to struggle like I did. You bet I was proud.

So why not search for the perfect man to go along with everything else in my life that I was celebrating?

Today, you can scroll through pages, spending hours swiping left and right, looking for the person to complete you and complement your every desire and need. Heck, I was going to be sixty years old inside of a year. This "chapter" of my life was going to be my last. The thought was uncomfortable. I wasn't the retirement type. You know, Florida or Phoenix. Shuffleboard and early-bird specials. Totally not me at all. As sixty crept closer, to be honest, I yearned for those years of returning from my mailbox feeling bad for turning *fifty* as I clutched a darn AARP magazine I'd never ordered in the first place, reminding me of it each month.

Can you imagine, eighty-four men to choose from? They couldn't all be bad. And yet, as I think back on that moment and how things would eventually turn out, I understand today that I wasn't choosing the *wrong* men. It's not even that my childhood had set me up for failure or to be victimized. It wasn't even that the odds of having one failed marriage set up the second and so on. Failure wasn't a problem for me; if anything, failure drove me to succeed.

Over the past several months I had suffered through so many disastrous dates, I should have found the common denominator and run from love. Put up a shield, a guard, understood the boundaries I had put in place, how and why they were crossed. But the thing is: you let that guard down for one second and evil, as I have come to learn, will find a way in.

There was a second man from the eighty-four (besides zero-chemistry guy) whom I had also met at a restaurant. It started off okay. But I knew right away there was something up with him. According to his profile, he seemed to be the ideal catch. He was a fairly nice-looking psychologist, and we had had intelligent, intellectual conversations over the phone for a week or so. But when we met in person, once again, there was no chemistry. He was tall, dark-haired, and handsome (you notice my type here?). Talking to him more and more, however, I realized he was a player. It was all about getting me into bed.

At the risk of sounding conceited, I am blessed with hazel eyes; long, flowing, thick blonde hair; and a good figure. I did not have trouble finding men. It was finding the right man I seemed to struggle with. There was one time when a man who wanted to date me actually threw himself on the hood of my car and begged me to go out with him, threatening to remain on the car until I agreed. I had to promise to date him. I lied and said I would.

What the heck was it?

Bad luck?

Bad judgment?

Of the five men on the shortlist Liz, her friend, and I created, one was French. Dark hair, tall. He was in the oil business and had been widowed a few years before.

"I just sold a huge cargo of oil and want to come down to OC to celebrate," he told me one night on the phone in his super sexy French accent. He had already sent me flowers. A teddy bear. He'd posted actual handwritten letters to me in the mail. I was interested in him, even though he lived in San Jose, more than a six-hour drive north.

And then, well, and then he thought it a romantic gesture to send me a pic of his penis—which was not okay with me. So I ended it.

One of the dates I set up from my OurTime top-five list turned out beyond dreadful. His online profile claimed he was six feet tall. During a text chat one afternoon leading up to our date, I asked him about that little tidbit on his profile page: "evangelist and private investigator."

Odd combination, I considered. *But what the heck. Who am I to judge?*

"I'm outgoing," he said.

Tall, dark, handsome, I thought, staring at his profile pictures.

In September 2014, we met at a restaurant in Irvine. Nice place. Cozy. Friendly. Lots of people. When I saw him for the first time, it was his height that struck me: five-eight, at best.

Six feet?

Staring at him, saying hello, I thought about it: *Okay, I'm not superficial. I can overlook this.*

He sat next to me on the same side of the booth the hostess put us in.

Somewhat strange, but . . . okay . . .

Over the next hour, he tried to kiss me on the cheek several times as we ate and chatted. His energy was aggressive, negative. I could feel it. Definitely not what you'd expect from a first date.

"I live in Pasadena," he said as we finished dinner. "Let's go down to the ocean and take a walk."

It was my opportunity to say no—to honor my gut instinct, check out of this date, and be done with him.

"That sounds nice," I said instead.

That's me: a people pleaser, an empath, a sympathetic listener. It's the way I was raised. Give people chances. Do not judge. Always expect the best from people because it's what God wants from us.

We dropped my car off at my place. I ran up to my apartment to grab a sweater and a pair of more comfortable shoes. Forgetful after a long day, I left my purse and phone upstairs. While I was gathering my things, he'd found a liquor store and bought a bottle of champagne. I had already watched him drink two glasses of wine at the restaurant.

He drove us up the coast and found what seemed to be the perfect spot on the beach. We walked out and sat on a towel he'd brought. He had two champagne flutes—I have no idea where they came from. Apparently, he was a magician, too.

"I'm good," I said. He poured me a glass.

"Are you sure? Come on. Have a drink."

"No, thank you."

I pulled my knees into my chest, staring straight ahead. The melodic pulse of waves crashing against the shore in front of us, along with a high moon, bright and perfectly round, reflected a diamond-like sparkle on the water. It was quiet except for those effortless sounds of nature lulling me into serenity. It might even have been romantic had he not proceeded to drink the entire bottle of champagne.

"I want to kiss you," he said, a slight slur in his speech.

"Not interested. I don't kiss on the first date."

He said it again.

"No." I was firm. "I want to go home."

He turned, grabbed my arms, and moved in for that kiss he was hyper-focused on getting. I didn't sense he wanted to hurt me. But he *was* forcing himself on me. So I made it clear by my body language that I did not want to be kissed or touched.

He didn't say anything—instead, he pinned me down.

I managed to push him off. When I stood up, he fell onto the towel. Without warning, as if he'd been hit over the head with an anvil in a Looney Tunes cartoon, this so-called evangelist passed out.

Thank you, God . . .

I found myself walking—no phone, no purse, no money—eight miles back to the penthouse.

Sitting down, hours after regaining my composure and taking a shower, I contemplated calling the police and reporting the evangelist. I knew the routine. And also knew how rigorous it would be, and how I would start the police interview by not being believed by law enforcement. It's just the way it is for a woman. I had escaped without being hurt physically.

I cut my losses.

And then, I logged into OurTime with the intention of deleting my profile. I was done with online dating. As I scrolled around, frustratingly searching for the settings page, I heard what had become a familiar *ding* from my inbox. A new guy had just responded to my profile.

I should have continued with deleting my account. I should have listened to what my gut was screaming for me to do. But something told me to click on the new guy's profile.

So I did.

And there he was: John Meehan.

2

BE WATER

My mother, Arlane, had instilled in us that we were put on earth to love one another and forgive. This was not some sort of saccharine, clichéd manipulation to force a value—or a moral code—on her children. Mom meant it. She believed it emphatically. My late father, Wayne Ambrose, a youth pastor and coach, reiterated Mom's virtue in every sermon he shared with the kids he mentored, as well as at our dinner table and in our little father-daughter chats, just the two of us. My parents raised three kids of their own but also took in eighteen foster children over a ten-year period. Weekends at our house were like school recess, with kids coming and going. Laughter. Playtime. Joy. My parents, Nazarenes, walked the talk. Nazarenes believe we are all born with a fallen nature—that every human being is inclined to evil—but atonement is available for everyone, through Jesus Christ. The concrete foundation of my parents' lives was built around this premise, along with unconditional love. They lived it. Love thy neighbor. Thy parents. Thy spouse. Forgive those who seek mercy.

As a child, I never thought of us as an uber-religious family, but as I entered adulthood, I realized that perhaps we were. I never saw us as being restricted in any sort of *Footloose* way. But now, as I look back, I realize I would have been judged had I chosen to dance, wear makeup, or show any skin. So perhaps we were. My two siblings and I did not feel oppressed, however. The Bible wasn't rammed down our throats. We certainly weren't whacked in the butt with the Good Book when we got out of line. My parents promoted and lived the grace Jesus Christ preached.

I spent a good portion of my childhood in the hospital or at home in bed. I was born without the tube that connects the bladder to the kidneys. I suffered almost daily 105-degree fevers. My first surgery was at two years old. It failed. The next one was at four. Then a third at seven.

I recall a conversation between my parents and doctors in which the doctor whispered, "Debbie is not going have a long life." It wasn't a surprise. We had expected to hear this just about every time I wound up hospitalized. Talk of my mortality was routine.

As I grew into my teen years, still sick and not expected to see twenty, one doctor said, "She's been lucky. Even if she does live longer than her teenage years, Debbie will never be able to have children or be able to work."

Throughout it all, I was called the Miracle Child. Before each of my surgeries, my parents were walked into a nondescript, antiseptic-smelling room, sat down, and told there was a good chance I would not pull through. I had spent so much time throughout my childhood with doctors, all of whom had had a hand in saving my life (however negative and pessimistic they were about my survival), that I revered them. Doctors were lifesavers. Rescuers. They had given me my life back. Perhaps all of that is why I felt meeting, falling in love with, and marrying a doctor would be such a triumphant moment for me.

My parents believed in the power of prayer. Mom and Dad would occasionally stop me as I was grabbing something to eat, or just sitting in my room, and say, "You are the most optimistic and strongest person we know. Prayer works, Debbie. It truly does."

That affirmation stuck with me. I grew into a trusting person, believing that if I put my mind and soul into something, it was possible. Not a day went by when Mom or Dad did not encourage me in some form. But more important, when a setback or disappointment occurred, they taught me to view it as a life lesson—a learning situation that would make me stronger. When I got older, I could not allow any of the many disastrous dates I'd had to deter me from finding love again. It took me decades to figure it out, but in the spirit of what Bruce Lee once said, I think love is like water: it flows and becomes the thing—a glass, bowl, riverbed—in which it exists; it is different every time.

If I was to acknowledge a flaw from my childhood, it would be that need to present the perfect family image—think Norman Rockwell painting—to the world. It was my family's weakness. Mom was a music teacher and highly admired at our church. We projected a white-picket-fence portrait of a family loving and praising Jesus Christ. I'm just not sure it was as blissful as the painting would suggest. If you looked at us, the Ambrose family, you wouldn't think there were any issues inside our ideal American household. And no one's perfect, but Mom and Dad had a long-term marriage and I never witnessed any marital problems. I never saw them argue; they were forever kind to each other. Yes, when my sister, Cindi, got out of line, she got the belt, and I never did. Why? I can only guess. And look, after several marriages, divorces, and four kids of my own, you might think I don't understand love. Or that I was hardwired for love's failure during my childhood, as if there were some dark secret kept hidden and buried in our house. But I believe I was raised by two amazing human beings, both of whom believed what they believed and didn't stray from it. I saw kind, wonderful, caring parents, and I felt loved and supported.

You learn a few things about yourself when you're bedridden for much of your early life. For one, I developed an obsession for reading, specifically romance novels. Reading took me out of a doldrum funk I could easily fall into and helped me come to terms with the fact that I would never be able to experience love or family, or have the life most others woke up to every morning and generally took for granted. The novels allowed me to step out of my life and enter a fantasy where meeting the perfect man and living a fairy-tale life with my soul mate one day were possible.

I also loved reading encyclopedias and medical journals, as well as creating and building 3D models. At the age of five, I drew at least 150 different floor plans for miniature houses with crayons. I would search throughout the house and garage for items to build dollhouse versions of my favorites. These were the first times I can recall designing something from nothing and making it real. I would add miniature furniture and dolls. One of my designs was made out of sticks and fabric remnants Mom had saved from her sewing projects, including—get this—a fur coat made out of clippings from our cat.

When I turned seven, Mom signed herself up for a night-school course in interior design. I was more excited than she was. I couldn't wait until the assignment came in each week. Mom said I actually completed every assignment for her—and she wound up with straight As.

When the doctors told me my illness would prevent me from being able to work, it was crushing, of course. But after the years passed and I survived, my drive to do whatever I wanted in life became an inherent part of who I am. Nothing was going to stop me from achieving my goals.

And I've worked hard. The design firm I built has sustained me and more than forty employees for more than three decades. I've won several local, national, and international awards. I've been named designer of the year and have worked in Egypt, Dubai, and China. Despite what doctors told me about not having children, I gave birth to four healthy kids. Giving up was not going to be part of my life. I could have, after all, turned out many different ways, yet my early life experiences helped me develop optimism and tenacity.

Before we became best friends, my sister, Cindi, who was two and a half years older than me, had a way of making me uncomfortable at times. I felt as though she was forever annoyed with me. Maybe she resented me for getting all the attention because of my illness? I do know a good part of her frustration was rooted in her need for independence. She insisted on overseeing every aspect of her life without input from anyone, especially me, her younger sister. I understand why today more than I did then. I had been saddled with health issues for most of my early life, so what kind of life experience could I offer my older sibling?

When I say Cindi was beautiful, it is not a lazily chosen adjective. Cindi was knockout gorgeous—the kind of girl who truly turned heads. She had the body of a supermodel; every curve and proportion were as perfect as they could be. I recall her long legs, tiny waist, and ideal-sized breasts. Add all that to shoulder-length, thick, blonde hair and light olive skin and, as you might imagine, boys idolized Cindi as much as girls were jealous of her.

Still, my sister carried a certain amount of ambiguity, mystery, and pain within her that she did not want to talk about or share. She was a perfectionist and very hard on herself.

In high school, Cindi excelled in athletics, pushing herself to be the best. She graduated in 1970, three years before me, so we spent a year together in high school. As I got older, into my teen years, I was always known as "Cindi's sister," not Debbie. I was happy with the person I was, and most would say I was easygoing, positive, and funny. I know now that those attributes were grounded in sincere gratitude for just being able to have the life all those doctors said I couldn't have.

"Cindi, you see the glass half empty and I see it half full," I said one day. She was just about ready to graduate and already talking about marrying her high school sweetheart.

Cindi shrugged off the comment. That was my sister: *Thank you, but I am who I am and I will do whatever I want to do.*

As complicated as Cindi was, she was never jealous of anyone, especially me. There was no sibling rivalry between the two of us. When I became homecoming princess, she took me aside and said, "Wow, I'm so happy and proud of my little sister. Come here, I want to show you something."

We stood in front of the mirror in her bedroom, and Cindi taught me how to wave properly. It was one of those magic moments, and for hours afterward I pictured myself sitting on the back of a Corvette convertible, moseying through the parade route in our town while doing the ridiculous wave Cindi and I had spent hours practicing.

Unlike me, Cindi argued with our parents all the time. She was a renegade. While I managed the chaotic living conditions one way, she went in a different direction altogether. I think this is why she married so young. The way Cindi navigated her life and dealt with our parents made an impression on me. I was there on the sidelines, feeling as if it was my duty to be the peacemaker while also taking care of Cindi by defusing any problems with our parents before they got out of hand. With so many foster children coming in and out of our lives, we never felt like the center of attention in our own home. Our parents' love was spread thin. On weekends there would be twenty to thirty kids—most of them from the youth groups at church—roaming in and out of our house. I protected my sister, maybe more from herself than anyone else. If I knew Cindi had gone out drinking, I would make sure she got into the house and in bed before our parents found out. I didn't want any conflict. Cindi got the belt from Dad many times, and I did my best to protect her from that. I knew something was wrong, but it never occurred to me until much later how wrong it was. My parents and Cindi also screamed at one another frequently. The less our parents knew about what Cindi was doing, the better off we all were.

My sister had several boyfriends throughout high school. She could have had any boy in the school she wanted. At seventeen, Cindi walked into the house one afternoon, a boy on her arm—no warning, no prologue, no indication whatsoever that she was in love.

"This is Billy," she said.

That was how we met Billy Vickers. He was good-looking—tall and thin with long blond hair. I recall him being happy and even a bit cocky. Early on, Billy came off as gentle and kind to my sister; he seemed to be the perfect boyfriend. We all got along well. Six months after meeting Billy, Cindi asked everyone to convene once again, this time without Billy. She said she had an announcement to make.

"Please, everyone," she said. "I need all of you to gather around me."

We all looked at one another. Mom, Dad, our biological brother, several foster brothers and sisters, and me.

"Yes, what is it, Cindi?" our mother asked.

Cindi was glowing, and I could tell she had serious news to share. Knowing Cindi, I knew she had not gotten us together to ask what we thought about Billy; Cindi was speaking her mind and we were going to accept—and deal with—whatever it was.

Was she pregnant?

"Billy and I have decided to get married," she announced.

This was the best way for her to get the heck out of our house.

We were happy for her. If that was what Cindi wanted, no one in the family was going to try to talk her out of it. It was 1969. Life was vastly different than it is now. The average new home was $14,950; gas was $0.49 a gallon; the minimum wage was $1.60; and the average yearly income was $7,850. Women often married right out of high school. Cindi, we all believed at the time, had found her soul mate. Today, I know for certain that her goal was to get out of the house and away from my parents, and she needed a man to rescue her.

Cindi and Billy's wedding took place on her eighteenth birthday, November 21, 1970. It was a big wedding. I was the maid of honor and remember the day as a celebration for everyone in the family, not only for my sister. We joined in her happiness and supported her.

My big sister was now a wife, and I knew it would not be long before she would be a mother. Cindi talked all the time about having kids right away. Kids offered her the opportunity to make things right in her world.

In 1974, when I was nineteen, I worked forty hours a week at a local Marie Callender's restaurant while putting myself through college. I was supposed to graduate high school that year, but I made it a semester early and started college right away. I guess I was in a hurry to grow up.

Marie Callender's caters mostly to travelers and locals, providing food and drink, a cozy atmosphere, lots of pies, and homestyle cooking. I had a small apartment by the beach in Newport at that time. I would go to college and then to work, come home from work, prepare dinner, and watch television. My nightly routine. I had a roommate, but she was never around. She spent most of her time at her boyfriend's, so I basically lived alone.

One night I came home to an empty apartment, as usual, but noticed the living room window was open.

Strange, I thought.

I walked over and looked at it.

Fingerprints?

They were visible. We didn't clean the windows, so there was plenty of dust.

Maybe my roommate had left the window open. Later, I walked into my bedroom to change clothes and get ready for bed, and saw that the top drawer of my dresser, where I kept all my lingerie, was open.

I stopped in my tracks and remembered a scary phone call I'd received a few days earlier. A man's voice, whispering, "I've been watching you sleep."

"Who are you?" I'd asked.

He hadn't responded. Instead, he'd described what I was wearing to bed that night.

"I love your pink teddy; it feels so soft. You look amazing in it."

It had been an exact description.

That whisper—it's something I will never be able to forget. Haunting. It had injected fear into me immediately.

"Please, please . . . stop this . . . who are you?"

"I got into your drawer and I have some of your underwear in my hand right now."

He'd hung up.

Now I trembled with fear.

What is happening?

I called my roommate.

"Have you been here going through my drawers? Did you open the window?"

"No, Debbie, why do you ask?"

I explained.

"Call the police."

As I thought more about it, I wondered, *Is there someone just messing around with me? Playing a joke?* These thoughts reflected my desire to find the silver lining in any situation and my tendency not to take events as seriously as I should. It had become easy to write such situations off as something I did to myself, or some sort of foolery. I was a nineteen-year-old, working in a restaurant. My mind was mush most days. It was a survival mechanism I had utilized as that sick child whenever I was stressed. Unconsciously, it forced me to tell myself that this guy was someone I had perhaps dated. *Was he playing a game? He's going to come forward and say it was all a joke. Maybe it was my roommate's boyfriend and they had decided to prank me.* I didn't call the police. Of course, I go over this now and it scares me to believe I was so naïve and my fear level was so low.

The next day, I walked in from work and saw the same exact thing: the window and lingerie drawer were open.

I called the police this time.

They showed up and asked me questions. I told them about the call, the way I'd found the apartment two days in a row. Suddenly, as the police made me see the situation for what it was, I felt like this was all building up to a big event targeted at me.

"We'll look into it. Lock your doors. Lock your windows. Keep an extra eye on yourself as you go to and from school and work. We will begin investigating immediately."

I received more calls in the next few days, and they became much worse—they were more graphic and detailed. He knew what I had done that day. What I'd worn at work and later that night. Where I'd gone. When I'd walked in the door. It was clear this man was stalking me. He knew every move I made. I felt violated and fearful all the time. I wasn't just looking over my shoulder; I felt like I was in a prison wherever I went.

I'd spent years thinking I was going to die from my health issues, but hearing this man describe my life, knowing he'd been inside my apartment and stolen my intimate personal items, frightened me so much more than facing death as a child ever had.

I decided to move in with Cindi and Billy. I slept in my baby nephew *Ben*'s room. I had been at their house about two weeks. One night, at about 6:00 p.m., I came home from work, put my stuff down, and headed to my room. Ben, Billy, and Cindi were out. I was alone.

As I walked into my bedroom, a man came out of the shadows, grabbed me, and wrestled me down, face-first, onto my bed.

"I've been watching you," he said—I recognized his whisper. Unforgettable. Intense. He was breathing heavily. There was no doubt it was the same man who had been calling and stalking me. And now, I knew, he was going to rape me.

He held me by the waist with one arm and pushed my head into the pillow on my bed with his other. I felt paralyzed. I was shaking and crying, and my heart was beating faster than I could ever recall. I instinctively knew he was going to kill me after he was done.

I turned my head when he released his grip and saw that he had a knife. The type a hunter carried, with a serrated edge.

"Be quiet," he whispered. "Don't fucking move."

I did what he said.

God must have been watching over me, because at that moment I heard Billy open the front door.

I screamed.

Billy came running for my room.

My attacker ran off and out the back door.

Billy followed.

As it all happened, the assailant's mask somehow came off—I'm not sure if I ripped it off during the struggle or if he took it off himself—but I saw his face. He was a guy I'd seen every day sitting at the bar at Marie Callender's. He was always very quiet. He hadn't creeped me out while sitting there, but there had been something about him that rubbed me the wrong way. I just couldn't put a finger on it.

After the incident, I moved in with my mom and dad. I needed to be with them, which was perhaps an instinct from back when I was ill. The man was arrested and charged after the police were able to connect him to a fingerprint lifted from a pay phone near my apartment. But it didn't matter. He had destroyed any type of confidence I had in those everyday people I came across during my life. At best, I was nearly raped; at worst, I could have been murdered. After surviving all those medical problems, the thought of losing my life to a strange man in an act of extreme violence made me truly yearn to be protected. At all costs.

3

DOCTOR'S ORDERS

I stared at John Meehan's photograph on that October night I'd decided to delete my OurTime profile.

After a bit of hesitation—and I know now that was my intuition screaming at me to run the opposite way—I decided, *One more date. Why not?* Liz and I had this saying: "One and done." You went out with a guy once and generally that was it—no spark, no chemistry, not interested. You had given love another chance, but Cupid was nowhere to be found. This would probably turn out the same way. So be it. One more date, I delete the account, and move on with my life.

As I poked around John's profile and looked at his photos (full-body shots on the beach; one with him and his dog, who I later learned had passed away before we met; another of John just hanging out inside a house), I thought he was gorgeous, movie-star handsome, and looked like someone ten to fifteen years younger than his fifty-five years. Muscular. Hazel-green eyes. Six feet, two inches tall. He had a thick shock of dark brown hair and a Colgate smile, both of which complemented the sexy jawline of a superhero. Shallow as it sounds, no matter what anybody says, we are attracted first by looks. If there is no physical attraction, we move on. It's like buying a house or looking for an apartment: You log on to Zillow and immediately scroll through the photos. If you don't like what you see, it's on to the next house.

I sat back and read through his profile. Even on his profile page, he came across as charming and delightful: the perfect guy. A doctor. A father. He'd just returned from serving in Iraq as an anesthesiologist.

What was there *not* to like about the guy?

I replied to his message, which was your basic "Hey, how are you? Great to meet you."

For a few days after that first message, John and I exchanged emails and texts. He sent me photos of him with his children. A picture of him wearing scrubs, with a colleague, inside an operating room. Pictures of him on the beach, on vacation. Those abs and that tan. I could tell he adored his dog from the love he showered on it in the photos. I sent him photos of myself.

I cannot understate how much it meant to me that he loved his dog. My youngest daughter, Terra, had dedicated her life to her dogs and cats. Everywhere Terra went, her Australian shepherd, Cash, was by her side, along with her two other dogs. I felt that anyone who displayed that sort of adoration for a pet, as John did, was a good person at heart.

We began conversing every day.

"You are *so* my type," John wrote back.

Admittedly, this message from him was a turn-on.

Texts and emails quickly evolved into long phone calls. He told me all about himself. Still a bit guarded, I shared what I thought was appropriate about my life.

Our conversations flowed naturally. He asked lots of questions. He came across as witty, smart, funny. I recall asking him about his ex-wife one night.

"Terrible person," he said. "Very cold. She's got a lot of money. We had a major custody battle and it broke my heart. The joy in my life is my children. I speak with them every day."

"I'm so sorry, John. Tell me about your kids."

"My oldest girl lives on campus at Princeton. She's twenty-two, studying to become a doctor. My nineteen-year-old girl is in Colorado attending military school."

After a couple more days, I felt I had gotten to know John well enough to meet in person. I had no concern about telling him where I lived. Security in the building was taken seriously. A guard stood at the entry gate. When you stepped inside the foyer, another guard checked you in. From there, without a key fob you weren't getting upstairs or gaining entry through any door leading to your condo. In addition, we'd spent hours on the phone, sharing stories of failed relationships, dreams, and the admiration we had for our children. I never sensed one sign of anything out of sorts with him—no red flags popped up after anything John said during our calls. He seemed genuine. There was a street edge to him I picked up on, but I liked it. Here was a doctor, an anesthesiologist who held life and death in his hands, a guy who helped people manage and not feel pain. That meant something to me.

"Do you know Houston's, in Irvine?" I suggested to John during one of our extended telephone conversations.

"I do," he said.

"I live nearly right next door. We can meet at my penthouse and walk over."

Houston's is a great first-date location. It's directly off the 405. It has a patio with Adirondack chairs and a romantic stone firepit for sitting and talking, while sipping expensive cocktails. It has a fairly respectable sushi bar, a $46 steak (which isn't too pricey, considering it's in Irvine/Newport Beach). The restaurant website is clear regarding attire: no "hats, tank tops, flip-flops." In addition, "team athletic" garb is "too casual." But the best part of meeting there was the location: a block away from my penthouse, four hundred steps, a five-minute walk. Based on all the great conversations we'd had over the phone, I didn't expect anything to go wrong, but if I sniffed anything out of order, I could ditch John and be home fast. Walking eight miles home had taught me a few lessons about dating.

So, several days after John and I first met on OurTime, the doorman, who doubled as security in my building, called up to my penthouse to let me know John had arrived.

After I took the elevator down and walked into the lobby, my first reaction to seeing John was that he looked so much younger than he did online. He reminded me of an older guy who still attended college. My second reaction was that, although he was strikingly attractive, he needed some help in the clothing department.

I wasn't nervous about meeting him in person, because we had spoken and texted so often by then that I felt I knew the guy. We'd texted real-time photos of ourselves. Nothing sexy or intimate—just your average, everyday duck-face snaps and smiles, along with zany pics of us doing mundane daily activities.

"Debbie?" John said when he saw me.

"Hi, John," I responded, sticking out my hand. "Would you like to come upstairs for a glass of wine? You can meet my daughter."

"Sure, that would be nice."

I poured some wine and we sat outside on the balcony. John stood for a moment and took in the incredible view of the Pacific Ocean and the city of Irvine lit up at night.

He turned from the ocean view and stared inside the penthouse. "Wow, Debbie, this is a really nice place. It's absolutely beautiful." It was as if he had never seen anything like it before.

We spent an hour or so upstairs. John spoke to Liz for a time. Liz worked on the sales side in the medical industry, so they swapped stories about doctors they both knew.

After a few minutes of chatting, I piped up, "We should get going."

John never touched me on the way to Houston's. He didn't put his arm around me or try to hold my hand.

John opened the restaurant door for me.

We decided to sit at the bar. I began judging him as we walked in and I got a better look. The first moments you meet someone, nerves are bubbling. After I settled down a bit and we felt more comfortable with each other, I noticed that he was wearing old shorts and a dress shirt, teetering on crossing the restaurant's dress code line. I wrote it off as a guy living the beach-bum life while not at work. It did not bother me as much as it should have. Usually, I'm not glib in that way; I go through life looking at what people wear, sizing up their lives based on appearances. I'm a designer by heart; it's my absolute obsession. Seeing life in terms of color coordination and neatness is something I focus on because my mind cannot shut it off, and I get paid to do it. The other aspect of evaluating one's appearance, a first impression, if you will, is rooted in my childhood, I'm certain. I had no control over my life and had no social life whatsoever as a child. As I grew into adulthood, beating the odds and overcoming life-threatening medical issues, it became important for me to notice people and how they presented themselves. I had fought long and hard to live, so I presented myself the way I felt inside: joyful and grateful.

"This is nice," John said as we approached the bar.

"It is," I responded.

Looking at him just before sitting down, I thought, *Have I finally met a great guy?*

Despite his rumpled look, John came across as the perfect guy. He checked every box.

4

CARELESS WHISPER

Before we even sat down at the bar, I sensed a romantic spark, a connection—that all-important-to-me chemistry—between us. Each moment after, that energy grew. John pulled out the chair for me and made sure I was snug up to the bar before he unfolded my napkin with one hand—snapping it open like a French waiter in a foreign film—and placed it on my lap.

"Thank you," I said as he sat down.

A true gentleman.

It was such a stark contrast to what I had experienced on other online dates. Before heading downstairs to meet John earlier that night, I had had a brief chat with Liz. At the same time, we had both said, "One and done!" And we laughed. I had expected it to be the case with John.

"You're welcome," John said.

Jazz played softly through the overhead speakers. People around us conversed quietly. It was a beautiful California night: seventy-two degrees with a salty, warm ocean breeze you could feel—and smell—around town. The stars in Southern California during that time of the year are brilliant. You look up and think diamonds have been tossed across black velvet, as far as the eye can see. The atmosphere alone was romantic. John was courteous and a gentleman. I felt comfortable and very safe. Sharing an experience with the right partner allows us to notice all the naturally beautiful trimmings around us, like those stars and the music, and it makes them better. You smell the flowers. You take in the subtle nuances of the atmosphere. It felt right sitting next to John, enjoying drinks, a light dinner, and stimulating conversation.

We laughed and shared stories. There was not one awkward moment during dinner. He came across as confident, radiant, sincere, and compassionate. A happy, seemingly honorable human being who cared about family.

John had told me previously that he worked long hours at several area hospitals and clinics and had just started dating again. He'd mentioned something on the telephone about being overseas.

"I just came back from Iraq a few months ago," he explained.

"Wow, that must have been intense, John."

"I mostly tended to the impoverished and war-torn victims and soldiers on the front lines," he added.

"Incredible."

"I've spent time in Afghanistan, too, back in 2002, doing the same work. It's exhausting and emotionally taxing but something I need to do."

"That is all very honorable, John. Extremely giving of you."

He nodded and took a sip from his drink.

"I did a stint with Doctors Without Borders, the internationally renowned medical aid provider, over there, as well. We helped very sick people. One of the scariest times was when we traveled from one area to another in a helicopter—and it crashed. This was many years ago. I injured my ankle and back." He pointed to both. "Still hurts to this day."

"Oh, my goodness, how noble," I said in response.

"It was very rewarding. I'd do it again in a minute." He paused and stared into my eyes, which I know sounds a bit ridiculous and clichéd. But John made me feel as if I were living in a fairy tale—and he was my prince. It was as though he was focused entirely on me. He seemed interested in what I had to say and how I felt. And he acted like nothing and no one else around us existed.

After a moment, still looking at me, he said, "You are so beautiful, Debbie. Do you know that?"

I was more flattered than I'd felt in a long time. John was interested in *me.* Who *I* was. Part of me expected a weird or disappointing comment or two, but as the night progressed and we spoke for four hours, it didn't happen.

The subject of God came up at one point. John explained that he was a believer, a devout follower of Jesus Christ. He added, "I worship at Mariners."

Oh my, I said to myself. *What a coincidence.*

"Mariners? On Newport Coast, Bonita Canyon Road Drive in Irvine?"

"Yes," John replied with a pop in his voice. "Why do you ask?"

"That's where my children and I attend, John."

"It's a small world, Debbie, isn't it?" He smiled.

We laughed and clinked glasses.

John told me he owned two houses. "One in Palm Springs, the other in Newport Beach." So, as I thought about it, the connection to Mariners made sense, because according to him, he had a home practically around the corner from the church. And Mariners is one of those Joel Osteen–lite megachurches. It's not as big as Joel's, but the church is a large, warehouse-sized theater where ten thousand–plus people can worship together. Christian bands take the stage. There's a big screen projecting Bible passages and song lyrics. Because of the church's size and three different service times on weekends, it made sense that we'd never run into each other over the two years John had been worshipping there.

The time at the bar passed without effort. But there came a point when we needed to leave. John got up from his seat and stood next to me. I expected him to make a move. Go in for the kiss, which I might have been receptive to in that moment. But he didn't. Instead, John continued being the gentleman he seemed to be and won me over with grace. All those other cads I'd dated were now forgotten. John seemed to be everything he made himself out to be, without much effort—just conversation and charm. I didn't get a sense he was overdoing it; he wasn't overselling himself as a salesman would a used vehicle. His stories felt real, not forced or made up.

"I would love to continue the conversation," John suggested. "I really don't want this night to end."

The feeling was mutual. I was enjoying myself. He had not tried anything aggressive or untoward the entire night. He had not said anything even remotely strange or of a sexual nature. I wanted to know more about him.

"Yes, I agree. I was thinking . . . why don't you come back up to the penthouse? We can have an espresso and talk some more."

John smiled. "That sounds wonderful."

I had no intention for my invitation to come across the way it perhaps sounded: *Come up to my place* . . . Inviting John back up to the penthouse was completely platonic. For starters, I assumed Liz was going to be home. Not only was Liz a good judge of character, but she could act as a buffer. Nothing sexual was going to happen, because I have never slept with a man on a first date—and would never do so. In addition, John had not given me the impression at dinner that he was after anything more than conversation and getting to know me better.

Opening the door to my penthouse, I called out for Liz to let her know we were back.

No answer.

I put my keys down.

"Liz?"

John stepped in behind me, and after checking my phone, I realized I had not seen an earlier text from Liz letting me know that she had headed out to dinner with a friend.

John and I were alone.

"Sit down," I offered. "Make yourself comfortable. I'll make us an espresso and round up some cookies."

"That sounds wonderful," John said, sitting on the sofa.

We sat and talked for a time, enjoying our coffee and cookies. John didn't even make a move toward me.

I had an early morning of appointments and clients.

"It's getting kind of late, John. I'm going to freshen up and use the restroom. I'll be right back."

Coming out of the bathroom several minutes later, I proceeded down a short hallway. I was in a good mood and thought I'd ask John about seeing him again. As I passed my room, something caught my eye.

I stopped, looked into my bedroom—and there was John.

Fully clothed, sprawled out on my bed, smiling at me.

I stood in the doorway. "John, let's go back into the living room and enjoy whatever is left of what has been a wonderful night." John had been such a gentleman up until then that this sudden change in behavior shocked me. I had not expected it.

John patted the bed beside him. You know the move: *Come on over here and lie down . . .*

"You have no idea how good this feels," he said, referring to the bed.

"John, listen. I am not going to sleep with you. That is not who I am. You must be confused. You must have gotten the wrong message."

John's face changed to one of venomous disappointment. Without another word, he hopped off the bed. I could tell he was angry. Not upset or mad. But on the verge of rage.

"I am fucking out of here," he said, not looking at me.

I stepped out of the doorway.

John stomped past me. Opened the door. And left.

5

APPROACHABLE DREAMS

Cindi and I grew apart after the attack. I got married to my first husband on July 30, 1976. I was so young and naïve. He left me for his secretary after four and a half years. I was pregnant when he left. That fairy-tale fantasy was quashed. Although my ex-husband and I later became friends and he always remained an excellent father to Brandon and Nicole, the two children we shared, by the time I was twenty-four, my life had become a combination of obstacles and rewards.

I was scared and struggling to make enough money to survive. As fate would have it, a friend, who happened to be president of a building company, approached me one day and asked if I would consider designing several model homes he was constructing. I had gone to school for design. I had even flipped several homes and designed the homes the children and I lived in. So I jumped at the opportunity to prove myself and get some practical experience. Knowing I needed help, I hired the best model home designer in the business to train me. And from this, my interior design business was born. It grew quickly, but I worked long hours and struggled constantly.

I had dreamed of being a stay-at-home mom—cooking, cleaning, doing the laundry, and embracing the June Cleaver persona of doting wife and soccer mom, while happily-ever-after took care of itself. When I'd lived that life, before my divorce, I'd had the same focus I'd had while building miniature playhouses from household items as a child. Security. Family. Now, newly single with two small kids, I was forced to survive on my own.

And it was around this time (the early 1980s) that I realized there was something going on with Cindi. But I did not want to pry, understanding and respecting how private she wished her life to be. There was a certain part of Cindi's life she didn't share or want me to dig into. I accepted that, along with her wish to deal with personal issues on her own.

Cindi had withdrawn almost completely, falling under the spell of—I would learn later—her husband Billy's obsessive, abusive control. I watched as Cindi grew unhappier every time I saw her, never really knowing the true underlying issue or what was going on inside her home.

It took a long time, but she did eventually begin sharing just a bit of her personal struggle. And I grew concerned. Billy was paranoid, she'd say. "A manipulating bastard of a husband and a useless, angry father."

"Oh, Cindi," I'd say. "How can I help?"

"I'm not sure you can."

It felt like a shock, but now that I look at it through life's experiences, I realize the signs were always there—one of which included Cindi spending very little time with our family and me.

Billy isolated Cindi from everyone.

"He criticizes me for everything," she'd admit.

I came to find out that Billy used guilt as a daily weapon to quash her self-esteem. He did not respect Cindi's needs, especially when she wanted time for herself or to go out with a friend. Every time Cindi walked through the door, Billy presumed her guilty of doing something she shouldn't have. The marriage was toxic. My sister was exhausted all the time.

As the truth became clear, I decided to keep a close eye on Cindi. Billy was horribly mistreating her. He was jealous and controlled her life in every way, including what my sister wore. He told her she was not allowed to get her nails done or wear makeup. If any skin showed after she was dressed, Billy went ballistic, demanding she cover up. We would go to the beach and Cindi would have to wear a shirt on top of her bikini. When Cindi and I went to the gym, Billy waited in the car outside and watched Cindi through the big plate-glass windows.

Cindi's demand for privacy about what was going on in her home was rooted in our being that "perfect" family when we were kids. She had a perfectionist gene in her. Her makeup, hair, and body had to look faultless all the time. Even when it came to her kids, Cindi exhibited some rather extreme behaviors, like blow-drying her children's hair and picking tiny pieces of lint off their clothes.

I was young and foolish, already nursing a broken heart from a collapsed marriage I'd thought was going to last forever. Part of me, then, thought Billy was so in love with my sister that his only concern was to protect her. This was the early 1980s, mind you. A different time entirely. You could not just pop on the internet and begin researching problems in your life or find online support groups. For the most part, you were on your own.

The fact was, Billy had been manipulating and abusing my sister from almost the moment they were married.

"I feel so trapped," Cindi would tell me.

Cindi, our mother, and I would get together every Wednesday and go shopping, visit model homes, and have lunch. Cindi was negative the entire time we spent together. I would think, *Life is too short to be that way. Billy could get help and change.*

She was living in a prison, however. Afraid to leave. Afraid to stay. The marriage was broken beyond repair.

The homes I design are what I call "approachable dreams," meaning that my aesthetic is similar to what you might find in a glossy lifestyle magazine. One technique I learned immediately was to coordinate everything by color, which sounds rather simple and obvious, but in practice requires a lot of thought and preparation. I would spend weekends scouring used bookstores looking for old coffee-table books. It didn't matter what was inside the covers; it was how the books looked. A blue and beige scheme, for example, works with cream as a pull-in color. So I would search for blue, beige, and cream books. When John Meehan first saw my penthouse, I had black velvet dining chairs, a glass cocktail table, and expensive fine art on the walls, including two Salvador Dalí originals. My daughter Liz had a collection of expensive bags and purses. Design was not only my job; it had become my life.

Managing my way while making a name for myself, I had been accepted into this new world of designers, real estate executives, and high-end builders by the end of 1983. I had worked hard to be welcomed into this group. I had proven myself. My name had spread throughout this community as the one to call if you wanted a home designed to sell. I had moved on from divorce and being nearly raped and killed. I had a nice place of my own. Cindi, on the other hand, needed my support as her marriage continued to crumble. Whenever I saw her, it felt as though Cindi was jealous of my newfound freedom, the money I was beginning to earn, and how happy I had become after the blow of my marriage's collapse, as I dived headfirst into this new life of work and kids. I didn't need a man. My business and children fulfilled every need.

By January 1984, Cindi told me she was planning to divorce Billy. And although her plans weren't finalized, she already considered herself separated, even though they still lived together. And she was contemplating moving in with me. I had a nice house in Laguna Niguel. She knew—and explained to me—that a divorce from Billy was going to be contentious and nasty. Billy was not going away without a fight.

"But I'm going to be okay," she promised. "I'll get through it."

Around that same time, I had been invited to an upscale nightclub in Palm Springs for a big, swanky party promising to be populated by celebrities, sports megastars, and elite businesspeople.

Along with the invite came the direct suggestion for me to bring a "few beautiful girlfriends" to the party. Today, that request reeks of sexism and misogyny, but back then, it wasn't unusual. It was a time when parties were an extension of the workday. And, of course, there was no social media. No dating apps. No internet business community. Men and women socialized and met at parties. Business deals were made at parties. People were introduced and connected. It was a time when you actually stuck your hand out, looked the person in the eye, and spoke face-to-face.

I called Cindi. "I want you to go on a trip with me."

"Where to?"

"Palm Springs, Cindi, a big party with really great people. Come with me, please? I've been invited. It'll be incredible for us both."

I'd wanted to share my success with Cindi ever since I started my own business. Mortality wasn't something I obsessed about every day now that my health had stabilized, and my life was fun, for perhaps the first time. I was over the divorce and had been meeting exciting people. When I did date, the men I went out with were wealthy and powerful. Independence felt like a gift, which I was embracing. Cindi was still depressed and angry. Maybe even more so.

But Cindi agreed to go, and just like that, there we were inside this posh nightclub, stargazing and having a pleasant time. Cindi thanked me for getting her out and back into the social scene. She was grateful. Radiant, I recall. My big sister was coming back.

As the night progressed, Cindi was happier than I had seen her in a long time. To perhaps justify her decision to divorce Billy, Cindi talked that night at the party about how cheap Billy was, focusing on an issue beyond his abusive behavior.

"I could never buy anything. I don't even dream of having a nice home. I'll never go where I want to. Never do things I want to do."

"Soon, Cin, you'll be able to," I told her.

"I like him," Cindi said shortly after we arrived. She pointed to a guy on the opposite side of the room.

There stood this gorgeous Black man flocked by people. He was tall and well built, with light brown eyes and a million-dollar smile. He had a star quality about him.

"Go talk to him," I told her.

To my surprise, Cindi put her drink down and made her way toward the guy.

It was Hall of Fame running back Marcus Allen, who would later go on to play sixteen seasons in the National Football League for the Los Angeles Raiders and Kansas City Chiefs. Watching him, I could tell he was immediately captivated by Cindi. And as they talked the entire night away, it was clear to me that he was infatuated with my sister.

Cindi and Marcus started dating soon after that Palm Springs party. And about a month later, Cindi called to say she was moving in with me.

I got to know Marcus fairly well. He was good friends with O.J. Simpson and gave him my phone number. At the time, O.J. was one of the most likable and popular celebrities on the planet. "Juice," everyone called him. People loved the guy.

"Let's go out," O.J. said after a few calls.

He had come on to me pretty strong at first. He made me laugh. He was charming and easygoing. Since O.J. lived just down the street from me, he mentioned the idea of hanging out together at the Ritz-Carlton in Dana Point, south of Irvine; he said we could take walks, go out to fancy-pants restaurants, and dance the night away. It's a beautiful area, a part of Orange County where the rich and powerful pamper themselves and live, to be frank, extraordinary lives. It wasn't quite my style, but I was learning to accept that I had, in some respects, earned a place among this crowd. It was the celebrity lifestyle that turned me off. I liked the people, but not the spotlight.

I was flattered that O.J. Simpson had asked me out. It was tempting. Something, however, told me dating a high-profile, professional sports superstar was not going to be good for me. Relationships, I had learned the hard way by then, should teach us where we need to grow. The best relationships promote growth in both partners, either together as a couple or on their own, as the relationship blossoms. I would forever stand in the shadow of O.J.'s life—the blonde on his arm. Why even go on one date if I didn't think taking it any further was possible? I remember thinking, *He could be fun.* And maybe for a fleeting moment, I considered being that next blonde he always seemed to find. But I was not someone who dated a person based on status or wealth.

"I'm sorry, O.J., but I cannot go out with you."

He accepted the rejection. We remained friends for a time.

Cindi would sometimes come out with puzzling comments. One day, not long after the Palm Springs party, she said, "It's all your fault, you know."

"What is, Cindi?"

"Your husband leaving you. You didn't listen to him, take care of him . . . he went out and found somebody who would."

"I was a good wife and mother, Cindi."

One story about Cindi I heard many years later from a mutual friend was that Cindi woke up one morning to Billy's hands around her neck. He was choking her. Days later, she overheard Billy on the telephone talking about buying a weapon.

"A gun, Billy?" Cindi asked after he hung up. "Why are you buying a damn gun?"

"Protection," Billy told her.

I came home from work one day. It was the last week of February 1984. It was dark outside. Walking in, I heard noises inside my home. A faint cry coming from my living room.

"Cindi?" I said, stunned. There she was in the corner of my living room, balled up in a fetal position, whimpering.

"I . . . cannot . . . live like this."

I got down on my knees and hugged her. "It's okay, Cindi. It's going to be okay."

"I cannot live this way anymore. He's out of his mind, crazy. Something is going to happen."

This would have been a great opportunity to share the details about the gun. But Cindi kept it to herself.

Soon after the party and meeting Marcus Allen, Cindi called her lawyer and pushed for the divorce to be fast-tracked. She also left her two children with Billy and, at first, stayed at our parents' house. She confided in me that she felt she had no choice but to leave the children with Billy because he had threatened her life if she took them. But Cindi would go over to the house often to see them and to try to keep the divorce proceedings as amicable as possible.

Cindi then moved into my house. Spending so much time with her, I saw firsthand how scared and shattered she had become, trembling and crying constantly.

"It's going to be okay, honey," I kept telling her. "We're going to get through this together."

Billy had broken my sister.

On March 7, 1984, I woke up to my phone ringing.

"It's me," he said. Billy had a strange, high-pitched voice, but he could sound intimidating, like a bully, when he wanted to. On this day, however, he sounded so different. He was quiet. Calm. Stoic.

"What is it, Billy?" I expected and braced myself for the worst.

"Everything is going to be okay," Billy explained. "I have a plan."

He hung up. I stood and stared at the phone for a minute.

What is he talking about?

Back then, nobody talked about mental illness—the undiagnosed elephant walking around society, a ticking bomb ready to explode. By then, I thought Billy could be irrational and unstable. *Crazy* was the term generally used: *Oh, he's just crazy—he'll get over it.* It was easy for me to blame Billy's odd behavior on the forthcoming divorce and the contention between him and my sister. Divorce changes people. It makes partners say and do things they would never have considered before the marriage disintegrated.

Was Billy letting me know that he'd accepted the divorce? That "plan"? Wasn't it up to him and Cindi to figure out a way to live as a family separately?

I stared at the phone for quite some time.

Something didn't feel right about the call. Yet, what was I supposed to do? You must understand, the last outcome you expect is violence. For the most part, we were kept out of Cindi's personal life. She came to me and opened up at the end of the marriage. During the 1980s and even into the 1990s, it was taboo to bring the problems inside your home outside and share them with family. And forget about a therapist. I never considered calling someone and telling them about Billy's seemingly irrational behavior. And keep in mind, the story about Billy getting his hands on a gun came out after the fact, many years later. I look back at times like this, when certain things didn't "feel right," and wonder why I didn't do things differently. It might seem as though my decision-making process in these moments was counterintuitive. But that's in hindsight. It's not reality. The fact of the matter is, I had my own life, my own problems, anxieties, and difficulties to deal with on a daily basis as I raised two children alone.

"I'll get through this," Cindi would tell me in one breath. "I'm scared," in another.

All I felt I could do was be there for her.

6

SECOND CHANCES

When I look back on my life, especially my childhood, I have no question that, for whatever reason, God gave me a second chance. Every medical expert my parents sought advice from agreed I was not going to survive into my teens, get married, have children, or ever have a career. There I was in 2014, fifty-nine years old, and I had proved all of them wrong, having accomplished nearly every goal I'd set my mind to. There had been plenty of physical and emotional pain along the way, perhaps more than one person is supposed to endure, but it was through the pain of intensely dark moments that light and grace were exposed to me, empowering me to keep going. And when I reflect back on my childhood, I cannot imagine where I'd be had I given up and curled into the medical diagnosis of death so many tried to force me to accept.

After John stormed out of my apartment, I struggled to sleep. I stared at the ceiling of my bedroom, thinking, *What the heck just happened? Why did he get so upset?*

The guy was calm and carefree one minute, and the next, after apparently not getting his way, angrier than a wet hornet. I had enjoyed the evening and liked him, but after such an unpleasant demonstration of uncontrolled emotion, I never wanted to see John again. I certainly didn't expect to hear from him, and while finally falling asleep, I considered the way the night had ended as a blessing in disguise. John Meehan wasn't part of the Great Plan in store for me.

One and done.

The first thing I did the next morning was go to see my daughter Nicole. Nicole has been a dream child. Smart, talented, funny, witty. Her common sense is so exceptional that I feel embarrassed when I listen to her, because she makes me realize how out of touch I am with the zeitgeist. Nicole and I have always been close. I was a single mom for the first nine years of her life. She had a front-row seat for the hard work I did to keep our heads above water. I would bring her into the office with me. By the time she was sixteen years old, Nicole was working for Ambrosia. She received no special treatment; she started at the bottom and worked her way up. Many years later, after she secured an executive position, I understood that the passion and work ethic I had demonstrated all those years had influenced her. An example took place one night as I was walking out to the parking lot, heading home after a long day. I happened to look back at the building and noticed there were lights left on upstairs. For me, working an eighteen-hour day when I had a deadline to meet was the norm, so I assumed I'd left them on.

I walked back inside the building to shut off the lights. As I approached the switch, a noise startled me.

"Nicole?"

She was still working. I had no idea anyone else was even in the building.

"Hi, Mom . . ."

"What are you still doing here? It's almost eleven o'clock."

"I had no idea how late it was."

She had lost track of time while working. I knew in that moment the work was in her blood. It was part of who she was.

The morning after my date with John, I opened the door to Nicole's office without knocking and sat down across from her with a thud.

"What's wrong, Mom?"

"Well, I am *so* disappointed."

"About . . . ?"

"You know that guy I went out with last night? I really enjoyed him. He seemed so nice, kind, perfect almost. A doctor. Two homes. Kids. He did all this volunteer work in Iraq and Afghanistan. He was considerate all night. We talked, Nicole, for *four* hours straight at Houston's."

"And . . . so, where is the 'but' in this, Mom?"

I explained what happened at the end of the night.

"Forget him. He showed you who he was."

We talked about her kids and a few work-related issues. Then it was time to get myself in gear and focus on work. Before stepping out of Nicole's office, I said, "I will not be going out with him again—I am certain of that." I needed to hear myself say it out loud for the simple reason that John Meehan had seemed like the perfect gentleman and guy for me right up until the last moment of the night.

"Good," Nicole replied.

Ambrosia is where I lose myself. Creating designs takes me out of my head and into that creative space where I am entirely engrossed, concentrating only on what I'm doing. Some call this transcendent state "flow," where time disappears. That was the space I needed to be in.

My phone buzzed around noon.

A text from John.

"I'm not sure what came over me. I just didn't want the night to end. The date had gone so well."

He had been having such a good time. He said he'd overstepped clear boundaries. "Given a second chance, I would *never* let that happen again."

I sat back in my chair and stared at the text. Who was I to refuse somebody trying to make amends, apologizing and striking at the core of my soul, politely asking for a second chance? John's apology hit me so deeply, I can see now, because he had checked every box. He was once again that kind and thoughtful man I'd spent the better part of an evening with.

"I accept your apology, John," I texted back without much thought. "I believe in second chances. Yes, let's go out again."

When I got home that evening, Liz was in the kitchen preparing something to eat. She said hello and asked about the date the previous night. Her tone, I sensed, contained a hint of disapproval.

Before I could even answer, she said, "I didn't like him. There's something about him, Mom. I don't know. I can sense it."

"Well, I *do* like him, Liz. So we are going to have a problem. Because I am going to see him again."

Liz shook her head in disappointment. Knowing my daughter as well as I do, I could tell her thoughts were ricocheting chaotically like a pinball. It was not alarming to me that Liz would reject John. For lots of reasons, Liz did not like the guys I dated. Yes, she was an excellent judge of character. She had a keen sense of who people were. But Liz could also be assertive and overreact at times. Most of us in the family knew this. But then again, none of my children liked the men I dated. I understood, of course. They had witnessed firsthand the pain men had inflicted upon me. They had been there during most of the abuse I had suffered at the hands of men, emotional *and* physical. In my later marriages and several relationships leading up to meeting John, I'd been hit and screamed at in front of them. They knew men had stolen and manipulated thousands and thousands of dollars from me. They had every right to have an opinion based on what they'd experienced. And they are my children: it's inherent in them to want to protect their mother. But I am my own woman. I listen to their advice, complaints, and judgments before I make major decisions, weighing what they have to say. I do not allow them, however, to make decisions for me—and I expect each one of my children to respect those that I make.

John called that night and we talked for an hour. I had read that guys would troll dating sites and pick certain women they liked and plagiarize their profiles to match almost exactly what was written on their own profiles. That is the height of manipulation and deception. Dangerous stuff. But I was certain John was not one of those men. He was the man he presented himself to be—save for that one unusual moment late into the night—and the man I wanted to get to know more.

7

TRAGIC ENDINGS

After Cindi and I came back from that Palm Springs weekend, my sister had a bounce in her step, a renewal about her, which I had not seen in years. She was full of life. She believed the days ahead would be calmer and she would have the life she'd dreamed about for so long. She would be out from under Billy's unyielding control. Free from walking on eggshells, terrified to say or do the wrong thing. Can you imagine how my sister felt all that time—the threat of this guy hanging over her head every single day of her life?

That time leading up to Cindi and Billy's wedding is somewhat of a blur because I had been so ill; Cindi was always gone, away from the house as much as she could be. I had just emerged from lifelong thoughts that I would die. I know now, however, that Cindi was hiding. Billy was her rescuer. All she had wanted to do was get out of the house.

My early childhood, along with being a witness to Cindi's life, would influence my later dating and relationship choices. It set me up for some of the hardships I would endure. We cannot choose our childhood. Yet we can decide, once we're informed, to change the way in which we look at the past and move forward from it.

The night I found Cindi cowering in the corner of my apartment was sobering on many levels. First, it showed me how serious her suffering inside that marriage had been. Second, I understood for maybe the first time that she was terrified of Billy. She was not just a wife looking to get away from a mean husband—but a woman running from abuse.

There was no way for me to know how much stress she was under at home and what was actually happening, however. It's easy to look at it all in retrospect and see "signs." But at the time, Cindi was still very much a private person, hiding most of the heinously abusive behavior from all of us.

Likewise, that call from Billy, during which he told me he had things figured out, was a portent, though I could have never foreseen what was about to happen. I approached Cindi about the call.

"Cindi," I said. "Billy called. Strangest thing . . ." and I explained what he had said.

She looked at me with this intensity I had never seen.

"He is crazy, Debbie, you have no idea. You have no idea what he has done or what he will do to me."

"Cin, what do you mean?"

"He's always threatened to kill me if I ever left him."

How was I supposed to take this? Literally? Figuratively? How many husbands had said the same in the heat of a divorce? I was confused and scared. The best I could do was keep Cindi at my house and protect her.

"You'll work for me as my bookkeeper," I said, hugging my older sister. "You're so strong. You've done the hardest thing imaginable. It's all going to be okay, Cin. I promise you. I am here for whatever you need."

"Really?" she said, referring to the job.

"Of course, honey. I am going to make sure you are taken care of and you get through this."

We cried together, shedding tears of joy and, for Cindi, freedom.

Meanwhile, Marcus Allen would send a limousine to pick Cindi up for dates. The polar opposite of the authoritarian she had been living under for so many years, Marcus treated my sister like a lady. He was kind and empathetic. She was enjoying every minute of her life away from Billy, who seemed oddly quiet; he was not stalking her—as far as we knew—or calling at all hours and bothering her. Had Billy accepted this new way of life for the two of them? I often thought that perhaps Billy had surrendered and had an epiphany; perhaps he had realized how much destruction he had caused and had decided to leave Cindi alone and move on.

"I have a plan."

Cindi and Billy got together and signed papers to put their house on the market. Within a week they had an offer and accepted it. The morning of the sale, March 8, 1984, Cindi put a turkey in the oven at my house, picked up Ben, and dropped him off at school. She was going to see Marcus that night and celebrate the cord being cut. Billy was going to be legally out of her life.

"I'm going to spend the rest of the day packing up the house and paying bills," Cindi told me that morning. "I'll be fine."

We hugged and said our goodbyes. "Things are moving along, Cin. I am so happy that the house sold so quickly. What a blessing it is to have that out of the way."

I wish I could recall exactly what she said in response. But knowing my sister, it was something along the lines of "Have a good day; I'll see you later." Cindi had come a long way in such a short time. She was slowly coming out of her shell of not sharing her deepest feelings and fears. We were sisters again. Close. Helping each other get through the pains of life.

When I walked in the door later that day, the smell of burned turkey was the first thing I noticed. It's funny how smells trigger memories and emotions. Today, whenever I smell burned poultry, I think of those hours after I walked into my house on March 8.

"Cindi?" I said, going from room to room. "Hey, Cindi? Where are you?"

I was curious about how her day had gone. I knew she would run into Billy over at the house, and I didn't want her to think she had to do anything alone ever again. I had told her that if she sensed an issue with Billy, she should call or just leave.

"I will," she had promised.

This next moment I remember as if it happened yesterday. I grew immensely concerned. I started to peel carrots in the kitchen, helping out with dinner. The turkey was going to be okay. We could cut off the burned sections. Who cared, really? My two oldest children, Brandon and Nicole, had come home from their day and were in their rooms hanging out.

As I peeled, I wondered what was keeping Cindi. And the last thing I wanted to do was phone the house and get Billy on the line.

Cindi will be here any minute, I told myself.

Then the phone rang.

I stared at it. You know this ring—when it sounds different, as if telling you something. It was that kind of moment.

I walked over to the phone slowly and picked up the receiver.

"It's Mom." Her voice was, I recall with absolute clarity, stoic and resolute. My mother is a funny person. She can make me laugh with a few words. But that day, her voice sounded so different.

"Mom? Hi. What's going—"

Before I could finish, she said, "Debbie, something's happened."

And, well, I knew. The next thing out of my mother's mouth is really all I hear when I reflect back to the four words that changed my life forever.

"Your sister is dead."

I fell to the floor, screaming. "No . . . no . . . no . . . no!"

The kids ran out of their room to see what was happening.

"Mom?" Brandon said.

"Mommy?" Nicole said, both of them staring at me on the floor.

The tears started and never stopped that night. Sitting on the floor of my kitchen, my back against the wall, a vegetable peeler in my hand, I asked my mother what happened.

"Billy shot her."

How could this happen now, when Cindi was finally happy? We were closer than ever and she deserved a new life.

My parents sent someone to pick me up.

Cindi and Billy had sold their house, but they hadn't yet closed the deal. So Billy was still living in it. He had waited for the right time. Cindi was sitting at a desk they had in the kitchen facing the wall. She was going through bills that needed to be paid. He walked up behind Cindi and shot her in the back of the neck, killing her instantly. He'd borrowed the gun from a friend two weeks earlier. Billy had planned the entire murder. He'd spent weeks waiting for the right time.

After killing Cindi, Billy shot himself.

When I arrived at my parents' house, Dad was sitting, crying. My brother was in tears. My mom was emotionless, holding herself together, going from person to person, making sure they were okay. She was strong and, oddly, already at peace with her thirty-year-old son-in-law murdering her daughter.

I looked at her. "Why aren't you crying, Mom?"

She actually smiled. "Because it's okay. Cindi is at peace. She's in heaven. We will all get through this."

I had a keen understanding of forgiveness. The Nazarene Church had taught us all to forgive sin—dine with the sinner if you can, the same as Jesus did, and you will be free from the bondage of anxiety and hate. But my sister was gone. Dead. Her life had just started. Why should I even *consider* forgiving the person who took all of that away?

Would we get through it? How could we accept such a tragedy and move on? The feeling was worse than anything I had dealt with throughout my life: divorce, life-and-death health issues, the abuse I had suffered myself at the hands of the men I had met after my own divorce. My sister had been murdered. The signs, leading up to her death, had all been there. None of us had had any idea what to look for or what to do.

Living through this tragedy changed my outlook on men even more. The wrong guy, I now knew, could kill you. I had been attacked—nearly raped and killed—inside Cindi's house, and now she had been murdered. What was I missing? What signs had I not seen? Trusting a man was going to be harder for me. But once I had given in to that trust, on the other hand, once a man had broken through the barrier, it was going to mean so much more to me.

Billy survived. He was in bad shape, but alive. And yet, as our lives changed forever on the day he murdered Cindi, the situation between Billy and my family would get far worse.

8

LOVE IS IN THE EYE OF THE BEHOLDER

My second date with John Meehan was on October 18, four days after I had first met him face-to-face. It went even better than the first. The third date went even better. John was a complete gentleman, kind and considerate of my feelings, time, needs, and boundaries. I kept thinking, *He got the memo.* I wasn't about to hop into bed with the guy because he was gorgeous and a doctor. I needed a man to woo me. Treat me like a lady. Respect me.

And John took on that role as if he'd invented it.

On one particular date, about a week after meeting John, we ate at Eddie V's Wildfish, in Newport Beach. Live jazz. Casual attire. The best seafood in town. John dressed in what I had come to terms with as his regular day-to-day garb: shorts, a collared shirt with its sleeves rolled up, and sneakers. Not quite a beach bum, but not quite a guy with money, either. Somewhere in between.

John sat to my right. He did not take his eyes off me. He grabbed my hand (more than once), kissed it, and said, "Debbie, I believe in love at first sight. I don't need you to say anything in response, but you need to know something: I *will* marry you."

He dropped me off at my penthouse that night and kissed me goodbye. A gentleman the entire night. He said, "You know, you are everything I have been searching for my entire life."

I closed the door, leaned against it, and looked up toward the ceiling like a teenager after her first kiss.

Is this actually happening?

People have asked: Why didn't you see what was going on? The red flags? I have often asked myself these very same questions. But judging my behavior then by what we know now is unreasonable and unfair; it's far easier to see what was happening *after* the fact, reanalyzing it all. At the time, John's subtle quirks were easy to overlook.

Two nights later, on October 20, John arrived to pick me up. He was an hour late and was driving a different car than he had two nights before. He seemed disheveled and different. Something was off.

"Sorry, Debbie . . ."

"It's okay, John. You're entitled to be late. What's with the new car?"

"When I was in Iraq, my house back here was broken into and they stole all my belongings, including my cars. I've had to rent cars until the insurance company comes through and settles with me."

During that date, after he calmed down, John was, once again, extremely attentive. We kissed several times as we walked around Balboa Island. He dropped me off at the apartment. Before I stepped out of his rental car, he kissed me again. I could sense he wanted more.

"I have an early day tomorrow, John."

"No problem. I'll see you again soon."

Within two weeks of our first date, John was at my penthouse every night.

"Hey, Debbie," John would say when I came in from a long day. He was generally waiting for me to get home. He'd run up to me as I'd walk in the door.

"Close your eyes," he said one night.

"John, come on . . ."

"Just close your eyes."

"Okay."

"Now open your mouth."

"What?"

"Just do it."

I figured if I trusted him enough to leave him in my penthouse alone, I could open my mouth without knowing what was going to happen.

"John . . ."

He put a long-stemmed rose in my mouth; grabbed me; flipped on his favorite song, "Both Sides, Now," by Joni Mitchell; and, without saying anything, danced with me. For weeks, my dream guy greeted me this way. I'd step in the door, stressed out from working all day, get a rose, and then a dance.

"I set up the surround-sound system with your favorite songs," he told me one night. "Some of mine, too." He laughed. Then he grabbed one of my hairbrushes, keyed up a song I loved, and proceeded to lip-synch the entire thing.

It occurred to me within those first few weeks we dated that, for an anesthesiologist, John had more time on his hands than I would have thought. But I never gave it that much attention. Inasmuch as I took responsibility for my own professional schedules and workload, I accepted that his own career duties were his and his alone.

"Had the day off," he'd say after spending an afternoon hooking up a new television. Or cleaning the condo. Or cooking me my favorite dinner.

I didn't have any reason to question him. On the days when he'd worked and we'd planned to meet at a restaurant for dinner or a drink afterwards, or just at the penthouse, John was usually dressed in his scrubs. I was under the impression that he had always just come from a procedure. Those around me noticed this more than I did during this period, but it wasn't a big deal to me. When John worked, he worked long hours. He went from the hospital to my penthouse or wherever we'd meet for dinner. His scrubs were dirty and his fingernails were more like a mechanic's than a doctor's, but I try not to judge people on specifics like that, especially when I am not at work. Why would I question the way John presented himself? I believed he was genuine. He might have seemed frumpy and poorly dressed. But the guy, according to him, was always working.

Love is blinding in so many ways. We're able to overlook the obvious and accept what our heart works hard to convince us is the life we want.

"You make me a better man, Debbie, do you know that?"

His comments felt genuine. I was more than flattered.

John left handwritten love letters on my pillow, as well as wildflowers he'd picked while we were out walking or driving. There was a general feeling of authenticity in everything he said and did. Heading toward the end of October, John was saying, "You are the love of my life, Debbie."

And I believed him. He gave me no reason not to.

It seemed like the fairy-tale romance novels I'd read during the time I was sick and bedridden.

I texted John one day during the third week of October: "So, you *are* the real thing?" I included a smiley-face emoji.

"Best thing that will *ever* happen to you in your entire life," he sent back.

I smiled. Felt warm and fuzzy inside. Went on with my day.

Sexually speaking, John was an amazing lover. Intimacy in this regard seemed effortless to him. He was affectionate and very unselfish and giving in bed. In fact, he was the most affectionate man I had ever been with. We spent hours in bed. It was as though I were the only person in the world to him. In the moment, having had so many romantic failures, I believed with all my heart that I had gone through all that past pain to get to this blissful place with a real man, who was completely in love with every part of me.

It had been only a few weeks since we'd met, yet it felt as if I'd known John forever. We seemed to click on every level. As the days passed, I reflected on the life John and I were sharing. We savored every moment together. On some nights, when I worked later than usual, we'd meet by the beach for a dinner John had prepared. Then we'd take romantic walks along the shoreline. In retrospect, it seems almost surreal, even corny. Living it, day to day, however, I was caught up in being courted and treated with respect after experiencing some form of disappointment from most of the men in my life. John worked hard to make me believe that true love was not only real but possible.

He opened doors, paid the bill when we went out, and greeted me with a card and kiss on so many nights that I cannot recall him ever missing one. He wanted to hear all about my business, my children, my day, and whatever else interested me. The utter laser-like focus he demonstrated, and his interest in what I had to say, was refreshing. John didn't go on about himself. He was more interested in listening to what I had to share. Driving to work some mornings, I would think, *Here's a guy working twelve-to-fourteen-hour shifts at a high-stress job dealing with lives in the balance, and he is able to leave all of it at the hospital, and give me his full attention.*

It wasn't all about me, though. John would tell me about his childhood, his past accomplishments, his children, and his dreams. He opened up to me. He loved to talk about his time in Iraq and his career of putting people to sleep so they do not feel pain. He grew up in San Jose, so we took a trip up the coast in my car (a Tesla I had just bought was his favorite vehicle) to his childhood home.

"Good memories there, Debbie," he'd say. "Things got worse, much, much worse, after we moved out of that house."

One afternoon, a gorgeous California Sunday, John drove us to San Jose to show me the gravesites of his parents and brother.

"My one sister and one brother, along with both parents, are dead," John said as we pulled into the cemetery. He sounded shaken by this, as if the pain of those losses was still raw. "My mom remarried when I was a teenager and I have one half sibling."

"I'm so sorry, John."

"My brother's death was the worst. We were close. I was always tagging along with him. He was a rebel, though, and, unfortunately, got into hard drugs at an early age."

"What happened, honey?"

"I was living in Ohio at the time. He was so out of control. He lived in California, up here near San Jose. I came out to visit and talk to him. To see what I could do. I remember the first time I saw him. He pulled up with these two girls, all of them high as kites. I told him he needed to get his act together. He was married, Debbie. He had two young kids."

"My goodness. I am so, so sorry."

"I stayed several days, tried my best to help him, but I got the sense he was so far out of control there was nothing I could do. Sometime later, maybe a few weeks, I got a call. I was back home in Ohio. He had overdosed. I was devastated. I couldn't function."

"How old?"

"Forty. So young. He had a cocktail of various hard drugs in his system. They found him on his back. He'd choked on his own vomit."

I was stunned by this. I'd heard of it happening, but always to someone else, somewhere else. Nothing this close to me.

As we talked, holding hands while walking toward the graves, John revealed something else: "I was going through a tough time in my own marriage and started taking prescription drugs myself in order to sleep. I've had so many injuries, from Iraq to sports and accidents, I am still on medication. But it's controlled, you know. I only take what is prescribed."

"I get it, John. Thank you for being honest with me."

This is what a healthy relationship was supposed to involve: two people who trust each other sharing their deepest secrets.

After leaving the cemetery, we took a walk. I felt this was the guy I was supposed to be with. He had outdone every other man I had been with long-term. I'd had several boyfriends in the years before I met John, but marriage was not something I had even considered with any of them. Some were terrific guys, but I didn't fall in love with them. Others were fun to be with. Heck, I even dated a couple of movie stars and multimillionaires who would have been—on paper, anyway—great catches. Yet there was no connection. I dated Jeff Moorad, a sports agent who became the CEO of the Arizona Diamondbacks and the San Diego Padres, for about eighteen months. But none of those men made me feel like John did. John was different. I connected with him.

There was an overlook and cliff along the trail we were walking on that day. John steered us toward it. He looked out into the distance and became quiet.

Then he turned and stared at me.

"What is it, John?" I asked.

"Debbie," he began, grabbing my hands in his. "I want to marry you—I'm just being honest. I am in love with you."

I did not hesitate. "No, John. I need time. It's only been a few weeks."

"You make me a better man."

That night, when we got back to the penthouse, we slept in my bed. We did not have sex. Instead, John kissed every inch of my body and gave me a back rub.

After that wonderful day and relaxing night, John began asking me twenty to thirty times a day, "Please, Debbie, make me the happiest man in the world and marry me." He'd leave poems and love letters for me around the penthouse. As I think back on it all today, it stirs up so much pain and confusion and shame. Should I have questioned a guy asking me to marry him nearly every day? Based on the way he treated me in the beginning, it's mystifying to consider that John was anything other than what he presented himself to be.

"I've squandered love so many times in my life," he'd say. "I took love for granted so many times. But, then again, I think now it was all part of a plan leading me to you."

9

EVIL SEEMS TO ALWAYS SURVIVE

Billy remained in intensive care for two weeks and in a coma for days. My mom visited him in the hospital. Crazy as this might sound, she asked us all to go. It was difficult and confusing, all the mixed feelings I had, after losing my big sister, my best friend, by this man's hand. She was a wonderful human being who had been taken away from us for no apparent reason other than "If I can't have you, nobody else will." And my mother wanted me to go stand by the bedside of the man responsible for this? This may sound as though my mother was out of her mind. But she lived her faith, unquestionably, by the book. She believed, unequivocally, in forgiveness.

It all seemed so pointless, sad, and all-consuming. It angered me, of course. What could I do about it, however? My mom was a devout, Bible-believing Christian. This is who she was.

I cannot say that I wished Billy had died. Nor can I say I didn't. You go through so many different emotions when a tragedy of that magnitude occurs.

What about Cindi's kids? Now they've lost both parents. If he lives, what will they think of their father? Am I supposed to hate him? Can I hate anyone? Is forgiveness even possible?

"We must forgive," my mother kept telling me. "It's our doctrine. It's what Jesus wants from us. I forgive Billy. I will stand in support of him. He went mad. He snapped. Jesus loves the sinner, hates the sin."

Stand in support of him? Really?

My mother and I were in two different places over this, for sure. Part of me hoped he lived, and another part of me wanted him to die a miserable death in that hospital bed. I was confused and angry. If Billy passed, some of the pain he'd caused would have no choice but to leave with him. It wouldn't bring my sister back, but it would save us the heartache of sitting through a trial, hearing details about her murder, and reliving Cindi's entire life with Billy. If there was one clear truth then, it was that Billy was taking his case to trial and pleading insanity.

This made me even angrier. He wasn't even admitting what he'd done and being remorseful.

In the weeks following Cindi's murder, Billy started to talk about what happened. Knowing Cindi was going to arrive in the afternoon and clean up, pay bills, and pack her belongings, he had sent the kids over to our mother's house. Her murder was 100 percent intentional, carefully planned and carried out. *Can premeditated murder even be considered insane?*

It's such a strange experience to relive this time now. The parallels to the Nicole Brown Simpson case, which would happen years later, are alarming to me. Nicole, O.J. Simpson's ex-wife, was brutally murdered with her friend Ron Goldman on June 12, 1994. O.J., who had emotionally and physically abused Nicole, stalked her and threatened to kill her numerous times; he was arrested and charged with both murders but was later acquitted. The fact that Cindi and I had met O.J. and Marcus Allen and knew them years before Nicole's and Ron's murders was beyond surreal. I go back to it all now and it's as if I were talking about someone else's life.

Thomas Avdeef, the deputy district attorney, described Billy as "a jealous, moody man who knew that when his wife moved out and opened her own bank account the day before the shooting, it was 'the end of the road' for their marriage."

Prosecutors claimed Billy was so full of rage over Cindi leaving him that, two weeks before the murder, he sought out a gun and planned her murder.

Simple facts backed up by evidence. All of it inarguably true.

Billy was living on his own after getting out of the hospital. He had fully recovered months later when his trial began. Investigators explained to the jury how Cindi had separated from Billy and had been living with me, and Billy had kept one of their children at home so as not to disrupt their son's life during the divorce and selling of the house. How she returned to the house that day and Billy, waiting for this opportunity, walked up behind her and, while she wrote out monthly checks for bills, shot and killed her with a gun he had borrowed from a friend.

Does that sound like a man out of his mind? Does it sound like a human being who deserves forgiveness?

Defense witnesses, as far as I can recall, claimed Billy was jealous of Cindi's popularity and beauty. Then Billy made the absurd accusation that Cindi's public ridicule of him in front of friends and relatives for his poor grammar, looks, and baldness was too much to take. As a Christian, I try not to judge, but in my view, Billy had married out of his league. Cindi was much smarter than he was, and it riled him.

Billy's defense tried to turn the tables on my dead sister. Ridiculing her memory, besmirching her character. Spinning the entire situation into something that made Billy sound like a victim.

Disgusting.

My mother spent almost an entire day on the witness stand, defending the man who had premeditatedly murdered her daughter. "I not only like Billy," she said, "I *love* Billy," while noting how much she hated the crime he had committed.

Love is one thing. You can love *and* let go. But my mother portrayed Billy and Cindi's marriage to jurors in a way I didn't recognize. She blamed Cindi for their problems. Jurors were, I recall, crying by the time Mom was halfway through her testimony.

Billy's attorney, James Riddet, addressed jurors with this gem: "We don't quarrel with the fact that he shot the gun . . . [He] definitely snapped and shot his wife. But he should never have been charged with first-degree murder."

Billy's defense focused on the charges—they claimed that Billy had been overcharged by a radical prosecutor out for vengeance.

I felt repulsed by the idea that Billy was not owning up to what he did, was not begging for forgiveness, and was not praising God for giving him an opportunity to show his faith in action. He was not remorseful in any way. He was attacking Cindi and now controlling her memory, just as he'd controlled her life when she was alive.

After four days of deliberations, the jurors deadlocked seven to five in favor of finding Billy guilty of manslaughter, they were unable to reach a verdict.

He was acquitted of both first- and second-degree murder.

Manslaughter?

I walked out of the courtroom in tears, in shock, and having to live with the fact that Billy Vickers, who had tormented my sister the entire thirteen years they were married, was now spitting on her grave. Meanwhile, my mother was smiling, telling us that God had spoken. God had forgiven Billy and given him a chance to repent—and because of that, our family should forgive Billy, too, and accept him back into the fold. It was something that should have caused a rift, a great divide, between my mother and me. But it didn't. What can I say? I love my mother. I respected her decision to forgive based on her faith. Did it hurt or strain our relationship then? Of course. Would I allow it to come between us? No. I, myself, am a forgiving person, as I have maintained. And the fact that my mother had and would continue to support the man who killed her daughter was not going to change who I was.

10

BALBOA ISLAND

Philanthropy has always been a passion of mine. Because I have been blessed with so much in life, I believe giving back is a way to spread goodness into the world, if only in my little way. I can honor the second chance I've been allowed with charity. To that end, the people I deal with on a daily basis have money. And most rich people, despite what many might think, are more than willing to give. You just have to give them a good purpose and reason.

I've always believed that God opened the door to my career success. And I made a promise to God when I was a young adult that I would always give back and do whatever was within my means to help women and children. Since that time, I have been part of many charity events and raised hundreds of thousands of dollars for Human Options, Project Playhouse, Children International, Feed the Children, World Vision, and Working Wardrobes, along with several other charities. At one point, I gave money monthly to up to seven kids and sponsored surgeries for handicapped children. Some years I gave more than I made. I don't say all this to boast. It is with modesty that I mention it because it plays into what was happening in my life.

So it meant a lot to me when I invited John to accompany me to one of my biggest charity events of the year.

"I am one of the sponsors of an annual charity event for breast cancer awareness," I said to John a few days before the event. "I want you to come."

"I'll be there," John said. He gave me a peck on the lips. "Right now, I am off to work. Another long, long day of procedures." He stopped. Paused. Focused his attention directly on me. "But I am honored to go with you."

This type of intimacy stirred me up. John Meehan said and did all the right things—and I believed him.

Inviting John to this event was a way for me to begin introducing him to the people in my circle. If we were going to be a couple, I wanted everyone to like John as much as I did.

The cancer benefit was an event my company had been a part of every year. It was such an important night for me. I respected the people from my business community. They were decent, caring human beings. They gave of themselves and were unafraid to open their checkbooks. I have always believed that if you are blessed with wealth, giving what you can to those who need help is not only a noble and charitable gesture, but an important factor in your psychological and spiritual health.

On the night of the benefit, with all my colleagues and friends mingling and socializing in sharp business attire, John arrived late. Zigzagging his way through the crowd, he found me.

John looked different. Kind of off. Totally wiped out. He worked hard, so I could understand. Yet I was stunned when I saw what he was wearing.

"My goodness, John, what do you have on?" I said as he approached.

"Sorry, sorry . . . I've just come from work."

John was wearing his scrubs—to a cancer charity event, mind you. He looked dirty, as though he had been working on a car instead of anesthetizing patients all day. I was embarrassed and, frankly, hurt and angry. Looking around, I noticed some people snickering at us. It was beyond embarrassing for me. I had built John up to several people I knew. What's more, my reputation was on display here. Although it might sound trite, as we were all there for charity purposes, I worried about what others thought about me. People judge. They make choices—especially in business—based on what they see and feel. I realized, perhaps for the first time since I'd started dating John, that not everyone was going to feel the same as I did about him. The fact that he didn't see the importance of this event in my life was sobering to me and insensitive on his part.

What in the world was he thinking?

We made it through the night. It took me a few days, but I was able to write the incident off as the childish awkwardness John often demonstrated. The absentmindedness of a guy perpetually running late, rushing to see his girl after an exhausting day as an in-demand anesthesiologist.

The other side of this was, not much anybody said seemed to bother John. By the end of that week, I was telling myself, *Busy doctor . . . how could people judge a guy for that.* He had shown up to dates wearing scrubs many times, saying, "Just came from surgery, Debbie, sorry—I needed to see you and didn't have time to stop at home and change."

As shocking as John's showing up at a cancer benefit in dirty scrubs had been, I wanted desperately to believe John was honest and a man of his word—that he had literally run from a surgery to the benefit and hadn't had time to change. We had been dating almost three weeks by then. I told myself it was an anomaly. Maybe even that John's showing up dressed in scrubs exhibited how confident he was and that he didn't care what people thought. I was falling in love with this man. At such an early stage of love, we are willing to overlook the obvious and convince ourselves of just about anything.

As November approached, I started thinking about Thanksgiving. At the same time, John would not let up about getting married. Only now, I was considering it seriously. I'd had other marriages under my belt; one more, to the right person, did not scare me. I wasn't open with him about my feelings, but inside I was thinking that John Meehan, a doctor, someone I found to be empathetic, honest, caring, and fun to be around, *was* the man I wanted to spend the rest of my life with. Liz, Terra, Nicole, Brandon, and my nephew Ben, however, were speaking loud and clear: "Something is up with John; he's not who he says he is."

I endured a near-daily tongue-lashing from them, especially Liz. She'd scream at me about her distrust of "Dr. John." Yet the more someone tells me not to do something, the more I want to do it. I wasn't about to be told what to do by my children.

Liz brought up the first time she walked into the penthouse and John was there, alone, waiting for me to come home. Her first thought was, *Oh, yeah, this loser.* She said that John had a creepy vibe about him, that he was "kind of moping around the penthouse" and his eyes, especially, were "going from one corner of the room to the other, as if he was scanning the place, thinking about something." Liz had been in her office inside the penthouse one day. John had walked in. He had stood near the safe. "What do you have in the safe, kiddo?" he had asked.

"None of your business," she had said.

"Get the creep out of the house or I am not living with you any longer," Liz had said later that night.

So I decided to rent my own place. Liz could stay in the penthouse and I would have my own space. Liz was not happy with that decision, especially because she knew John would eventually move in with me. And she assumed he would ultimately break my heart.

So, a few days before Thanksgiving, I rented a house in the harborside community of Balboa Island in Newport Beach, an incredibly gorgeous area of town accessible only by bridge or ferry. The home was directly on the ocean waterfront. I paid the entire year's rent, $78,000, up front. Moving into a beach house had been a dream of mine. I had always wanted to live on the ocean, and here I was, finally seeing that dream become my reality. In realizing my dream, however, what was I doing choosing John over my kids? Was this the right decision? Would I lose my children in the process of gaining a man? My children and I were very close. Would doing this drive a wedge between us? I believed in John enough, however, to not only do it, but feel that one day the kids would understand and come around to him.

Balboa Island was the ideal location for John and me to live together one day. If I was going to seriously consider marrying the guy, I needed to live with him first—just not immediately. My children would have flipped out—and totally disowned me—had he moved in right away. That I couldn't live with. The beachfront house, however, solved two problems in my life at the time: one, I needed to be on my own, not living with my daughter; and two, my life with John, however it proceeded and however I managed it, needed to be private. John would spend just about every night at the new house, of course, but my plan was for him to move his belongings into the beachfront house slowly. As far as I could tell, he didn't have much stuff, anyway. A point I asked him about one night.

"Most of my belongings were stolen, Debbie."

"Really?" I said.

He explained that it had happened while he was overseas.

"I'm so sorry, John."

As we discussed the beachfront house, I told John one night, "I want to put your name on the lease." I had not yet finalized the lease.

"Can't do that," he said.

"Why?"

"Tax issues. It'll just cause us problems."

"He's hiding something," Liz said angrily when I told her about the lease a few days later. Ben, my nephew, was there. "He's not who he says he is," Ben said.

Meanwhile, I traveled to Vegas a lot for work at the time, so I could see Terra with almost as much frequency as I'd seen her when she lived in Irvine. Our first conversation about John, as the relationship turned serious, was an honest one.

"I'm dating someone, and I really like him, but Liz can't stand him."

"Typical Liz."

Terra called Liz right after we got off the phone.

"Listen, Terra, he's a scumbag. I have this really bad feeling about the guy. He does strange shit. Looking around the apartment at Mom's art and asking me about the safe and . . ."

"Really?" Terra said. She wanted to develop her own opinion of John, so she listened to Liz with a bit of skepticism.

Terra had her dogs, went to church, and listened to country music. She'd had a somewhat carefree life growing up. I'd made sure of it. Terra was extremely pretty—blonde, green-eyed, curvy, and petite—but her beauty extended beyond her looks. And if anyone doubted how important Terra's dedication to Jesus Christ and her faith was, all he or she needed to do was look at her foot, where Psalm 23 was tattooed:

The Lord is my shepherd, I lack nothing.
He makes me lie down in green pastures,
he leads me beside quiet waters, he refreshes my soul.
He guides me along the right paths for his name's sake.
Even though I walk through the darkest valley,
I will fear no evil, for you are with me;
your rod and your staff, they comfort me.

Terra is an avid hiker with a gentle demeanor, but don't let her size or manner fool you: she is a firecracker. Terra met her boyfriend *Tony* at a pet store outside Vegas, where they worked and lived. Both fans of *The Walking Dead*, they formed a bond through their mutual love of animals and the series. Terra suffered from a lot of stomach issues. The pain was brutal at times. She also suffered from PTSD, due to a previous boyfriend who was a methamphetamine addict. He had driven a car into her, purposely striking her, and she had been banged up badly. And while Tony became what Terra called her "safe person" and made her feel comfortable and protected, he was often out of town for work, which caused even more stress at times.

Respectful and open, Terra would give anybody a chance, which she definitely got from me, and try her darnedest to withhold judgment. But she was also especially protective of me, particularly when it pertained to men.

"Mom," she had said more than once about a man I dated, "he goes to church with you. He claims to be Christian, and yet he's obviously going through the motions and lost during the church service. He doesn't get involved or have a personal relationship with God. He's doing it all to manipulate you."

I'd shrug off comments like that.

My daughter doesn't know what she's talking about.

Terra and I chatted by phone before she left Vegas to come visit for Thanksgiving.

"Why is a guy like John, if he is so great, still single?" she asked. She was worried John was one more in a long line of guys using me for my money.

"I don't know, honey. Why am *I* still single? It's part of life . . . *My* life, I should say."

And even as open as Terra was, I knew that when she arrived for Thanksgiving she'd be scoping John out, looking for what was wrong with him. Not only were Liz's phone calls getting to her, but the one thing that always bothered Terra, as it should have, was how men had manipulated me most of my life. She was on the front line and witnessed a lot of it. The tendency to manipulate, I must admit, was something I overlooked where it pertained to John. As my kids were trying to point this out during my early courtship with him, I routinely pushed it aside and focused on how much love John was showering on me.

But at the time, I thought Terra, Liz, and Ben simply didn't know John like I did. They didn't see how much he cared about me and how he treated me with respect when we were alone. *My children and John will eventually like each other*, I kept convincing myself. I was engrossed in the loving, funny, smart, and charismatic side of John. I didn't see *any* bad side. He told me his clothes and belongings were stolen. I believed him. He said he owned two houses I couldn't see the inside of because one was rented out and the other was disgusting and dirty due to a roommate and he was embarrassed by it. I believed him.

John had a reasonable answer for everything. Being in love—and believing in love—allows you to accept those answers without question.

I was rebelling, consciously and unconsciously, against my children's constant judgments of the men I had dated. I was determined to do what *I* wanted and prove to them that John was a solid, stand-up guy.

You don't know or understand John like I do.

"You're moving far too fast, Mom," Liz said. "Repeating the same old mistakes you've made. You're acting on your heart, not logically."

I told myself the kids didn't see or want to get to know the day-to-day John Meehan. He treated me better than any of my past husbands ever had. I was certain that if they could only see *how* John loved me, they'd get it.

Thanksgiving was going to be the perfect opportunity for Terra and the rest of the family to get to know John and see for themselves that although he might come across a little odd, he was a good guy overall, with my best interests at heart.

11

A GROWING DIVIDE

John and I started moving into the Balboa beach house the week of Thanksgiving 2014. I felt comfortable and safe around John during that time. He'd worked overtime to convince me of this. He could make me feel as if I were the only woman on the planet. I cannot stress enough how focused he was on me when we were alone. All of us step into a relationship with baggage, obviously. Our childhoods shape the people we are not only in public but also inside the day-to-day bubble of intimate relationships. John began to open up, allowing me to understand why he did some of the odd things he did. As I got closer to him, I felt his quirks and eccentricities were a by-product of his upbringing.

"My father was a playboy," he said one night as we sat outside the beach house, staring at the ocean. "He was really good-looking. He managed a poker club at night and was a lawyer during the day."

John's grandmother's maiden name was Anastasia, and he indicated that his father was connected to organized crime through Albert Anastasia, an alleged crime boss/hit man from the Gambino crime family. John threw the name around like he not only knew Anastasia's descendants but was associated with the current family. I found his stories fascinating.

While we were moving some of John's belongings into the beach house, I came across a certificate John kept in a box. It stated that he was a licensed nurse.

"Why does your diploma say 'nurse,' John?" He walked over. Took it in his hand and stared at it. He was perfectly calm.

"I have an additional doctorate degree somewhere. You have to go through a nursing program to become an anesthesiologist. Thirteen years of higher education at four different colleges, this is part of my educational pedigree." He put the diploma in another box. "I'm a licensed anesthesiologist in several states."

"Oh, my goodness. You've done a lot of schooling."

"I have, Debbie." He leaned over and kissed me. "Now," he said, "when are you going to marry me and make me the happiest guy in the world?"

I smiled.

It was easy to accept any explanation John provided. He'd explain away a predicament I'd bring up, grab me, plant a kiss, and then digress into another subject, which always included marrying me. I fell for it every time.

The growing divide between John and the kids, however, was hard on me. John was angry that Liz and Ben were questioning who he was.

"They say you're not who you say you are," I'd tell John after talking to Liz or Ben.

"Fuck them, Debbie; they know *nothing*!"

It made him livid that they would question his past. I felt torn. Caught directly in the middle. I wanted them all to like one another and give each other a chance. John had issues with my view of Nicole as one of the best human beings on earth. Raising my two older children alone, I made each go to work when they turned sixteen. Ben came to work for me as well. I would have them do different jobs within the company, starting at the bottom. The character they displayed was both admirable and unlike what I had ever seen in children the same age. To give you an example: I would tell them they'd done an excellent job and deserved a raise.

"No need," they'd say.

"You mean you do not want more money?"

"No."

It was gratifying to see their work ethic and integrity blossom. So, when John said negative things about Nicole, like she was being nice only because she wanted my money, I became angry and lashed out at him for not knowing anything about the person he was judging. Growing up Nazarene, I was taught that to judge people was a mortal sin. It made me so mad when John used a broad brush to paint my kids as being considerate only because they wanted my money.

"You're very wrong, John."

"I hope so, Debbie."

With Terra's arrival for the holiday, I worried about a big blowout among John, Liz, Nicole, and Terra (even based on Terra's willingness to give John a chance before making a decision about his character). I didn't want the others to pull Terra any farther over to their side and gang up on John. It would be an ugly argument, with John complaining about spoiled, entitled kids wanting to get hold of my bank account, and the kids telling me John was after my money and lying to me about who he was. I would be forced to take sides. It was unfair and childish of them. They needed to back off and give John the chance to show them who he truly was. *Just spend some time with him, with us, see how he is around me. Notice how caring and loving he is to me.*

The plan was for Terra, her boyfriend Tony, and her dogs to stay at the Balboa oceanfront house with me, especially because the penthouse didn't allow pets. John would stay at his house until Terra left, and then return to the beach house. I told John he couldn't spend the night while they were there.

When Terra arrived a few days before Thanksgiving, we were still moving things from the penthouse to the Balboa beach house. John was outside the penthouse, trying to secure a bed to the roof of my car. He was struggling on his own but, in typical macho male behavior, stubborn about accepting help. Terra's dogs came through the door and immediately began roaming around the penthouse, energetic, nervous, and sniffing.

"They are so anxious," Terra said to Tony.

"I know," he said. "Interesting."

The dogs became even more stirred up as soon as John approached. They acted odd, as though there was something about him they did not like.

John was at least a foot taller than Terra. She looked like a doll next to him.

Terra looked up at John. "Hello."

He only nodded in response. He already had a budding resentment against Terra and my other children. He felt it was him against them. I had told him about their trepidation, distrust, and dislike of him. He hated it.

"We're here to help with the move," Tony offered. He had a cast on his arm but said he could still help. Tony had once worked for me in one of my warehouses. A strong kid, he could assist even with one bad arm.

"I've got it under control," John insisted. He didn't want help. He had wrestled with a queen-size mattress by himself and would not accept the fact that he needed another man to finish the job. "I know what I'm doing." Terra later related that he sounded frustrated, threatening, and bitter.

But more upsetting than John's refusal of help was his avoidance of socializing. He was meeting my daughter and her boyfriend for the first time and all he wanted to do was go back to moving. He had no interest in trying to disprove what they thought of him.

"Is this guy actually for real?" Tony asked as we watched John struggle with the mattress.

That night, I took John, Terra, and Tony out to dinner. I thought it would be a good opportunity for Terra and John to talk and get to know each other.

As we ordered food, Terra and John started a conversation. I listened and liked the way it sounded. Terra was doing her thing of interviewing a guy I was dating.

The restaurant was jam-packed. It was loud, but I could hear them.

"You're a doctor, right, John?" Terra asked.

"I am," John said.

Terra described stomach issues she had been living with for quite some time.

"I think you're dealing with an ovarian cyst," John suggested. He seemed to be in a good mood. Guarded, but talkative. "That's what it sounds like to me."

Terra told me after dinner that night that she considered John to be "really smart and knowledgeable" about medical issues. I was so happy to hear he'd impressed her in that regard. This was further evidence to me that Liz had not given John a chance. Terra was judging him based on what she felt after spending time with him.

That said, there was something about John that still rubbed Terra the wrong way, and she didn't trust him completely. (Plus, later, when Terra went to an ob-gyn, the doctor told her, "It's not an ovarian cyst, for sure." Tests revealed she had a stomach ulcer.)

And, to make matters worse, later that first night, Terra came out of the bathroom and made a beeline toward me. She was yelling. She had found a few shirts, John's toothbrush, his shampoo, and some additional hygiene products.

"Why does John have some of his stuff in the bathroom? You told me he wasn't moving in. You guys have known each other what, two months?"

John heard Terra scream at me and made his way into the bedroom.

"Hey, hey, hey! Don't you raise your voice to your mother like that," he told Terra. "That's disrespectful."

Terra started crying—and screaming at me even louder.

This shocked me. I had never heard Terra yell like this. Part of me was embarrassed; a bigger part of me was hurt. It didn't make sense to me that she was so upset by a toothbrush, a few shirts, and some other nonessentials.

"What do you want from me, honey?" I said finally, defending myself. I turned to John. "I got this. Thanks." He walked out of the room. "Terra, I love the guy. He loves me. He does spend nights here. He just left those things, but we're not at a stage where he's moving in here right now."

The Balboa house was a short distance from the penthouse. The day before Thanksgiving, while I was at work, Liz took a walk on Balboa Island—there was a boardwalk just nearby—to check up on things because she knew John was spending most of his days there when not working. Terra and Tony were out and about, visiting family and friends. I understand now that Liz was looking out for her mother when she walked over to see what John was up to when no one was around. This was something Liz would start doing routinely. I can truthfully say that by then John and Liz hated each other.

"I walked by and there he was, on the couch, playing *Call of Duty* on your seventy-one-inch plasma television, which I assume he does all day long," she called to tell me. The house was all windows, right on the boardwalk. So she could easily—even stealthily—check things out without going into the house. "If he is a doctor, why the hell is he home like that?"

"Let me handle it, Liz. John's different, but he loves me like no other man has. You just are not getting it. He works so much. He's not allowed a break like everyone else?"

I was kind of appalled by Liz's call and her "spying" on John, looking for something wrong. So the guy was sprawled on the couch playing a video game. John was a kid at heart. This behavior fit his character, actually.

"He looks like a loser, Mom," Liz said. "He looks homeless. He creeps me out. His scrubs are always dirty. And why the hell does he wear them all the time?"

It's true. John did not have lots of clothes, and the clothes he had were old and worn out. After Liz brought up the issue, I asked him why he wore his old, dirty scrubs every day.

He claimed his entire wardrobe had been stolen while he was in Iraq. Feeling sorry for him, I took him to Brooks Brothers and bought him an entire new wardrobe, most of which he never wore. Instead, he opted for those scrubs all the time.

"Get over it," I told Liz. "He is perfect and makes me happy."

Terra made a point to get to know John as best she could while she was in town. She told me he would talk about serious things, that he'd come across as informative and knowledgeable, but she noticed that he never looked her directly in the eye when he spoke. To the point of it being weird.

He would give her short answers, never elaborating on what he said. She had to ask a lot of questions to get to know anything about him.

I had to agree. John asked many questions about me, the kids, my family. Probing questions. But it felt as though he was reluctant to share much about himself.

"Why is he using your cars all the time, Mom?" Terra asked me.

I told her that John's belongings had been stolen while he was in Iraq. I left out no details John had passed along.

"There's something not right about that story, Mom," Terra said.

I didn't see it. I took John at his word. Why wouldn't I?

On that same day before Thanksgiving, after I got home from work, Terra was helping me unpack. I had planned a nice family holiday. Liz, Terra, Nicole and her husband and kids, Brandon and his family, Ben, my mother, John, and me. I fantasized about sitting around the table having pleasant family chatter, passing the food, everyone happy and laughing. My kids smiling. The grandkids playing. John proving to everyone that he was a stand-up guy. I call it a fantasy because it was easy to dream of the perfect family, the same one I'd always thought I had myself as a child.

As Terra and I unpacked boxes, she confessed that she had returned for the holiday because she'd had serious concerns about John. She was worried I was in over my head. That he had ulterior motives.

Terra had gone to my hairdresser while she was in town. I had sent John to her for a haircut before the cancer benefit. The hairdresser had told Terra that she had met John and had reservations about him.

"There is something off with that guy," the hairdresser had told Terra. "I do not think he is genuine."

Terra confided that she had a sinking feeling John was high on drugs.

John had issues with his back and his arm. He would often go to the ER for pain management. I didn't think much of it other than that John was doing what he needed to do to take care of himself. The guy was a doctor. He said he'd been going to the ER for many years, especially after returning from Iraq. The injuries were all related to his time overseas.

John had actually gone to the hospital while Terra was visiting. And when he came back, she said, "He was just so . . . happy. I had not seen him like that since arriving. He was different, Mom."

I knew Terra had lots of friends who were frequent flyers in hospitals, so she knew how people doctor-shopped for pills. I was naïve about drugs. I never did drugs, and didn't think I had ever been around people who used drugs. I had no foundation for how people behaved when high. So it was easy for John to hide what was, I found out later, an addiction to Adderall, OxyContin, and Ambien.

I asked Terra what had made her take such notice of John's ER visit.

"It was how John had complained about his arm and the description he gave," she said.

"Elaborate, please," I said.

"I had friends with arm issues and theirs were related to shoving drugs into their veins," Terra explained.

As we continued to unpack boxes and talk, Terra and I stood inside a doorway. John and Tony, Terra's boyfriend, were off somewhere else inside the house.

"Honey, why are you having all these concerns about John? I thought you were getting to know him. What's going on with you?"

Terra could sense the frustration in my voice: *Why are you and your sister giving me such a hard time about this?*

I felt Liz had been poisoning Terra. Not allowing her little sister to make up her own mind. Liz was on a mission, I felt then, to prove John was a charlatan, a cad who was using me. I grew concerned that Liz would embellish stories to make her argument more concrete.

"Mom, I just don't know," Terra said honestly. I know my daughter and she is earnest. "There's something bigger going on here with him."

We talked for about five minutes and Terra concluded her concerns. She made me stand and listen, telling me things she thought I needed to hear. Most of what she said is a blur today because I was a bit manic, protecting John at any cost. Wanting to be the parent and wanting to be with the man I was falling deeply in love with.

As we talked, John came up behind me. I could instantly tell he was angry. Apparently, he'd been around the corner listening to the entire conversation.

"Hey, listen to me, you little shit," he said to Terra. "You just want her all to yourself. You won't give me a chance. I know what's going on here. You and Liz, you don't want to see your mother happy . . ."

As soon as John opened his mouth to speak, Terra lost it. She yelled as loud as she could at John.

John reacted with reserve, reiterating how entitled my kids were. How they were repeating behaviors I had explained to him and getting between me and any man I dated.

"Terra, please stop yelling," I said. She was getting angrier and louder.

After Terra went at John for about five minutes, she packed her stuff, grabbed the dogs and Tony, and started toward the door.

"I'm leaving!"

"I do think it's best you stay somewhere else," I said as she walked out. I was so hurt and shocked by how she yelled at John and me.

Sometime later that night, after going over it in my mind, I called her. "Listen, Terra, I don't think it's a good idea for you to come for Thanksgiving tomorrow." It was a difficult decision.

The entire situation turned even more chaotic from there. John ranted all night about Liz and Terra. He said he didn't want either of them over to the house anymore. I got a sense he didn't even want me to see them. I was so torn. John was my boyfriend. My life, really, by this time. My daughters were adults. In his view, they were acting childish. It broke my heart.

Soon after I hung up with Terra, she called back, yelling, "How can you choose him over me? What is going on with you? You're going to choose *him* over *me*? I thought holidays were about family, not boyfriends."

A therapist I sometimes consulted with over the phone had told me to set boundaries with my kids. It would help us all. Part of me believed this was what I was doing.

Terra stayed away from our holiday dinner.

Liz showed up, but not to eat or mingle. She was there to tell me off.

"What the heck, Mom . . . this guy is not who you think he is." John looked on. "Why are you doing this to us? Something is not right. Then you go and disinvite Terra? And you text me and tell me to kill myself? Do I even know you anymore?"

I was shocked. Apparently, the night before, Liz had received several texts from my phone. I say "my phone" because I didn't write the texts. One of them included "Kill yourself . . ."

My kids were smart enough to know that I would never talk to them in that manner, nor would I ever suggest such a thing. Liz felt John had taken my phone and sent the texts, then deleted the conversation. She was wrapped up in her anger. I, on the other hand, saw chaos. The situation was out of control: John and the kids despised each other. To me, all the dissension was based on John's and the kids' refusal to get along and the kids' disapproval of any guy I dated.

When Terra and Liz were told they weren't welcome for Thanksgiving, they felt John was driving it all and I was going along with him. He had, in fact, told me he'd appreciate their not coming over. It forced me to choose. My therapist had also told me the kids could not treat me any way they wanted. I had started talking to her before meeting John because I was interested in how to have a healthy relationship and choose a healthy man.

My mother, who had no problems with me dating John, later told me how impressed by John she was after spending time with him on Thanksgiving.

"He was very, very nice," she said. "The one thing I noticed was how he was dressed, however. Very tacky. The guy never dressed up. We would always dress for the occasion. It was a special day. And he was there looking pretty sloppy. Looking at him, my first impression was, well, the guy works hard and it's okay for him to dress the way he wants to on his days off."

"Terra and Liz do not like him, Mom."

"I think he's a great guy," my mother told me during the dinner. "He's very nice and courteous and kind."

The day after Thanksgiving, Terra returned to Vegas. We didn't speak for some time. We'd never fought like that before. She'd never raised her voice to me. I could tell she felt strongly about John. As December came, I hoped what had happened at Thanksgiving would be forgotten as Christmas approached. Maybe we could all get along and spend this special time of year together.

The situation among us all, however, was about to get far worse.

12

THE BULLY PULPIT

I felt Billy premeditated the murder and got away with it, but I had mixed emotions. I disliked what he had done; he had caused us all so much hurt and pain. But did I hate him? No. Also, Billy's boys loved their father, and I couldn't decide whether him being in their lives was something that the boys needed or not. I was hoping Billy would make it up to them somehow, or at least try to, by being there for them and loving them dearly. Whether or not he actually did, I still don't know.

As 1987 came, and Billy would soon be released from prison, it became hard for me to fathom that my mother and father still had a relationship with this murderer. Mom had visited Billy in prison and talked about how she expected us to accept the fact that when he was released, he would be invited to family get-togethers and parties. We were to help Billy renew his relationship with his children.

Imagine: the man who had killed their mother was going to be given a second chance to have a relationship with her children. This, to me, seemed beyond just forgiving Billy. It was as if we were rewarding him. None of it felt right.

The Nazarene faith pushes the idea that the Holy Spirit acting as God's Spirit can transform us into being more like Christ. Living a sin-free life is a pillar of the faith. Disobedience to God is an ultimate sin. My mother and father took this belief to an extreme level regarding the man who murdered their daughter, and yet they hadn't done that, for the most part, with

Cindi when she was a teen, struggling to be accepted and carving out her own place in the world.

My life, without Cindi to lean on for support, was in a free fall as I worried about the day Billy would be released from prison.

In 1985, Billy had pled guilty to voluntary manslaughter and was sentenced to five years, yet in the summer of 1987 (when I was thirty-two years old), after spending just two years and nine months in prison, Billy was released.

Of course, he showed up at my parents' house not long after and was warmly accepted back into the fold. I didn't understand it then, and likely never will. I can explain this only by saying my parents were dedicated to living in the shadow of Christ, regardless of what anyone else believed or thought of them.

My dad was one of the best men you could ever know. He had learned he had cancer a year after my sister was murdered. At the time Billy was released, Dad was struggling healthwise but insisted nobody know about it. My dad was someone who helped people on a daily basis. He was told all the time, "You have the gift of love." Every day he made a difference in someone's life. I still get emails from people telling me how he had touched their lives. I understand how this contrasts with the way he treated Cindi. Yet I can only state the facts about my life. Some of it still doesn't make sense to me.

On the day Billy was released, my parents opened their arms to him. My parents' assertion that it was okay for the man who had murdered their daughter to step back into our lives after serving less than three years held a hidden message for me. I understand this now. Those types of experiences set us up in life. They rewire our brains to think differently. Although what my parents did was not malicious or something they set out to do in order to confuse or traumatize me, this was yet another instance when I felt I wasn't enough. It led to the gradual deflation of my self-esteem. I was their only daughter now. But *still* not enough.

I went through the motions of being okay with the situation so as not to upset my parents; I had been conditioned to be obedient in that way. But

I felt inside that Billy's early release was wrong on so many different levels, and unjust. I was also scared of this man.

"Debbie!" Billy said, walking into the house, approaching me. Billy and I had gotten along before the problems within my sister's marriage and the abuse came to light. At one time, I had even considered myself his "little sister." And he had seemed to love and embrace that aspect of our relationship.

A once skinny guy who hadn't been too tough upon entering prison, Billy showed up after prison looking very different. He was buff and had put on twenty-five or more pounds of prison muscle. Oddly enough, he also had a tan, as if he'd spent the past three years vacationing in the Caribbean.

He walked over and hugged me. I could smell him. An acrid, musty aroma of the outdoors, unappealing and foreign. This man was a stranger to me.

"Let me look at you," Billy said. "I've missed you, and everyone, so, so much."

He acted as if he'd headed off to war and come back to a hero's welcome. He'd committed a calculated murder and, boom, just like that, thirty-three months later, he was standing in my parents' living room, hugging me, smiling, celebrating his release. People wonder how I was able to get involved with abusive men, marry guys who would later turn out to be entirely different from what they projected during courtship. This is one reason: My parents didn't teach me to have boundaries with people. They promoted forgiveness and love at *any* cost.

Walking around the house, Billy did this weird thing. He began to point out items—knickknacks and the like—and say, "That is mine. That one over there is mine. This one, here, that is mine, too."

I looked down at the carpet, not knowing how to react or what to say. My sister's killer was walking around the house, as if taunting me, throwing what he had done in my face.

Then, "I want them all back."

"Sure, Billy," I said.

What else was there to say to that?

As he sauntered about the room, I felt as though we were in one of those movies where the bully comes back to town and subtly intimidates everyone who played a part in sending him away; the room was filled with this unspoken and unacknowledged hostility, thick as humidity. Billy was running through a mental Rolodex of who had supported him, who hadn't, and how each of us had acted toward him throughout the past three years.

I had reason to be angry. I had spent thousands of dollars on his children and had been there every day for them while he was serving time in prison for killing their mother, and now he was walking around the house claiming ownership of cheap knickknacks.

One item he came upon, a small rabbit figurine, was worth more to me than maybe anything else in that house. Billy knew this. Cindi had collected figurines, and that one in particular had been her favorite. Before Billy had been released, I'd walk over to it and think of my sister. How this cheap piece of ceramic had made her feel so warm. As time passed and I accepted my sister's death, I'd smile at the memories it brought.

"I especially want *that* one back," Billy said, standing by it, smirking, running a finger over its contours like some cartoonish villain in a James Bond film. He knew this would break my heart—and intimidate me.

Billy sat down on the sofa and slapped the cushion next to him. "Sit down, Debbie. Let's catch up."

I sat.

"You know what I miss most?" Billy said. He didn't look at me. Grinning, he drifted off and stared into the air. "Women! I want you to take me to meet women, Debbie. Where is the hot spot to go these days?"

"Um, I don't know, Billy . . . the Red Onion, maybe."

"Let's do it. Tonight."

Where is your concern, remorse, regret, sorrow? Repentance? What about your kids? You haven't even asked about them.

Stepping into my role as Miss People Pleaser, I said, "Okay, Billy, I can take you there."

We went out. I watched the man who killed my sister try to pick women up for several hours before I told him I was ill and had to go home.

I stayed as far away from Billy as I possibly could and ran into him from time to time over the years. My mother stayed in constant contact. I preferred not to find out any more about him than I needed to know, which was not much. I've heard he had developed cancer in recent years. I also know that one of his children stays in touch with him and the other does not. The relationship with his kids has been challenging, to say the least.

13

THE BREAK-IN

It was a beautiful morning in December. That warm breeze off the water, the sounds of the surf, both were always soothing to me. It made me feel as if everything would eventually be okay. Everyone would come around. We'd be a family. No more fighting. No more finger-pointing at John. No more questions. Just love.

John was pushing marriage on me every day. He was also begging to move into the beach house.

"We need to get married, Debbie. Then your kids will believe my love and my loyalty to you. It's the holidays, the perfect time. Let's just do it."

"I need time, and if I decide to go through with it," I told him repeatedly, "I want a prenup."

I was feeling stressed from the kids' refusal to let me live the life I wanted. They had been extremely critical, although I understand today that they were trying to protect me from myself. Like many people in my situation, I wanted to see what I wanted to see. Love can temper our deepest intuition, which I rely on more these days than I did then. Also, I had no idea the kind of power a controlling partner, whose goals are manipulation and exploitation, could have over a person.

"Fine, fine," I said one day, caving in. The holiday season was in the air. I was in a festive mood. And I was tired of John continuously asking me.

As soon as the words left my mouth, I had a terrible, sick feeling. It felt wrong.

That was my gut speaking.

I wish I had listened.

"You will?" John said, surprised at not hearing the same emphatic no once again.

"Yes, but I do not know when. Soon. I promise. Let me figure it out."

John and I went to church one Sunday in early December. The end of the week was always my day of reflective prayer and reconciliation. I felt being in that building, worshipping, singing, seeing people I knew, was my saving grace—an antidote to all the negative, cantankerous banter around me that the kids were exacerbating. John seemed to be interested in the service and even cried a few times, which made me think at first that he was feeling the power of prayer. I didn't say anything, but I also developed the strangest feeling that he was going through the motions of it all to please me, not because of an inherent devotion to Christ.

When we walked into the house after church, I was stunned to see a woman with wet hair, sitting in one of the wingback chairs by the fireplace. She was gazing out at Newport Harbor through a window, drinking a glass of—oddly—Ovaltine, the open container next to her on the coffee table, while reading a tiny Bible. She did not look at us.

Is this really happening?

I was instantly triggered. Whisked back to when I was almost raped and killed in Cindi's house. My pulse sped up. I started to shake.

John yelled at me, "Go outside and call the police."

"What?"

"Go, Debbie, now . . . do it."

I dashed out the door and dialed 911. After hanging up, I walked back into the house slowly to see what was going on.

When I came around the corner, I saw John first. He had the woman's head pushed onto the countertop in the kitchen. He must have grabbed her out of the chair and muscled her into the other room. He held her hands behind her back.

"What the fuck do you think you're doing?" he said through clenched teeth. "The cops are on the way."

The look on his face. It was not of someone scared or enraged by an intruder. I had a fleeting sense—easily overpowered by my fear within the situation—that John was acting. He seemed compassionate and empathetic while singing and praying in church, and he seemed loving and caring with me, but now he was being violent?

Again my instinct was speaking—and again I was stuffing it down and away, not wanting to face the truth.

I noticed she was wearing my clothes. All white: socks, shoes, sweatpants, shirt.

"John, don't hurt her," I said.

John had the situation under control. So I decided to walk around and see if anything was damaged. I made it into the bedroom and noticed she had used my shower. It was the oddest feeling. Someone had broken into my house to take a shower, eat, drink a glass of Ovaltine, and read a Bible? It felt so surreal.

The police showed up and asked the woman where she lived, what she was doing, and how she had gotten into the house. She spoke very little, saying, "I broke the skylight and jumped onto the bed." Her voice had this flat monotone, and she stared out at no one and nothing in a trancelike state. She wouldn't look at me or John.

One of the officers came over to explain my options.

"I do not want to press charges," I said. John deferred to me since it was my home. But here I was, once again, giving someone a second chance. I felt sorry for her. Her demeanor and overall appearance, in my opinion, suggested she was obviously homeless and bereft of the common conveniences we all take for granted. She clearly suffered from mental illness. I could tell by the way she had responded to questions, her cavalier attitude to what was taking place, and the shallow gaze that indicated she did not comprehend the seriousness of the situation. It broke my heart to think she was wandering the streets, with nowhere to go, nothing to eat, and nowhere to sleep.

"Are you sure about this, Miss Newell?" the officer asked.

"Yes, of course I am."

As the police were taking the woman away, John whispered something to her.

I felt bonded to John after this. He'd rescued me. He'd been there when an intruder came into my home. He'd taken care of the situation without a second thought.

"Thank you, John."

He took me in his arms. "I will always protect you, Debbie. You never have to worry about anything while I am by your side."

I felt secure and comforted. John made me believe there was someone in the world whose focus was on me only. I was his everything. He would move mountains to keep me safe.

After things settled down that night, John and I sat on the couch. My head was on his shoulder. He kissed my temple and said, "We need more security here. I need to stay with you all the time and you can never be alone."

"Did you know her, John?" I blurted out. I just had this feeling. It was that whisper as the cops led her away: *What did he say to her?* I had this sense, based on the way he treated her, that they knew each other somehow, that maybe she had followed him to my home and, learning where he lived, decided it was safe to break in. Perhaps she was someone John had been trying to help. He had told me by then that philanthropy was important to him. He'd lost so many people to drugs and alcohol abuse, and giving back made him feel those losses would never be in vain.

"What? Of course not."

"I didn't think so."

"Debbie, we need to get some security here and we need to do it immediately."

It didn't take much convincing. As much as I empathized with the woman, I felt violated. It's a frightening feeling. That someone could break into your home and go through all your belongings and be there when you walked in. It had happened to me twice in my life. I did not want to know what might happen a third time.

By this time, John was staying at the Balboa beach house several nights a week, though he hadn't moved in officially.

"I need to be here every night. I am moving completely in," he said. "I won't be going to my houses at all. I am going to protect you, Debbie. I will watch the house whenever I leave."

"I agree, John."

He called a security company and had them install cameras throughout the inside and outside of the house, allowing him to make sure I was protected any time I was alone, wherever he was.

"I need to know the love of my life, the reason I am on this earth, is safe. Debbie, need I remind you? A rapist stalked you, took your panties, and then attacked you."

"You're absolutely right, John."

When I first saw the cameras, they seemed a bit overwhelming and invasive. It felt as if someone was always watching me.

"I've been thinking," John said a day after the cameras were installed in the bedroom, in all the hallways, overlooking the front door, and in the living room and kitchen. "I want cameras installed inside the warehouse, too—and in your office, where you keep important papers and your work."

Ambrosia Interior Design had a large warehouse in Irvine, where we stored valuable art, furniture, and other expensive items.

"You think that is necessary, John?"

"You saw what happened here, Debbie. Yes, it is."

"Okay, let's do it."

14

I JUST DIED IN YOUR ARMS TONIGHT

I'd like to be able to say I had some reservations about 24/7 surveillance inside my home and that I did not completely accept the idea that it was being installed for my own good. But the person I used to be was someone who chose to push aside her deepest fears in the face of love. There was this faint hint in the back of my mind signaling that John had set this up for his own reasons—and yet I talked myself out of it and never confronted him with my anxieties, I realize now, because I was afraid the answers would blow my fantasy to bits. I had been taught to push fear to the side and focus on forgiveness whenever a problem with someone arose. This is part of my psychological DNA. John was my opportunity to love again. Call me ignorant. Naïve. Delusional. Ask yourself, *Why did she stay? Why didn't she listen to her kids? Why did she believe John?* Those might be fair questions. I had come from a place where, on the day my sister was murdered—in a premeditated, cold, and callous act of profound evil—my mother was smiling, behaving calmly, and telling us it was all going to be okay. My sister wasn't yet buried, and my mother was already talking about forgiving her killer. That attitude is the foundation of my Christian faith. Am I blaming my mother and father? No. I am only pointing out the blueprint for life they imprinted upon me. We are a product of our upbringing. You could say, even, that despite my childhood, almost in defiance of it, as my gut and questions about John kept bubbling up, it became more and more difficult for me to ignore them. I was valiantly trying to face the truth and overcome my bias at the same time. But the fact remains, in a controlling relationship, the person controlling you works overtime to keep you questioning your own beliefs. Before you know it, you are thinking the way he wants you to—and have no clue that he has brought you to this place.

John continued to ask me to marry him every day, multiple times. "I cannot wait to be married to you. I am *so* in love with you."

"John, please. When I am ready."

I'd bring up how much the kids disliked and distrusted him.

"They're just jealous. They want your money. They're waiting for you to die so they can swoop in and take all of your money." He kept feeding gasoline to the fire between me and my kids.

"That nursing degree, John. I don't understand." This kept bothering me. The certificate I had found. For whatever reason, I could not shake it.

"I have a PhD, which gives me the right to the title of doctor. I have advanced training in anesthesiology."

"I see," I answered. Although I was still questioning these things about John, his consistent charm and casual way of explaining away my doubts became easier to accept. This was John's job: to convince me that all my reservations were in my head.

Just before Christmas, I had some business in Nevada. The idea of slipping away to Vegas, even though I was going to be working, was so welcoming. The storm within my family seemed to be worsening. The only one out of the bunch seemingly on my side was my mother, along with my two best friends. One I worked with, so I could discuss everything with her, and the other one lived in Santa Barbara, so I could pick up the phone and share my frustrations.

"I'll be gone a few days," I told John.

"I'll drive you. I don't want you going alone. I can take some time off and just hang out in the hotel room and watch sports while you work. I actually could use a break from work myself."

"Don't think we're getting married in Vegas, John," I warned him. "It's way too soon."

When we arrived in Vegas, I had to complete a frame walk, which is exactly what it sounds like: a building is in its skeletal stage of being built, which means the framing is up, and a bunch of us walk through to make sure the framing meets my client's specs. John said he'd run errands while I worked.

We kissed.

"Okay, I'll see you later, then."

John dropped me off and left in the Tesla. I assumed he was going back to the hotel to watch sports, get some rest, and then run those errands he'd talked about.

When I returned to our hotel room, I was astonished and overwhelmed by what I saw. Champagne on ice. Flowers all over the room. Rose petals sprinkled about the room like confetti, leading to the dining area.

"John . . . I don't know what to say."

He stood, looking at it all, smiling.

This sort of romantic gesture struck the core of my soul, melting my heart. This was the guy none of my children knew. The tender, caring, thoughtful man who loved me without stipulation or judgment.

"Say you'll marry me, Debbie?"

We sipped champagne in the room for an hour or so. Then we went downstairs to the casino and had a peaceful, romantic dinner. From the moment I walked in the door after a long and tiring day of work, John had transformed the night into pure bliss.

I can be impulsive. Spontaneity sparks something in me. I make some decisions (apart from those involving my business and children) based on emotion rather than logical thinking. I wish I'd thought through some of those decisions more and stuck to my gut feeling that I should wait to marry John. I also still wanted a prenup before we actually made it legal.

My one regret is that I never pursued my increasing ill feelings with any enthusiasm. I allowed John to talk me out of the way I was feeling.

"Come on, Debbie," John said. He moved in closer to me as we finished dinner. "Let's go to the courthouse right now. Make me the happiest man on the face of the earth. What do we have to lose? I want to grow old with you and die in your arms."

John told me that he'd driven straight to the courthouse to get the paperwork for our marriage all set up after he'd dropped me off at work earlier that day.

In that moment, I was taken in by John's romance and boyish innocence. I believed every word he said.

"Okay, let's do it."

The next thing I knew, we were standing in a chapel, holding hands, as the woman in front of us read marriage vows for us to repeat.

When I watch the video of the ceremony, I can see how nervous, yet totally in love, I was. I can understand why people shake their heads and judge me for marrying John after knowing him for only two months, especially with all the issues he and my children were going through. You can tell yourself you'd have done it differently, but nobody really knows what they would do in someone else's shoes.

We got married in a clichéd Vegas wedding chapel (although there was no Elvis impersonator holding the Good Book in front of us) with faded, grimy, whitewashed walls. We stood in front of a trellis covered with fake-looking plastic plants. The ceremony had an impetuous, spur-of-the-moment feeling that I cannot believe I agreed to. I see myself in the video but don't recognize who I was. I was anxious. John beaming. Here I was, at war with my children over John, and marrying the guy. Part of my motivation for marrying John that day was, of course, wanting to make my own choices: *I'll do what I want to do and nobody will tell me differently.* It was the same type of thought Cindi had had when she married Billy—only I hadn't seen it then.

John wore black slacks. His shirt was untucked. He looked as he always did, sloppy and uninterested in presenting himself as the professional he claimed to be. I'd given in to the idea that John was this happy-go-lucky guy who worked long hours and didn't much care to dress like a doctor or made a lot of money. I empathized when John said material things did not interest him.

As John put the ring on my finger, he let out this laugh, as if all of his "work"—the pecking away at my emotions, the daily marriage proposals, the flowers and rose petals and all the favors for my mom—had finally produced results.

"I pronounce you husband and wife. You may kiss your bride."

And just like that, in ten minutes, John Meehan and I were married.

Debbie Meehan. It didn't even sound good.

Before we left the dirty chapel room, I looked at John and said, "I cannot tell anyone. You understand that, right?"

He nodded his head in agreement. "This is our secret until I feel the timing is right."

"I understand, Debbie."

"And one more thing, John: I need a postnup."

"Okay, Debbie. Whatever you need. I am just honored and happy to be your husband."

That postnuptial appointment, which I'd made as soon as we got back to Balboa Island, was canceled. I had to travel once again for work. You know how these things go: *I'll do it when I get back.*

But I never did.

My children rarely liked anyone I dated, so their input mainly went in one ear and out the other. This made it easier to tell myself that if they didn't approve of, or like, John, it was on them. Also, their opinion and advice could be confusing and inconsistent. For example, I dated one guy over whom Liz threw such a fit that I broke it off, because she'd made it nearly impossible for me to date him. I then went to her and explained that we had broken up.

"Oh, darn, I liked him," she said.

Conflicted feelings. Never the same message.

With Nicole, Brandon, and Terra, I could tell if they didn't like a man, but they didn't voice their opinions as loudly or as often as Liz did. They spoke from their heart and generally left the matter alone and allowed me to make my own mistakes.

Even though I did not see the "bad" John for the first five months of our relationship, I was unsure about my decision to marry him. I knew it was not the right thing to do. Call it my intuition kicking in, or whatever you want. Something had been telling me to hold off. Going through with the wedding, however, is not something I regret, although many observers might have a hard time accepting this. I know now that John used every manipulative skill in his playbook to get me inside the chapel on that day. I was vulnerable. He had played my kids against me. He had made me feel loved and appreciated beyond belief. I was being controlled. The relationship was never about me.

Aside from my kids claiming John was a charlatan and bad person, my life with him was almost perfect. A small earthquake happens; some people feel it and others don't. I've learned that is the way life works. I can blame my childhood. My previous marriages. The abuse I'd suffered at the hands of men. I can scream ignorance and denial all day long. None of it changes what I did. What happened. Or how I viewed the situation in real time.

About a month prior to meeting John, I had started seeing a therapist specializing in physical, emotional, and internal healing. I did this to make a list of traits I wanted in a man and to understand why I had made such poor choices in men over the years. I also needed help creating healthy boundaries with my children.

"What's missing on your list, Debbie, at least from what I can tell, is kindness," my therapist said to me during one session.

"Kindness?" I asked, confused.

"Yes. Kindness in a man and kindness within the relationships you're having with your kids. You radiate kindness. You're forgiving and caring and empathetic. You are able to comprehend the notion of someone else's pain, feel it, and understand how that person might be suffering."

It all sounded like me. I did feel that way.

"Because you're kind and empathetic, and feel for others, while also seeing the potential for *good* in others, it blocks you from seeing the red flags."

"That's interesting."

"You also trust way too easily. You admit that you're impulsive and that you wear your heart on your sleeve."

"I do, indeed."

In those days after I married John, I spoke to my therapist and told her about the marriage and growing issues with my kids.

"So John was asking and asking, pressuring you to marry him. You had fallen in love with him."

"Yes."

"You wanted to please him, right? Marrying him is the ultimate pleasing gesture."

"That is true."

"Let me ask you about arguments you two have. Tell me about that."

"He wins every argument because he is so persuasive."

We concluded that I hadn't wanted to marry John, but he had worn me down. He saw an opportunity in Vegas and seized upon it. He knew and understood my weaknesses. He knew how to pull directly on my heartstrings and use my vulnerabilities against me.

I thought my children would end up liking John because he loved animals and treated their mom so well.

Despite all that had happened at Thanksgiving and the dire state of my relationship with my kids, I thought, *When they truly get to know John, they'll feel the same as I do.*

I was overwhelmed with anxiety when we returned to Orange County and began our married life. Every time I went to that place in my head—*How am I going to tell the children?*—a voice told me to forget about it and be the parent in the situation. Establish firm boundaries. Speak your truth from a place of love. Demand the respect you deserve. There's an old self-help saying: "Say what you mean, mean what you say, but don't say it mean." This would become my mantra as the Christmas holiday drew near.

I needed to somehow explain to my children that John Meehan was now in their lives, and they would have to deal with it.

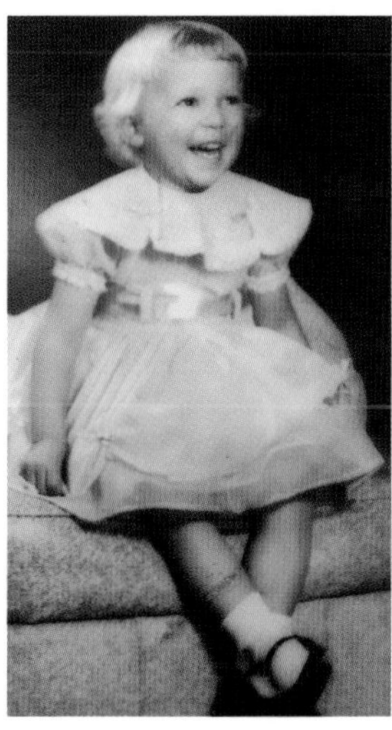

Left: Debra was a happy and seemingly healthy child, although she was born with a severe illness. *Right:* Growing up in the 1960s, Debra Newell, her brother, and her sister lived a quiet, religous life in Southern California.

Left: Debra was close to her sister, Cindi, and looked out for her in many ways. When tragedy struck and Cindi wound up dead, Debra was faced with reevaluating her strict religious upbringing and what God was asking of her. *Right:* Debra; her mother, Arlane; and sister, Cindi, whose own marriage to her high school sweetheart was anything but a fairy tale.

Being raised by God-fearing parents whose marriage, Debra says, was nearly perfect, set the bar rather high for relationships.

Debra with her parents and first husband. Though that marriage ended, Debra still believed the right man was out there for her.

From an early age, Debra's passion in life was design, which she turned into a successful career spanning some forty years.

Debra's two youngest daughters were very concerned about her dating John Meehan.

Narcissist and career con man "Dirty John" Meehan sent this selfie to Debra early into their relationship.

A cancer fundraiser Debra was involved with seemed like an odd place, Debra thought, for "Dr. John" to show up in scrubs.

Debra and John were married in Las Vegas after a business trip.

Debra had always wanted to live on the water, and the oceanfront condo she and John moved into was exactly what she had dreamed of.

Left: Trying to get John as far away from her and her family as she could, Debra purchased a house outside Las Vegas and allowed John to move in. Soon, John trashed the place.

Bottom left: John's manipulation and lies, which Debra began to discover a few months into the romance, were often in the form of handwritten notes he left for her.

Bottom right: After Debra decided to end her relationship with Dirty John Meehan, her favorite vehicle, a Jaguar, was stolen and set on fire.

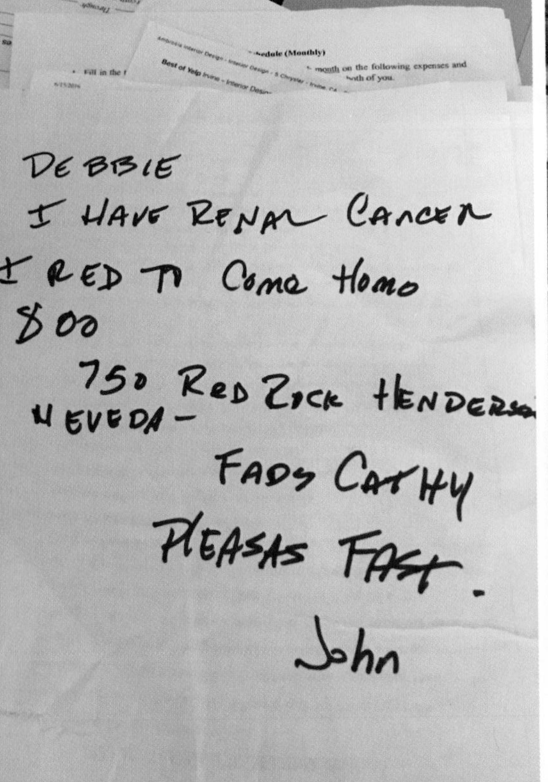

DEBBIE
I HAVE RENAL CANCER
I RED TO COME HOMO
$00
750 RED ROCK HENDERS
NEVEDA -
FADS CATHY
PLEASAS FAST.
John

Top: The apartment rooftop garage parking lot where John attacked Debra's daughter Terra with a knife.

Left: Debra's daughter Terra is a true inspiration: a woman who fought for her life in a parking lot and, despite her petite frame being up against massive John Meehan, walked away with her life. *(Photo courtesy of Terra Newell)*

Debra (*left*) with Laura Richards, a British psychologist and criminal behavioral specialist, who became one of Debra's close friends. Laura, a leading expert, is pushing awareness of coercive control, a domestic violence crime that those being victimized by don't have an understanding of. From almost the moment John Meehan stepped into Debra's life, he utilized his expert coercive control manipulation and skills to gain control of every aspect of Debra's life. *(Photo courtesy of Fiona Corrigan)*

Debra with her and John's golden retriever, Murphy. *(Photo courtesy of Fiona Corrigan)*

15

HURT PEOPLE HURT PEOPLE

I realize I sound as if I have never taken matrimony seriously. I can understand how some readers of this book will perceive this about me and judge. It's okay to judge me in that way; you have a right to. In defense of my life and how I have lived it, however, I need to say that I harbored high expectations for my relationships. I often looked to love as a lifeboat, a rescue option from a previous pain. As far as marriage, I believed my parents set the bar high. I understand now that repeated difficulty in a marriage is associated with a disordered personality. The dissolution of a marriage, frequent discord, and conflict in romantic relationships resulting in termination are certainly central in personality pathology. The fact that I kept trying, however, reflected a need in me. I'm not a quitter. A failed marriage did not sully my feelings toward the foundation of marriage itself. I believed in it—and still do. Because we carry into a marriage so much of who we are and what has made us into the adults we have become, it is fairly common for two people in love not to get along. Codependency is an illness, essentially; so many of us rely on others to make us feel whole and happy. It is easy to say, *Why didn't you see how vile a person he was before marrying him?*

The end of my first marriage had destroyed my dreams about Prince Charming riding into my life to save me. I was left with custody of both children and all the daily responsibility that entails. My children's father saw them every Wednesday and every other weekend.

Between my first and second husband, even after, I dated multimillionaires and actors, successful men who could have given me what I had worked so hard for myself. I modeled in New York for a season. I was asked to be in *Playboy.* I wasn't interested in getting married again. I was enjoying my life. I had even turned down a few proposals. I was finally getting to know who I was, digging deep within myself and, honestly, starting to grow as a person.

In 1986, six years after the divorce, I married my second husband. We had Liz and Terra together, and the marriage lasted twelve years. Because of the time invested in the relationship, its demise destroyed my heart in a far deeper way than in my first divorce. The relationship went bad after three years, but I stayed in it, believing the whole time that we could and would rebuild and repair.

In 2001, I met *Tim.* He was smart, handsome, charming, and conservative. He seemed to embody all the characteristics my previous boyfriends and first husband did not. I was enjoying the dating scene, and when a girlfriend offered to set me up with Tim, I begged off at first. I liked being single, and also didn't really have time for serious dating.

"He's a great guy," my girlfriend insisted.

This occurred after 9/11 had just changed the world. We were all so unsure of what was going to happen, wondering if there was going to be some sort of global implosion with a major war breaking out. We had a sense of being American that I could not recall ever feeling.

"Okay," I told my girlfriend. "I'll meet him."

Tim branded himself a devout Christian. He put me on a pedestal from the moment we met. He gave me the impression that he adored my kids and I was the center of the universe. I'd watch him treat my children as if they were his own. As we dated, I never saw one outward sign that Tim was anything other than the man he portrayed himself to be.

On our first date, Tim talked about his job in high-stakes finance.

"Interesting," I said. "That takes a lot of discipline."

Then he mentioned his wife. "Brain tumor," he told me, referring to how she had died. "It all happened so quickly."

"I'm so sorry."

My empathy, I can see now, has led me down the rabbit hole of believing whatever most men told me. I took people at face value. I was attracted to how Tim was raising his kids after his wife's death. He remarried and—no surprise—had immediate trouble with his new wife. Apparently, his second wife suffered from mental illness. So, when I met him, he was a bit guarded and came off as a kind, gentle soul who had been through tremendous tragedy and loss in a short period of time. What he had experienced was incredibly tough—and would be difficult for anyone. I was taken in by his compassion and love for others. We seemed like a good match.

Over the course of our first few dates, he shared intimate stories about his life and relationships. This told me how vulnerable Tim was. He was unafraid to go within himself and share the worst of what had happened in his life with someone he barely knew.

"He's sensitive and easygoing," I told my girlfriend, thanking her for introducing me to such a wonderful person.

After three months of dating, Tim said, "Will you marry me, Debbie?"

"Yes," I said, without hesitating. "But I want to wait."

If there was one thing I had learned—or so I thought—it was not to rush into anything. I thought I had my impulse to jump in and commit under control. Yet six months later, I gave in and there we were on a cliff, overlooking Dana Point, a breathtaking beach just south of Newport Beach, in Laguna Niguel, reciting our vows in front of friends and family. The sun shone brightly. The water smelled of seaweed and salt. The sand was warm and soft. People were dressed as if we'd had the wedding on an island in the Caribbean. It began as a glamorous, fun, glorious day. Perfect conditions for love and happiness to thrive.

That darn piece of paper, however. I had convinced myself by then that getting married changed things in a positive way. Marriage meant we were committed to each other for life. It was like signing a love contract. Again, I can understand that this sounds pathological. No one, however, was living my life. I had been through so many traumatic experiences that my emotions were stacking up inside my nervous system, without my realizing it.

I always wanted my marriages to be forever, but somehow things would happen that I had no control over—or at least I would realize that staying was so damaging to my children and myself that I chose to protect my children, as painful as it was. Moreover, I believed my parents' marriage was perfect. Yet as I look at it all today, I know that was the fantasy I had built to deal with the truth. I see how my need for love to rescue me was rooted deeply in the love I craved as a child from my parents.

The wedding itself was a portent of my new life; it had the feeling of this strange party to which I hadn't received an invite. Tim spent no time with me after the ceremony. He danced with all the girls who worked for him and hung out with that same crowd during the reception. I felt a disconnect the moment I became his wife. I was under the spell of finding my knight in shining armor. It was magnificent up until the moment—the *exact* moment—we were married.

What in the name of God am I missing here?

As I look back on it, I recall only one incident that might have given me pause about going through with this wedding. I had surgery and couldn't get out of bed. I could barely move. I needed help. I was in a spare bedroom. Alone. Weak and dehydrated. I had beckoned Tim several times one night. Called out his name.

No response.

I managed to gather the strength to get out of bed and walk into our bedroom, where Tim was sound asleep. It was the middle of the night.

In a raspy, parched voice, I said, "Tim, Tim, please, I need your help . . ."

He woke up. Turned over. Looked at me and yelled, "Leave me alone! I'm sleeping." Then he turned around on his side and went back to sleep.

"I'm sorry, I'll manage," I said, walking back to the spare room.

After resting a bit, I walked into the kitchen, grabbed my medication and some water, which was all I had wanted, and went back to bed, riding out the illness alone. I thought about it later and concluded that perhaps I had caught him at a bad time and he was stressed from work. There was always an excuse or reason to overlook instances when a man showed me who he was and treated me poorly.

A few days later, Tim seemed to be back to the man I knew.

"I'm really sorry, Debbie. I hope . . . please . . . I really hope you don't leave me over what happened the other night."

"No, of course not."

We made up. I forgave him.

In retrospect, I know it was a sign of who he was, and I had rejected the truth. He had tried to be perfect, tamped so much of himself down to hide it from me, but it all came out that night in one fell swoop of anger and resentment. Whatever was going on in his life had nothing to do with me. But I was the target.

Hurt people hurt people. Generally speaking, those they hurt are the closest to them. I never really understood this until much later.

Our oceanside wedding should have been romantic and the start of a wondrous life together. He should have been staring into my eyes, enamored. We should have been holding hands, greeting and socializing. We didn't. And I made excuses for him.

Our first night together as a married couple, he came to bed and . . . went right to sleep. We did not have sex.

The next day, he spoke of a need to get home to be with his daughter, who was twenty-two years old at the time. It wasn't that he missed her or she needed help with a problem. To me, it felt like he had this weird desire to just *be* with her. Not to be *there* for her, but *with* her. That relationship, as time progressed, became stranger and stranger to me. He said one night, "I want her to live with us."

"Your adult daughter? She can be on her own. We're newlyweds. We just got married two days ago, Tim."

"I don't care. She is coming to live with us."

He babied her. That first day after our wedding, he wound up spending the entire day and night with his daughter at the house he owned, where she lived. The plan was for him to move into my home and for her to take over his home. But the impression he gave me was: *If you want to live with me, she is going to be living with us, too, or you'll have to live alone.* But again, none of this was obvious or even gave me second thoughts before we were married.

I called him that day, after he had left the house early in the morning, merely hours, mind you, after we were married. "Why not spend the day with me?"

"No, I am spending the day with her . . ."

"Um, okay. But we just got married."

"I know that, Debbie. But I want to be with my daughter."

He finally came home on the day we left for Canada on our honeymoon.

"I need to get home," he said a day after landing in Canada. "She needs me."

He was fixated on getting back as soon as possible to run to her. I found it beyond odd. It bothered me. I couldn't help but think, *He's different. He's cold and withdrawn. Not the person I knew before we were married.*

I could not believe the disparity. How much he had changed. He became this other person, who, I would soon learn in a very direct and hurtful way, was the man he had been all along.

It was as if I had seen signs of it leading up to our wedding but had chosen to overlook them for another chance at love.

16

SILENT NIGHT, HOLY HELL

That December of 2014, about three months into my relationship with John, who was now my husband, turned into one of the most stressful holiday seasons I can recall. Every holiday season was special for our family. My children, mom, and grandchildren looked forward to spending time together. We tried to make the holidays as classically American as possible. In the weeks before Christmas that year, I explained to my girls that if there was going to be drama over John, it was probably better that they didn't come. It hurt me because—if they chose not to—it would be the first year we would be apart during Christmas. It would not be the same. I was in so much pain wondering what the girls were going to do, especially when I did not hear back from them right away. It broke my heart, even as I believed I was taking care of myself. My family was supposed to be around me, sharing and celebrating all we were thankful for. I was in tears most days, thinking it wasn't going to happen.

This had not been a hasty decision on my part. I had discussed it with my therapist before telling the children how I felt.

"Love yourself and set boundaries," my therapist suggested.

Setting a boundary was a new concept for me. Something I had a hard time learning. We think we set limits with people in our lives and express our needs, but to stick to that plan is another thing altogether.

"Set some rules," my therapist said. "You have the right to do this. If they're going to come over, they have to be invited over. They can't just show up without calling first. You have a right to hang up on them or ask them to leave if they're going to yell at you."

I had never viewed my relationship with my children in this regard. Remember, my children had been through the same hell I had with my previous husbands and boyfriends, so there was guilt involved, reminding me that I owed them—that I should be their friend, not their mother.

"Tell them you deserve happiness, just like they do."

"It sounds so easy."

"Yes, Debbie. Explain that you are not going to be treated like you have been."

And during a session with Terra, we agreed to maintain boundaries where John was concerned. Terra wanted to see her nieces and nephews. She wanted to be around family. She did not want anything to do with John.

Our relationships are a manifestation of our past. Our brains become deeply rooted—wired—in former relationships. The self-doubt, a current flowing through that wiring, forces us—if we don't do the work and implement change—to look at the worst of ourselves. We project all those bad emotions onto others. We judge our partners and believe they are judging us. Our belief system about ourselves becomes distorted. We end up mired in codependency without realizing how deep we are in the muck. Recognizing this takes time, therapy, and difficult, deep emotional work. To become our best selves, we need to let the past go and believe we deserve the best. We need to stop looking at new relationships through the lens of old ones. All of this seems rather straightforward—heck, maybe even simple—to do. Few of us are able to put it all into play, however. I wasn't anywhere near that point then.

I'd rush home and tell John about any session I had with my therapist, outlining the advice she had given and what she had encouraged me to do.

Smiling, John would say, "I agree with her. She's 100 percent right. Take control of your life, Debbie. Right now, the girls are controlling you."

On Christmas Day, at my oldest daughter's house, Liz did ultimately show up. But she left as soon as John and I arrived, visibly angry. She was amazed that I was standing behind my decision to choose John over her and her sister.

Terra showed up some time after Liz had stormed out. She began talking about moving back into town one day. She was having issues with her boyfriend. Terra had fought to be taken seriously in their relationship. She also questioned her own feelings—was she being excessively sensitive and allowing the situation with John to affect her too deeply? I see now that I should have been more of a mother to her and empathetic, realizing not every human being responds to the same situation in the same way. John was clearly influencing the decisions I'd made and driving my reactions to the kids.

As far as anyone at Christmas knew, John was still my boyfriend. No one had any idea we were married. If they knew, it would have injected an entirely new level of contention between the kids and me.

I had gone out and bought all these presents for my grandchildren. John walked in with all of them and engaged with the kids immediately.

After arriving, Terra did not say much. She sat there watching John handing out the gifts. What upset her, she told me later, was that John acted as if he had bought the presents and that he sat down on the floor with the kids and helped open them. Terra claimed that she and I had discussed, specifically, that John wouldn't even be around the kids or play with them. She told me this had greatly offended and hurt her.

The way I recall Christmas Day is different. John sat at the dining table by himself, and the children came up to him. He was especially good with the children. There was a playful side to John that my grandchildren brought out. I found it endearing.

At one point, Terra started crying.

"Terra," I said, walking over, "you need to handle this. You don't have to hang out near John. Just go sit in the other room."

We *had* agreed on this during therapy, but I said, "What am I supposed to do? He's sitting right there. I can't make the kids not talk to or play with him. You just have to let it go."

Terra then moved to another room, away from the party. We could hear her crying. My mother sat and spoke to her.

"I just want to leave," Terra said to her grandmother.

"This is terrible," my mother answered. "All of our family meeting for Christmas and you're just sitting here, shaking and crying? You need to stop overreacting. Just enjoy the day and everyone else here."

Terra had terrible insecurity about the situation. She said later that she had felt as if "everyone was rolling their eyes" at her. She had a reputation in the family for being overemotional.

I didn't know this until later, but my mother had a longer conversation with Terra that afternoon.

"What's going on, honey?" my mother asked.

"It's him," Terra said. "John."

"What about John, honey?"

"I don't like him. There's something about him. I don't like him."

Meanwhile, the conversations I had with Liz during this time were volatile. She yelled at me almost every time I talked to her. Usually, something like "Mom, I don't care what you say. John isn't who he says he is. You are *not* seeing it."

Liz could not have been more astute or correct in her observations. But I couldn't or wouldn't believe any of it was true, especially because Liz had not liked or approved of any man I ever dated or married. Besides, I *had* married the guy. I *loved* him.

A tiny part of me had hoped I could announce that day that John and I had gotten married, but what should have been a time of peace and joy turned into an emotional fiasco. John, for what it's worth, didn't act in kind. He didn't get into an argument with the kids or become angry. He acted like an adult, while they acted, well, like children. John even played the "I'm sorry" card, which only made me love him more. For all his character defects, John could frost the charm over things as if he'd baked the cake. And I was falling hard for his suave way of making me feel like the only woman on the planet.

17

IMPOSTOR

Tim had put on some sort of show while we dated. It became clear on our honeymoon that the person I had married was not even close to the person who had wooed and tricked me into that marriage. I use the word *tricked* because it is accurate. If someone misrepresents himself, lies, and puts on a display of emotional and committed love in order to get what he wants, it is a trick, a manipulation. I own my part in falling for it all, be it from Tim or any other man I allowed into my life. I was fooled and didn't see the red flags because he—and the rest of them—hid them very well. They were so smooth that anyone would have fallen for their charm, good looks, success, and mind games. My biggest regret is that my naïveté and codependency allowed victimizers to infiltrate the lives of my children.

As we visited different places on our honeymoon, Tim displayed an impatience and an abusive nature I had never seen, except for that one instance while I was ill. He became critical and mean-spirited.

"Come on, Debbie, hurry up, you're not walking fast enough," Tim said more than once while we were in Canada. The incident that sticks out to me most occurred as we were checking into the hotel. I carried all our luggage as Tim walked in through the doors empty-handed, with mirrored shades and a swagger to boot, as if he were some rock star

"Tim, I could use some help here, please . . ."

"Don't talk now, I need silence," he demanded.

What have I done?

I was so upset that I decided I couldn't stay in a bad marriage, as I had done in the past. Tim should have been adoring me. We had just been married. Instead, I'm carrying our luggage wherever we go, and he is belittling me at every opportunity, in a constant state of irritation with anything I do.

How could I not see this? Why do these men show me love, win me over, and then abandon that caring personality and become monsters? It must be me.

Throughout our honeymoon, Tim didn't want to have sex. I had to compel him to consummate our marriage—and it was quick, uneventful, and loveless, and, honestly, made me feel as though I was forcing myself on him.

And here's the thing: we had decided to wait until marriage. Tim and I had refrained from sex.

This is what I have been waiting *for?* I thought after finally consummating the marriage for all of two minutes.

"This marriage," he said one day, "will be all about you making me happy. Do not forget that—ever!"

Most of our honeymoon Tim spent getting massages and playing golf.

"You should be happy about that," he said when I questioned it.

"I'd like to be spending our honeymoon with you. Making love. Doing all the things couples do on their honeymoon."

"Debbie, listen to me: you should be happy for me. I am doing what *I* want to do. You'll learn as time goes on to support this. Because this is how it's *always* going to be."

I spent our honeymoon crying, disappointed, and scared. I had not felt this alone in years.

Not again . . . please, Lord. What is the lesson You are trying to teach me? These guys start out so great and then this . . . what am I doing wrong?

Evaluating why I had been choosing these types of men, I focused on how perfect they all seemed during the courtship period of the relationship. I know now that this behavior is called love bombing. In a very sobering 2021 article in *Cosmopolitan* magazine, Lauren L'Amie writes: "Love bombing is characterized by excessive attention, admiration, and affection with the goal to make the recipient feel dependent and obligated to that person." Love bombing is a symptom of narcissistic personality disorder, and in many cases it is unconscious behavior. The high for the victimizer comes within the "getting the other person" period. Once the love bomber has the other person, according to Ami Kaplan, a psychotherapist quoted in L'Amie's article, "the narcissist typically switches and becomes very difficult, abusive, and manipulative." The narcissist shifts his or her behavior from idealization to devaluation. To give a bit of context for how real this phenomenon is, the term love bombing was first used to describe what cult leaders do to potential members.

With my first husband, I had waited nine months before agreeing to marry him. With Tim, I waited six months. Was that not long enough? Why was I making such poor choices regarding the time we dated before marrying? Would these guys have carried on with their charade for two years if I had waited that long?

The answer is likely no. I would have gotten through the preliminary stage and seen glimpses of who they truly were.

One day during my honeymoon with Tim, at the front desk of the hotel in earshot of several people, he made a demand.

"I want a massage. And I want you to find me a girl, and I want her to be very attractive and young."

I called one of my girlfriends back home as he was getting his massage with a young girl who, I should say, eerily resembled his daughter.

"I made a terrible mistake," I told my girlfriend. "This is not right."

That marriage was over before the honeymoon ended. I decided in Canada that I was going to annul the marriage when we returned. There was no way I could make a life with a guy who, after I had spent our honeymoon following him around on a golf course, shushed me anytime I started to say something, not to mention Tim's additional abusive behaviors.

I spoke up on our honeymoon as we got into a discussion about the relationship. We were on yet another golf course. Tim said, "Quiet, Debbie. You will listen to me. May take a bit, but you'll get it someday."

I walked off the course after a few holes. The one thing he did not ask me to do was carry his golf clubs, which I might have expected now while reevaluating it all.

I wasn't going to wait nine years to divorce him, as I had with my second husband, or even four-plus years, as I had in my first marriage.

When we got home, I dove into my work. I wanted an out, a release from this stranger I had married, a man I clearly did not know.

Tim called me at work one evening after we had settled in back home. Although I had already decided to end the nightmare, I had not told him yet.

"Where are you?" he said.

"Oh, I'm still at work. But the kids are with their father, so I am going to work a little later tonight. How are you?"

He ignored my comment. Instead, he said in this cold, stoic voice, "What. Is. For. Dinner?"

"Oh," I said, caught off guard. "I don't know. What would you like?"

"I *said*, 'What is for dinner,' Debbie?"

"I don't know." I thought for a minute. Then I added, "You didn't work all day; maybe you can come up with something?"

"You get home right now and you make me dinner."

"I'll be right home," I said. This was the first week after the honeymoon.

That first Friday night at home we spent married, I decided to have one of my granddaughters over to the house. She was two years old. My son, Brandon, was going to the gym to work out and would be gone about two hours. I was in the living room with her. Playing. Tim walked in the door and stopped, stood over us, and stared.

"You did not ask my permission for her to come over."

"Permission? She's my granddaughter."

"You are to ask me always. I might have made plans for us."

"You didn't, though."

He stepped closer. Put his finger in my face. "You are to ask for *my* permission from now on."

Everything I did was wrong. If I walked in the door and did not go greet him first before doing anything else, he scolded me. But he didn't just lash out. He'd grab me by the arm, march me upstairs, sit me down, and proceed to tell me off for fifteen minutes.

Even after all this, I decided not to annul the marriage right away. I don't understand why entirely, but I can say that I didn't want another failed marriage. Who does? Maybe part of me thought Tim might be struck by lightning and change back into the man I had first met. I put up with it for about eight months. We separated. He moved out. I thought maybe the divorce would be amicable. Yet, as work picked up and we spent time apart, it took me two years before I dredged up the nerve to file. By this time, it was clear Tim was obsessed with me. He'd sit in front of my building, in his car, about three parking spaces down from where I'd park, and watch me for hours. I'd leave the building and he'd follow me.

His response to my filing for divorce? To come after me for all my money. At the time, I had about forty employees. Business was booming. We had been together as man and wife for almost three-quarters of a year. I waited two years before filing. It was 2006, and a recession was soon to upend the American economy.

Divorce proceedings took four years. He outlasted me and won.

Tim was awarded $658,000, on top of $200,000 for all his attorneys' fees.

The timing was devastating. The perfect storm of personal and business implosion. The recession began. In total, I lost $7 million after the recession settled in. I had been building four businesses for two decades, working day and night. My companies had about $550,000 in overhead each month.

All of it was now gone.

I wasn't living beyond my means. I had a nice home, nice cars. But that was it. My focus was my work, which was where I lost myself and time seemed to cease. What hurt me more than anything was having to lay off all the great people I employed.

After the divorce was finalized, I did what I had always done when faced with adversity and failure: I cried, felt sorry for myself, and fell into depression for a time—but then, after living with those feelings long enough, I got back to work.

As I was building the business back into a fraction of what it once was, Tim levied my bank accounts and garnished any wages to take all he could from me. At the time, I was having difficulty keeping up with payments to him. I understood, for a brief moment, that he had likely sought me out, married me, and treated me like I did not matter in order to push me away so he could take my money. Yet it was not something I dwelt on. I did not look at people as inherently bad in this way, which is probably one of my biggest character defects.

I spent years building the business back up. I diversified my business this time: a moving company, a dress store, a furniture store, and, of course, the interior design end of it all. And despite what all my previous husbands had done to me and the losses I suffered, I would get married once again to another man I was about to meet. That fourth husband and all the ones before him, however, were nothing compared with John Meehan, who would make all of them combined seem like Boy Scouts. My losses in love should have prepared me for what was coming. Yet, in retrospect, I could never have predicted what was about to happen.

18

DISCREPANCIES

Terra and Liz were united in their desire not to have a relationship with me if John was in my life. We had just spent what was one of the worst holiday seasons I could recall, save for that first year Cindi was gone. Out of spite more than anything else, I dug my heels in: my girls were not going to control my life. I was going to love whomever I wanted and they would have to accept it or live with the consequences. Maybe John, who was on his best behavior at this point, was right? Perhaps the girls did not want any competition for my attention or money?

In January 2015, without my knowledge, Nicole's husband, Scotti, after talking it over with Nicole, Liz, and Ben, hired a private investigator to probe into John's life. They were determined to show me who John Meehan truly was and why I should cut him out of my life.

Meanwhile, I started to see a different person slowly emerge in my new husband. For one, I started noticing subtle discrepancies in the stories John had been telling me about his life.

"Three years," John said one night as we sat and watched television.

"I thought you said five years?"

John was referring to how long he'd lived in Newport Beach.

"I said three, Debbie! You're wrong."

He was so convincing that I wrote it off as a memory lapse due to aging.

Then we got to talking about his desert home in Palm Springs. I had this image, based on what he'd said, of a beautiful adobe home in the desert, surrounded by plenty of land and space. A perfectly manicured structure of light pink stucco, with posh landscaping and perfect cacti growing around the yard. But as John told me more about it one night, he painted a picture of a mobile home in a trailer park. Not that it made any difference to me, but the two versions of his home were so different from each other, I wondered what he was talking about.

"Look, Debbie, you're confused. I do not know why you are all of a sudden questioning what I told you. It's your damn daughters fucking with your mind, mixing you all up. They'll ruin us if you let them. I won't stand for this. Why are you interrogating me?"

"John, that's not what I am doing. I am just pointing out the differences in what you've said. It's okay. My mistake."

"The fifteen months I spent in Iraq were awful, Debbie," John said while we were out eating dinner one night in late January. "One of the worst times of my life."

I was sipping wine; I'll never forget the moment. As he casually said "fifteen months," the number struck me.

Fifteen months? I knew he had said something else previously. Who would forget the amount of time he spent inside the theater of war?

Several weeks before this, John had told me he'd been in Iraq for twelve months. It was eighteen months when I first met him.

"Fifteen months you were there, John?" I asked.

"Yeah . . . it was horrible. Like I told you, I had to kill five people."

"No, John, you left that detail out. You killed *five* people in the line of duty?"

How was it that a doctor, working for Doctors Without Borders, had been put in a position to kill five people inside a war zone? Was John now telling me he was Rambo?

"I've *told* you this," he responded, getting louder. "Five people! I don't want to talk about it any more than that. Why is it you are questioning me on everything I tell you?" He threw his napkin down on his plate and stood. Then leaned over the table. "Those fucking kids of yours are manipulating you to the point that you don't know what the fuck is up or down. I won't fucking stand for it anymore. This is bullshit."

He walked away from the table.

Ten minutes later, he was back.

"Is that when you injured your ankle?" I asked. I recalled that he had told me he busted up his ankle in a helicopter crash in Iraq, which was one of his excuses for going to the ER from time to time. That and his back pain.

"No, Debbie, I never said that. I hurt my ankle in a basketball game. Can we just eat and not talk about all this bullshit that your kids are bringing up and poisoning your mind with?"

Another detail I had heard incorrectly, apparently. The list of inconsistencies was adding up. I was beginning to think John was lying about certain things. I was scared to confront him about it.

John had moved into the beach house gradually, so I never figured out how little the guy owned. It wasn't as if he'd shown up one day with a truck full of his belongings after a trip to his house.

"I'll just grab whatever when I'm over there," he'd say, referring to his houses and storage unit. "Move things in a little at a time."

"Sure, John."

I didn't think anything of this. Why would I?

John had always talked about several luxury vehicles he owned, all of which, he claimed, had been stolen while he was in Iraq.

"Why don't you just buy another car?" I asked one day. It was now February, and he was still driving my Tesla.

"All of my money is tied up in stocks and in a trust fund for my kids, Debbie. You know this. How many times have I told you?"

The fact was, he had never mentioned this before. As it was, I paid for almost everything: his clothes, his rent, and any other expenses we incurred throughout our day. John paid for food, which made me feel as though he had some money. But he also had a litany of excuses for why his money was not readily available.

"How much do you have tied up, John?"

He shrugged. Turned his head and looked away. "Nine hundred thousand dollars or thereabouts."

"What?"

"Yeah, tell me about it."

In the coming weeks, he changed that amount and told me it was more in the neighborhood of $1.5 million.

"Why aren't you working?" I asked him.

John had not worked for the past several months. He'd leave the house and be gone, but I knew he wasn't going to work. I'd come home to a messy house and empty cartons of takeout and realize he had spent the day in front of our television playing video games.

"I need to renew my anesthesiology license, Debbie," John said when I pressed him about working.

"Well, why aren't you doing it? You need to work, John."

"I'm enjoying a little break here. I've been working sixteen-hour days for the past several years. Can't I take some time off? Do I need to kill myself working so much?"

I did not realize the behavior I noticed was a symptom of drug use, mainly because I had never been around people who were using drugs, but John acted differently at times, slurring his words, walking lethargically. Then he would snap out of it and appear normal.

It sounds naïve, especially as I look back, but I did not think at the time that John was hiding anything major or lying to me about anything big. He was isolating me from my children and anybody else who could possibly help me understand that everything he was telling me was a lie. He was an expert manipulator. I was easily swayed by John's constant demonstrations of love and affection. He worked doubly hard at it, especially after I questioned something he had said or done. More than that, I craved this sort of attention. John, you must understand at this stage of our lives together, was the solution to all of my relationship failures. A companion I had yearned for since childhood. He made me feel special in a way no other man ever had. In John, I saw none of the bad attributes my previous husbands had exhibited. I thought I was on guard for such faults and would notice immediately if another soul sucker walked into my life. Unbeknownst to me, however, John was building trust—while alienating me from my family—so as to gain access to every aspect of my life; this was his job, essentially.

What he was doing to me he had done to countless other women for over twenty years.

And my ride with John had not even begun yet.

During February 2015, whenever I was at work, John was home, rummaging through all my belongings, gaining access to my bank accounts, and taking notes about my personal life: my Social Security number; passwords; and retirement, savings, and checking account numbers. He was planning, it seems, the largest takedown of his life. I was his target.

As John formulated a complete profile of my life, those discrepancies in his stories were beginning to affect me. I could not shake off or deny certain variations in his stories. One does not mix up the amount of money one has in stocks and a trust by hundreds of thousands of dollars.

"Liz and Terra are using you for your money—why are you not seeing this?" John said every other day, if not several times a day.

I began to think he might be right.

"I don't know, John . . . my kids are not like that."

"Debbie, listen to me: you are too close to see it. I see it clearly. They are *using* you."

"Are you sure, John?"

"I am going to help, though. I am going to show you how to take care of your finances. I'm going to help you take care of your money." He walked over. Put his arms around me. Kissed me on the top of my head and hugged me. "I love you, Debbie. I'm your husband. I am here to help, not hurt, you. You need to accept that. I am not the threat here. Your children are making me out to be someone I am not."

"I love you, too, John."

After those conversations, I was always left feeling frustrated and confused.

19

HE HAS A KNIFE

After the Tim ordeal, I jumped back into the dating pool. This was just as talk about the imminent Great Recession was buzzing and America was struggling. Not only had Tim drained me of all my money, but for a long time I had trouble functioning emotionally. I did not think I could meet anyone more manipulative and abusive than Tim. Marrying him taught me to put up a shield around my heart. To protect it at all costs and not get into a serious relationship without first knowing the person inside and out.

I wasn't about to actively go out looking for love. I wanted it to find me. If it didn't, I was content being on my own.

On a plane heading to a business meeting one day in Sacramento, I happened to sit next to what seemed like an intelligent, kind, caring gentleman, *David*.

"Chemist," David said, initiating the conversation. "Water purifying is my specialty."

"Really," I responded, shaking his hand. "Good to meet you. Interior design."

David and I struck up a conversation and talked for the entire flight. There was a spark. We had a lot in common, along with an intense attraction. I should have known then and there to put the brakes on.

Walking out of the airport, I gave him my phone number.

As I sat in back of a taxi, heading to my destination, I thought, *That was okay. He seems nice.*

I didn't put much more thought into the possibility that such a chance meeting would turn into anything romantic. He seemed like a sweet guy. But if love was going to come at me again, it would have to grab me by the lapels and shake me into believing it was genuine and possible. The man would have to be more than special. I was scared of love but not opposed to it.

David called and called. I didn't respond for several weeks. I was apprehensive, I guess.

After thinking about it, I decided I wasn't in a good space to date anyone. It had been two years since Tim had totally destroyed me, but it had taken so long to get over how badly I was manipulated, controlled, and burned that I thought waiting a bit more would make me stronger.

"Yes, I'll go out with you," I finally agreed after the chemist called a few more times. It was as if I had no control over this part of me. My gut and heart said no, but I went ahead and said yes anyway. What was a dinner and some conversation with a guy I had gotten along with on a plane?

David wined and dined me. He was incredible to my kids. Thoughtful. Easygoing. The relationship wasn't difficult. It wasn't work. Any man I was with needed to be a role model to my kids. Whenever I started liking someone, that image of a happy family took over. The house. The Sunday dinners. The vacations. The nights watching television, talking, enjoying one another's company. I fantasized about the perfect American dream at the end of it. I believed. I didn't see those dark storm clouds approaching—I saw only sunlight and smelled the freshness in the air after the storm. Call what I was going through a personality flaw, or something I knew deep down but consciously rejected. All of this, however, is who I am. People will judge me. They will say I did not learn from past mistakes. That I was inviting all of this into my life. That I made poor choices.

All of that is unfair and untrue. I was victimized. Chosen and preyed upon, actually. It would take me several husbands and almost forty-five years to fully understand, but a behavior pattern called coercive control works in ways that the victim is completely unaware of. Those who are expert manipulators and controllers work hard at making you believe what happened is your fault. That you asked for it. Take a look at my life up to this point. Would anyone go out looking for the abuse and trauma I had endured?

David became a welcoming, warm breeze. He was fun to be around. Happy all the time. He didn't have any children, which was something I liked. I had my own kids. I had also seen how my previous husband allowed his child to influence our life together. A guy's having kids was not a deal breaker, but a guy's *not* having them was a plus.

We were getting along exceptionally well. Better than I could recall in any other relationship I'd been involved in for over a decade.

David was a big guy: six feet, four inches tall and 225 pounds of solid muscle. He played football. Within a few months we were living together in Orange County. Some nights he would come home after getting into violent fights on the field. He'd have bruises, cuts, or black eyes. I began to hear from people who knew him that he had a hair-trigger temper during games. He'd snap for no apparent reason. I wrote it off as his involvement with an aggressive, violent sport.

Six months after our first date, he was asking me to marry him.

And I was thinking about it, even though I did not want to be married again. It had been five years since my last marriage ended so bitterly and, frankly, expensively. I wanted to have fun in a relationship. Marriage, in my experience, could take the fun out of any relationship.

"I've waited my entire life for the perfect woman," he'd tell me. "That's you, Debbie."

I ate this up.

It seems beyond comprehension now, but after six months of the chemist being the nicest guy I'd met in quite a while, I felt we were madly in love. I caved and agreed to marry him.

I know you must be saying to yourself at this point: *What is wrong with this woman? Why is she jumping into marriages, one after the other, so quickly?* I realize those are fair questions. I was a sucker for that euphoric stage of falling in love at the beginning of a hot romance. When everything seems perfect and your feelings are intense and strong. I felt like it could stay like that forever, each and every time.

We had a small ceremony, and just like that, I was married to my fourth husband.

As in several past relationships, a different person emerged almost as soon as we had rings on our fingers. Hate me. Judge me, as I have said. Tell me I am suffering from personality disorders and marriage is my drug. This is my story. I own it. Every bit of what happened.

In David's case, it was a deep-seated rage issue I noticed after we were married. It was as if he now felt comfortable expressing this part of himself around me and my kids. But not toward us at this point. I noticed that when we were outside our home, his explosive anger would come out of nowhere. After we were married, a switch had flipped. I saw his temper, which I hadn't seen in any way before. Maybe it wasn't in our lives while we were dating, and maybe it was, but suddenly it appeared to be a prominent fixture.

David, Liz, Terra, and I went to the supermarket one day. It was crowded in the parking lot because it was near the holidays. By now I had built my company back up after Tim had tapped every bit he could, and I had money coming in once again. My kids were almost grown by this point; they were heading off to college and doing well. Things seemed to be okay.

Driving through the supermarket parking lot, with cars everywhere and people walking in and out of the store, I sensed my husband was becoming impatient. The anger was something, up till this point, I viewed as a part of him he kept confined to the football field. I never viewed it as something that might creep into our lives. I know now that rage is not an attribute one can shut down under certain circumstances and turn on during others; it is always there, percolating.

David pulled up near a parking spot. Put on his blinker. Facing us was another car, an elderly man driving. The old man had his eye on the same spot. It didn't seem like he was stealing it from my husband. I don't think he even saw us. Being as old as he was, the guy deserved the space out of respect, anyway.

After the old guy took the spot, David found another in the next row. It wasn't a big deal. He parked and we got out of the car.

As we headed toward the entrance of the supermarket, my husband said, "Debbie, honey, I'll be right back."

I wondered where he was going but didn't think anything of it. Maybe he had forgotten his wallet in the vehicle and had gone back for it.

"We'll meet you inside—find us, honey," I responded.

"Yeah, no problem."

My husband arrived after five minutes and seemed fine. We had a casual, peaceful shopping experience.

When we walked out of the store, several police cruisers were parked out front.

"What's going on here?" I said out loud to no one in particular.

A patrol officer walked up to us and asked my husband his name.

He told them.

"Please come with us, sir," the cop said.

They took him aside and began talking to him. Next thing I knew, they were cuffing him and placing him into the back seat of a patrol car.

Apparently, he had not gone back to our vehicle to get something he had forgotten. Instead, once we were inside the store, my husband walked over to the old man's car, took out a key or something hard and sharp, and proceeded to scrape up the man's vehicle from one side to the other. He then caught up to us inside the store.

I was grateful he had not beaten the poor old man senseless. That was the silver lining in the situation. But to me, what he had done seemed scary. He said nothing. He never ranted and raved about the old man. To the contrary, he walked over to his car calmly and destroyed it before finding us and shopping as if nothing had happened. Without visible anger or anything said.

What if I wronged him? What if I took something he didn't want me to? Worse, what if one of my kids did something he didn't like?

I began to live in fear.

As the months went by, things got worse. There was a van parked near our home for about two weeks, just sitting there. Someone had abandoned it, obviously. My husband would get livid about things like this. So he went out there one night and spray-painted the entire van.

Then I lent Liz's boyfriend, *Jeremy*, money to buy a car. Three months went by. He wasn't paying me back on the schedule to which we had agreed. I didn't care, actually. I was helping somebody out. He'd pay me back when he could. I wasn't worried about it. I'd been married to the football-playing chemist about eight months. By now we were living separate lives in the same house. He'd go out four or five nights a week. I'd do my own thing, working, seeing friends. It was not a marriage. Our sex life was nonexistent. *I'll deal with this*, I kept telling myself. *I'll work things out.* The last thing I wanted to do was go through another divorce.

Liz, Jeremy, and I were home one night. Sitting around, laughing, talking. A normal night. My husband walked in. He didn't say anything. Instead, he stepped in front of Jeremy, grabbed him by the neck, and began punching him in the face.

My daughter and I screamed. I jumped up and tried to pull him off. Liz kicked and hit him.

"Stop . . . stop . . . stop!" Liz yelled. She was all of a hundred pounds at the time. Five feet, two inches tall.

David continued to pummel Jeremy.

Blood spattered everywhere as my husband continually thrashed him in the face.

At one point, Jeremy managed to slip away and run into the kitchen.

Moments later, he came out with a butcher knife, like the hero in a horror film during the final showdown. Jeremy was prepared now to protect himself.

"Please, no, no, no," I yelled. "For me. Do not do this."

Jeremy had every right to defend himself. But I couldn't fathom any further escalation of this type of violence. Liz was crying, screaming for it all to end. My adrenaline was flowing and my heart was pumping vigorously. Anxiety was nearly crippling me.

"No, please," I said again, pleading. "You don't have to do this."

Jeremy stared at Liz and me for a moment, then looked at my husband.

Fearless, my husband had this look on his face: *Come on, try it. I'll kill you.*

"Do not do this," I said.

Jeremy looked at me, then at my husband. I could tell he was considering an attack.

"Just leave the house," I said. "Go. I'll call the police. It'll be okay."

He was bleeding so badly. His cut and bruised face had swelled up. Blood covered his shirt. He was missing a tooth.

Liz took her phone and threw it at my husband. Hit him. That seemed to break up the standoff and the intensity of the moment.

We ran toward the door that led out of the apartment.

As we got closer, my husband lunged at Liz, picked her up, and threw her. She landed against a wall.

He did this three times.

It was as if he had picked up a mannequin and tossed it across the room. Each time, she screamed out in pain.

I grabbed her by the arms and helped her out of the house.

I called the police.

They arrived shortly after and arrested my husband.

Of course, the marriage was beyond repair. I could not put my children in jeopardy of ever being victimized by his rage again. I felt their lives, and mine, were at stake.

A month went by, and we had not had any contact until he called me one summer day.

"What are we going to do?" he asked. "We cannot be in limbo here."

He happened to be in Florida working. Not having him around gave us all a bit of solace. The distance helped us cope with what had happened. He could have killed Liz and her boyfriend. This was clear to us in that room and, later, when we took Jeremy to the hospital, where we learned how badly he had been hurt.

I flew down to Florida to talk to him in person about moving forward with divorce proceedings. I did not feel as if meeting with him was going to put me in any danger. Despite what I had witnessed, he had never given me the impression he would ever hurt me personally. This, I know today, was a mistake in judgment on my part. Yet I knew nothing about domestic violence then, or the psychology behind abusers. I relied mainly on my own feelings.

"I'm here to talk, per your suggestion," I said when I found him at a trade show he was working. He knew I was coming. We had made plans to meet and get the divorce process started in order to finish it as quickly as possible.

"Well, I am working right now. And later, I am taking some friends out to dinner, so you will have to wait."

"I really need to talk to you if we're moving forward with a divorce," I said later that night, meeting him inside the hotel restaurant. He was with a friend. They were drinking.

He looked at me and shrugged.

"I need to know what you want to do—I want to move forward with a divorce. You need to talk to me."

"My friend is having problems. He needs me."

I walked away.

He found me. Furious, he said, "How dare you be so insensitive to my friend's needs when he's having problems."

"I came here to discuss us. I'm leaving tomorrow. It's Terra's birthday. I need to be with her."

He grabbed hold of me and backed me up against the wall. I was terrified.

Looking directly in my eyes, he hit me.

I went down instantly, my head throbbing and bruised.

I pulled myself up and ran to my room, checked out, and waited at the airport until I could find a flight. What alarmed me about the entire situation was how I had put myself in a position to be abused. I knew he was violent. Why had I allowed myself to be alone with him?

No matter how devastated I was after a relationship ended, I had never fallen out of love with the fairy tale. I continually believed it was possible. Part of my problem, I realized later, after my marriage to John Meehan fell apart and I was able to accept serious mental health help, was being so ill during my childhood. Everything I had learned about love was from books and my belief that my parents had a perfect marriage and we had a perfect life. My parents would tell me how strong I was. How wonderful our lives were. Whereas most people take being alive and waking up every day for granted, I truly believed life was a gift. I knew what it was like to wake up and feel as if any day could be my last. That alone had given me a sense of living life to the fullest.

The other part of this pattern is that there are predators who prey on the vulnerable. I had money. Maybe even a *V* for victim tattooed on my forehead that only very bad men could see. There are men all over the world who hunt for victims like me. They will travel from anywhere to anywhere to manipulate and control and scam women. Many of the men I ultimately married knew I was gullible. It made me vulnerable to exploitation and influence. Being someone who wanted to see the best in people—whether I met up with good or evil—was not something I could stuff away and disregard. It is at the core of my soul.

I did not have my football player husband arrested for hitting me. I divorced him in 2011, not long after that incident. He got nothing from me. It was a victory and, I believed, one more lesson in love.

I told myself, *Never again.* I was done with marriage.

Not long after, I heard David was close to being homeless. A guy like him ultimately will alienate everyone around him because he cannot control his temper and rage, unless he gets help. After we divorced, he came to me. I gave him $10,000 and a job. He lost his temper on the job one day. I went out to the warehouse and told him he needed to leave and that I never wanted to see him again.

Second chances, whenever I gave them, always seemed to come back to burn me.

20

PRIVATE EYES ARE WATCHING YOU

John knew I was disciplined when it came to saving money. He also knew I had put away $1,000 from every paycheck I had ever paid myself for years. I had about $80,000 in cash I kept in a safe inside our beach house, plus more cash stashed elsewhere in the house. Over the course of several weeks in February 2015, as we began our married life in the beach house, I managed to add another $20,000 to the safe for a total of $100,000 in cash there. No one in my family knew yet that John and I were married. It was my secret.

As John spent his days soaking up and writing down all he could about my life, along with the kids' lives, I worked nonstop. I'd pull my head out of the sand of my demanding job and, for a fleeting moment, think about how many inconsistencies were popping up in John's life story.

In late February, after John and I discussed the danger of all that cash lying around, I decided to let John take that $100,000, ten banded bundles of $10,000 each, and several pieces of jewelry worth tens of thousands of dollars I had stored in my home safe, and bring it to the bank. I was scared of having that much money inside the house. John had suggested many times that it was not smart leaving that much cash lying around.

"I'll open a safety deposit box," he suggested. "You should not keep that type of money here in the house. You saw how easy it was for that homeless woman to get in."

I thought about it. "Sure, John, thank you."

He was good about doing things for me. Servicing the cars, shopping, bringing me lunch and having dinner ready. He was also helping my mother. I believed at this point that John had good intentions. I saw his character flaws as quirks. We all have them. Up until this point, he had not done anything that would have led me to believe that my life—and that of my children—was in any danger.

I was rarely talking to or seeing Liz and Terra. John had done a good job of alienating them from me—as part of his master plan, I now understand. I felt guilty whenever the kids and I met up outside the house and John didn't know. I was betraying my husband—and my daughters.

John opened a safety deposit box at Chase Bank in Newport Beach. He put it in his name only.

"Here is my passport, Debbie," John said two days after opening the safety deposit box. "You go down to the bank, put this and your passport into the box, and sign your name on the account."

These were the subtle things John did that made me trust him and not question his genuineness. If he wanted me to go down to the bank and put my name on the account, after admitting that only his name was on it, this showed honesty.

I went to the bank and added my name to the account. The bank manager followed me to the vault where the box was located and watched me open it.

I looked inside.

There was cash in the box, but definitely far less than I had given John.

Driving back home, thinking how I would approach John about what I had discovered, I convinced myself there was some sort of mistake or misunderstanding. Maybe I hadn't given him the entire amount? Had he opened two safety deposit boxes? I wasn't overly concerned. We were married. John was a doctor. He had a trust fund worth $1 million. What would he want with $20,000?

When I got home, I asked John about the money.

"I took some of the cash out and put it in a safety deposit box I have in the desert."

"Why, John?"

"I have IRS problems, Debbie. I don't want them to levy your money. We're married. They could come after it."

"I'm not sure they could do that, John."

"I'll put it back, then."

A few days later, he told me the cash was back in the original safety deposit box. I explained that maybe the safety deposit box wasn't the best place for it. The bank would be better. Now that we were married, however, the government could come after my money, too.

"Just make sure you take it all out of the safety deposit box so they cannot get it," John said. "If it's in the bank, there's a record of it. Let's keep it somewhere else."

We shared an office at the beach house. I grabbed the cash from the bank deposit box and put it back inside the safe inside our home office.

In early March, I was working from home one afternoon. John was out somewhere running errands. As I was looking for a work file, I came across a piece of paper on the floor inside a closet. It had John's name on it.

"When I was incarcerated . . ." the letter began.

John had signed it.

It was the first time I had any inkling that John had been in prison. This was sobering and alarming because John had made a point to tell me, without being asked, that he had never spent a day in jail.

"Not one night in the clinker, Debbie," he had said jokingly.

"Well, that's good to know, honey."

We had laughed.

I read the letter further and realized John had done *hard time.* It made me suspicious of all those other details in his stories I was questioning. I took a photograph of the letter. I dug deeper into a box John had hidden in the back of the office closet and found several diplomas. As I was reading them, I heard him pull up. So I snapped photos of them and other documents and put them back quickly.

Before he walked in, I placed that small safe we had with the cash and jewelry inside a bag, then put the bag in a suitcase. My plan was to take it out of the house without John knowing. It was the first time it hit me that John Meehan might be scamming me.

"I need to go to the office for a while and work," I said immediately when I saw him. "A few things have come up."

He walked over and kissed me. "Okay, I'm going to lie down for a bit. I'm not feeling well."

I took the suitcase, got into my car, and headed off to the bank, where I had a second account, in my name only, with cash assets in the neighborhood of $130,000, which I had accrued before marrying John.

John texted me when I got to the office.

"Was there someone in the house you need to tell me about?"

I didn't respond.

Then, "Now I understand."

I still didn't respond.

"What's his name?" John asked.

I was scared and confused. What was he talking about?

About nine minutes later, John texted, "You missed the other camera I had put in."

Missed the other camera?

As I said, after that "homeless" woman had broken in, John had insisted on installing security cameras. He had an app on his phone so he could monitor the house when he wasn't around. What I didn't know was that he had installed additional, hidden cameras to watch me.

I drove over to the penthouse where Liz was still living. I took the money in the suitcase with me. I had not counted any of it yet.

"What's going on?" Liz asked.

I didn't want to tell her. I just asked her to leave me alone right then and told her I would explain everything when I could.

"John, right?" she said. "What did he do now?"

I sat and counted the cash.

I must have counted wrong. So I counted again.

Then a stunning realization: $56,000. A total of $44,000 was missing from the $100,000 John had said he returned. I knew then, sitting and thinking about it, that I had been a fool to believe what this man had been telling me. John was not the person he had purported himself to be. I had married a stranger. My kids, hard as it was for me to admit, had been right all along.

I said nothing more to Liz. Money can always be replaced. What John would soon take from us, however, we could never get back. And what I was about to learn about him—well, the lies he had told up until then would pale in comparison.

21

MURDER BY MAIL

Although fall is by far my favorite season, spring in Orange County is a pleasant second. Perfect temperatures. Sunshine and blue skies. Warm, soothing breezes, both day and night. The ocean is bathwater warm. There are not a lot of interlopers or tourists around. It's a time for those who live there to enjoy the beauty God has allowed them to be lucky enough to experience. I was grateful for what I had every day, even while John seemed to be disrupting my life, exposing who he was a bit more as each day passed. Regardless of the toxic situation, I never overlooked, or took for granted, the blessings in my life: healthy children and grandchildren, the opportunity to run my own business, friends, and family. Despite the journey I had been on, with Cindi's murder and so many disappointing relationships and marriages, I woke up positive about life on most days. How could I not? God had given me—literally—a second chance to live and had blessed me with so much. I was not going to look God in the eye and complain about problems along the way. This thing going on with John, was it another brick in the wall of my life? Perhaps I had John all wrong. Maybe he was genuine and all of these circumstances—the note about prison, the cameras, the discrepancies in his stories—were my own anxiety manifesting into paranoia. Was I worrying too much? Overthinking it all?

"Did you borrow any cash from my wallet?" I said during a call to Liz one day. I thought maybe she had swung by the office and, not finding me, had taken money out of my purse. This was not her normal behavior, by any means, but any time she borrowed money, she paid me back. It wasn't as if I thought she'd stolen from me.

"No," she said.

Accusing Liz of taking cash crossed a boundary—and she was absolutely justified in her anger. Although I didn't think she had stolen from me, I was upset that she might have taken cash without asking. John was working hard at embedding in my mind the question of whether the kids were focused on my money.

"Well, I am missing some cash and thought maybe you swung by. It's okay."

"Mom, please. You need to keep a better eye on your money. You think I went out of my way to stop at the office and borrow money from you without asking? Maybe it's the loser you're dating. How many places have you gone today—it could be anybody. But you call *me*? Accuse *me*?"

The one absolute Liz pointed out was that I routinely failed to see the danger in situations and overtrusted people around me, giving most people the benefit of the doubt—that is, except where my children were concerned. Although I was becoming more curious, perhaps even suspicious, about what John had told me about himself, I had been shocked to learn that he had been incarcerated. Yet I still did not want to believe my husband—not just someone I was dating, as Liz had said during the call—was stealing from me. Or that he was a pathological liar.

I hung up with Liz, thinking I had misplaced the money or spent it.

By now, John was leaving the house in the Tesla every morning, dressed in his scrubs. I assumed he was heading to work for the day. I was glad he was working again.

"I hate him, Mom. Hate him!" Liz said the next time we talked.

"Well, I am sorry you feel that way, Liz."

"Let me ask you: What is he doing when he leaves the house in the morning with your car?"

"Going to work, honey, come on. I don't know where, exactly, but he puts on his scrubs and he goes off to work. He travels to different clinics and hospitals."

"Are you sure about that?"

"Yes."

"Okay, then, would you mind if I put a GPS tracker on your car to find out where he is actually going?"

I thought about this. At any other time, I would have said no. It's a violation of privacy. But certain things John was doing at home had begun to gnaw at me. I was questioning him, without telling anyone. Plus, I wanted to prove to Liz, Terra, and Nicole that they were wrong about John.

"Sure," I said. "You put a tracker on my car if you need to put a tracker on my car, Liz."

"Okay."

After John had sent me that text about another camera in the house, I called him.

"I saw you remove the box," John said.

"What?"

"The box."

He explained that at first he'd thought I was an intruder who had broken in and taken the safe.

Again, this was one more way John talked himself out of what could have turned into an accusation. He was an expert at explaining things away and making me believe him.

Later that day, while John was out, I called Ben, my nephew. I knew from what Liz had been saying that Ben had taken a strong interest in trying to convince me that John was a con man, a dangerous person I should remove from my life. Ben was always looking out for me, and we were close.

"He's not who you think he is, Aunt Debbie. I have this feeling. I know people who are like him. Liz does, too."

So as March was in full swing, I decided to do a little digging myself into John's life, especially after speaking with Ben and Liz. On several different occasions toward the end of March, I found a few boxes of papers inside the house belonging to John—which told only part of his life story.

First off, John Meehan was never a medical doctor. Although he had been a nurse anesthetist at one time, I found out he had not had a license in years to even practice nursing. This shook me up when I saw it in black and white in front of me. Understand that a lot of what I found out about John was uncovered over a lengthy period of time. This was not an information dump, falling into place all at once, on the same day. From experience, I can say that when instinct speaks, listen. We all know when something doesn't feel right. In my case, my mind pushed that internal instinct aside and tricked me into thinking I was overreacting or worrying too much. Yet those sinking feelings—when a visceral response to a situation, or to something a lover or friend says, cannot be dispelled by thinking it away—should never be ignored.

One document I found scared me. In 2002, John had been found guilty in Michigan of assaulting a police officer. Finding this information sent me online to look even deeper into who John Michael Meehan actually was and what else he'd done. Each new revelation numbed me. But none of it, as it would turn out, was enough in the moment for me to turn my back on John completely. He was my husband. A lot of hurtful things people have said about me and my life with John fail to take into account that I loved and felt compassion for him. There was not one time during this period of our lives together when I ever thought my family and I were in danger. Could he be the greatest liar of all time? Yes, I considered that. Was he making up stories about himself? Yes. But I believed then that maybe he was embarrassed about this criminal part of his life. I asked myself continually, *Was John going to physically hurt me or one of my kids*? And not for one minute did I ever think that was possible.

The big piece of John's life I found in mid-March as I was digging through his belongings involved his brother's death. John had told me he had tried to rescue his brother as he fell into a serious drug addiction. John said he had headed west from Ohio, where he lived at the time, but arrived too late. His brother was already deep in his addiction. In fact, he wound up overdosing sometime later.

John said, "There was nothing more I could have done for him. Once an addict is in that deep, there's no way out. I tried to save his life."

I located a police report generated by John's ex-wife in September 2000, which had initiated an investigation into John's brother's death. The police report describing what happened spared no detail. I found it in a small box of John's belongings. I sat down at my desk and read.

"[John's ex-wife] found a wooden box containing empty vials of drugs" inside the home she and John shared. Several of the drugs were the same drugs used during anesthesia procedures. It was after this that John's ex-wife looked at John's correspondence with his brother via email and found evidence of what had actually happened.

John had been stealing vials of meperidine, Versed, and fentanyl from hospitals where he'd worked as a nurse anesthetist and shipping them to his brother in California. He'd also included instructions on how to administer the drugs.

Meperidine is a highly addictive form of Demerol, which is designed to relieve "moderate to severe pain." An opioid, it is used mostly during surgeries. At the age of seven, when I was in so much pain because of my illness, I was prescribed Demerol and suffered intense withdrawal symptoms, including violent shaking, when I was weaned off of it. I knew the dangers of this drug personally.

Versed is intended to make patients feel relaxed and sleepy before surgery. Fentanyl, a synthetic opioid, is of course used to treat the worst pain imaginable (generally at the end of life). It is dangerously lethal in the most diminutive doses; similar to morphine, fentanyl is fifty to one hundred times more potent.

After John's ex initiated the investigation with a call to the police, a search warrant was executed at the location to which John had moved after he split from his wife. In the attic of that house, detectives found a "Middle Tennessee School of Anesthesia" medical bag—which John had stolen—containing "30 empty vials of Midazolam" (the generic version of Versed), "four empty vials of Fentanyl, six empty vials of Meperidine, and three empty carpujects of Meperidine" (readily injectable doses).

John was arrested a short time later on an outstanding warrant for probation violation from a previous charge of carrying a 9mm Ruger semiautomatic pistol, which detectives had also recovered from the attic. John had been on probation at the time for "menacing." He'd threatened a woman he had been dating after they broke up.

As I sat in my office chair and took a deep breath, it felt like too much to take in. I read through it all, thinking, *Do I actually know this guy and what he might be capable of? Am I totally off base to think he couldn't hurt us? Maybe he is more dangerous than any man I have ever known.*

John had sent his own brother enough drugs to kill several elephants, literally, and had expected him (a drug addict) to take them without complication? Any one of those drugs, if taken in a dosage slightly higher than what a doctor would administer and supervise, could slow breathing enough to kill a person. As a medical professional, John had to know this. Theoretically, he had sent his brother a weapon he knew would kill him, along with instructions on how to load and fire it properly.

Questions plagued me. Dazed, I stood up from behind my desk. It was all there in front of me. On paper.

Had John killed his brother intentionally? Was John also taking these drugs? Were they in my house? What else is he lying about?

22

KILLING IS EASY

"What did he say?" Terra asked Liz during a call one night in late March 2015. She was referring to the private investigator's latest revelation about John—conversations I would not learn about until later.

Liz, Scotti, and Nicole did not want to tell Terra everything. Terra can be easily scared and triggered.

"John has several different Social Security numbers," Liz told Terra. "He was working as a nurse. He's no fucking doctor. He also has a storage unit in town with a refrigerator that has bottles of chloroform in it."

That comment stopped Terra in her tracks.

"What is he doing with chloroform? Why does he have it?"

Anyone who watches even a modicum of crime television knows that chloroform is used to knock people out. The image it summons is one of a man coming up from behind a woman with a handkerchief doused in the stuff and putting it over her mouth and nose.

"Why do you *think* he has it?" Liz asked with sarcasm.

"Why is he using different Social Security numbers?"

"I know, I know . . . this is so crazy. Just as we thought all along."

"I'm very worried about Mom," Terra said. "What if he does something to her?"

"Yeah, I know . . . but we can't think like that. We just have to get him away from her."

They discussed the GPS tracker Liz had installed on my Tesla. Liz had actually purchased two. She'd put one on the car and kept the other one to swap out. This way she could download data from one as the other collected more. She'd never miss anywhere John went.

"He just goes to all these random locations and I haven't really been able to put it together. What's weird is on some days he doesn't even leave the house. He's just there all day long."

Close to this time, Liz had a conversation with her boyfriend about the GPS tracker.

"You are crazy," he said after she explained. "Why are you even getting involved? The guy is fucking scary. Your mom will figure him out."

"You do not know my mom," Liz said. "She is too sweet a person. She needs my help."

Liz called me one day and mentioned the GPS tracker.

"I don't know all the places he works," I responded. "He travels a lot. Sometimes he takes the day off. That doesn't mean anything, Liz."

Before we hung up, I could sense Liz was frustrated and wondering, *Why are you not listening to me?*

What I learned later was how heartbroken Terra felt about everything going on. She was terrified for me, Liz, Nicole, and the kids, and was in the process of figuring out how to still have a relationship with me, despite how torn she felt. I viewed my children's behavior as extra sensitive, driven by their feelings about my past relationships; I had heard my children disparage so many of them that I felt as if they were doing the same thing now, when in truth they were actually warning me. They were expressing love and support. I never felt I was choosing John over my children, because I was hopeful that, eventually, everyone would get along. I thought time was all I needed. John was so loving, happy, and hilarious around me, and I hoped they would come to see that.

John was still adoring me with incessant acts of what I perceived to be love. I'd have a doctor's appointment and he'd be there, holding my hand, telling me it was all going to be okay. He'd bring me peonies, my favorite flower, three, four, five times a week when they were in season. I think what's confusing to most people who don't understand this part of my story is how hard John worked at making sure I rarely questioned his dedication or commitment to our marriage. And how manipulative he was when I did. To say he was doing everything for me would be an understatement. Any errand or chore I needed done during the day—having the cars washed and detailed, doing the laundry, grocery shopping, paying bills—he did without questioning it or being asked. I would come home to a house where everything was done. We would take romantic walks on the beach at dusk. Stop and stare at the marvelous yachts trolling the harbor. He'd hold my hand and ask about my day. He presented himself, even as I was hearing things about him and beginning to find out things on my own, as the perfect husband.

And I loved every minute of it.

John also had this convincing way of appearing vulnerable. Inside of John hid a little boy who exposed himself once in a while. It's strange to me now after all that's happened. But in the moment, I saw it as a gentle, loving quality. Cute, even. Just another part of John to love. When we were out walking and came upon a dog on the beach or in town, for example, John would get down on bended knee and pet it lovingly. To me, that kind of affection showed a person with humanity, compassion, tenderness. When my grandkids were allowed to be around him, he'd wrestle with them and chase them around the beach. He'd sit down and play in the sand with them, making castles while talking funny childspeak. He had this fun-loving, charming side to him. He also had a wonderfully comforting sense of humor. He made me laugh. You see, it's easy for those who hear my story (or see it dramatized on the Bravo series *Dirty John*)—and think they understand it—to look back through the lens of what they know happens in the end and say, *Why did she stay in it so long?* When it's your life, however, and you're living it from moment to moment, you cannot possibly see all there is to see. We also tend to glorify the good times and positive qualities associated with a person. We want it all to be okay.

Months before I met John, I was involved with a dynamic man who had a pleasant personality. *Ned* was one of those guys who was just fun to be around. Ned called me constantly. He always wanted to talk. "I've been praying for you," he'd say. Ned knew I was a devout Christian and spoke of how Christ was the center of his life. He'd send me Bible verses every morning and mention how grateful he was that God had brought me into his life.

"You're the only one for me, Debbie."

"That's sweet, Ned."

"I'm serious. God put our souls together."

We dated for a few months. Every day seemed brighter. God was the focal point of everything Ned said and did.

"I want to get to know you without physical emotions getting in the way," he explained several weeks into the relationship.

I had been wondering why he wasn't pushing to sleep with me.

"No sex until we're married," he said.

"I can honor that."

It made me love him more.

Ned lived seven hours north of Irvine, just outside Sacramento. So we flew back and forth once a week to see each other. He'd asked me to marry him and I accepted.

He owned a large company. I decided to surprise Ned one day: fly out, sneak in, and say, "Hello, I'm here." Thinking back on it now, I realize that something had been bothering me about Ned. I couldn't shake the feeling. My gut screamed that something was terribly off.

I stopped at the door into his office because I heard him on the phone. He was calling the woman on the other end of the line "sweetheart" and "darling"; then I heard him say he was looking forward to her and her son moving to California to live with him.

"Who are you talking to?" I said after walking in, standing over his desk.

He proceeded to talk to the woman as if I weren't there. After hanging up, he looked at me and said, "You have no right barging into my office like this."

"Who were you talking to? Tell me. Right now."

"Are you insinuating something, Debbie? You don't know what you're talking about."

I stood and thought back to this app I had just downloaded: LinkedIn, a social media site connecting businesspeople together. There was a request from a woman to connect that I had not paid much attention to. The only thing we had in common was my fiancé, Ned. While in Ned's office, I sat down and connected with her. She answered back right away. I asked if she had been talking to Ned just a few minutes before.

"Yes," she responded. "How did you know?"

"Call me right now if you can, please."

We talked and discovered Ned had been seeing both of us. What's more, there were other women, as well.

Several.

"I'm going over to your house and packing up my things, Ned. We're finished."

He looked at me and didn't say anything for a few moments. Then, "You know what, you're just not my type, anyway."

I found out later that on the day Ned had asked me to marry him, he had gone off, met up with another woman, and had sex with her.

This was my life. I never asked for any of it. I didn't "miss the signs," as some have suggested. I wasn't in denial, walking around wearing blinders, accepting any type of behavior because of a desperate need for love. Yes, I was searching for love. I wanted to *be* in love. But I'm not a weak, feeble woman, a bubbly blonde airhead who accepts whatever a man tells her. These men victimized me. You have no idea what it's like until you've been there.

John walked into my life and helped me get over Ned. I had met John just months after that incident in Ned's office. John made me feel as though love was possible again. He wanted *me*. He built up my self-esteem after Ned had torn it to shreds.

As March ended, my family was sharing so much about John with me, beyond what I'd discovered on my own, that I didn't know what to think anymore. Add to this a growing divide between the kids and me, along with my devastation over losing those close relationships. Having John in my life came with a high emotional and personal price tag. I was conflicted, still wondering what was true and what wasn't. Despite all the signs that John was stealing from me, pretending to be someone he was not, and secretly taking over my life, I didn't see all of it clearly. I didn't know what to do.

As part of my job running Ambrosia Interior Design, I'd jet off frequently to visit clubhouses and model homes designed by my company. Part of my job was to control the quality I demanded and had promised clients. John came along with me most of the time. We were in Seattle one day that early spring, walking around the city, visiting all the tourist sites. As we walked by this homeless man, he insulted me under his breath. But we clearly heard him.

"She's hot—for an old lady."

John snapped. He got in the guy's face and began screaming at him.

The guy said something else.

John grabbed him by the lapel and shook him. I could see rage bubbling up. The kind of anger I had witnessed in my previous, football player husband. It triggered me. John was about to pummel the guy.

I grabbed my husband by the arm and pulled him away, pleading with John to stop.

"What are you doing? Calm down." It was as if I didn't recognize him. His face was a sweaty shade of rose. His eyes were round and wide, and his fists were balled up.

"He's not going to insult my wife and get away with it."

"Come on, honey . . . he's not worth it."

We made it back to the hotel without the situation escalating into an incident, or John being arrested for beating up a homeless person.

John settled down and went into the bathroom. He came out with his medical bag, a syringe, and several bottles of medication. I knew that he'd injected testosterone. I'd seen him do it before. Watching him do it after this confrontation, however, made me question whether that drug was causing the explosive moments of rage I saw in him from time to time.

"Why do you do that?" I asked. "I know you told me, but I'm confused."

"So you think maybe this is why I got all heated up down there?"

"No, John. I just need you to tell me again."

"My kidneys," he said.

"Wouldn't that drug *hurt* your kidneys?"

"I'm the doctor, Debbie. Remember?"

He finished injecting himself. Then produced one of several prescription bottles of medication he carried around with him. OxyContin was a drug I'd seen him take every day. Now, if you want to call me naïve when it comes to drug addiction, okay. I was at the time. What I knew about opioids was minimal. They were prescribed for pain. Lots of people took them. John being a doctor, he knew what he was doing. That was where my interest in and knowledge of those types of medications ended.

"In case you're wondering about these, it's my bad back," he said, popping two pills. "It's gotten worse over the past few weeks."

"Relax, John. It's okay. I understand."

We went to see the film *American Sniper.* Clint Eastwood directed the movie, which focuses on an American sharpshooter in Iraq.

"That was so damn accurate," John said as we walked out of the theater. "That's *exactly* what it's like over there."

"Scary," I said. "You saw that type of thing?"

He looked at me with a profoundly intense gaze. "I've taken lives myself, Debbie. You know that. I've told you before."

"What was that like, John? It must have been heavy on your heart."

We had been married for a few months by then. John had told me little about his time in Iraq. I was under the impression that it was too emotional for him to talk about.

"Very, very difficult . . ."

He didn't seem to want to get into it, so I didn't press.

"Look, you can ask me all the questions you want to about my time in Iraq—I'm ready to talk about it with you. When we were first married, I wasn't. I hope you can understand that this is difficult stuff. But I love you, Debbie. I want you to know everything about me."

This wasn't shocking or alarming. It was one more way John made me feel comfortable around him. One more layer of control he was wielding secretly. Only I didn't know it. Now that I look back, John wanted me to know he had "killed" people in order to intimidate me and control the situation by scaring me. He understood the girls and Ben were not going to back off. People were figuring him out. He also knew I was beginning to question aspects of his life as well. Telling me he was ready to talk about those ugly details surrounding the lives he had supposedly taken in Iraq was John's way of saying he had no trouble killing people.

"How many?" I asked later that same night.

"Six."

He had added one since the last time we talked about this when we started dating! *A man would remember—without a doubt—how many people he killed in combat.* But I didn't call him on it. I added that comment to a mental checklist of discrepancies I was keeping. Holes in his stories were getting deeper. And yet as we walked around, talking, he spoke more about his supposed time in Iraq. He broke into a vivid description. Names and places. Feelings and thoughts. It was as though he were reliving it all as he explained.

Robert Hare, a Canadian psychologist, along with American psychiatrist Hervey Cleckley, created the Hare Psychopathy Checklist, a now rather common diagnostic tool used to rate a person's psychopathic or antisocial tendencies. I discovered the checklist long after meeting John.

I know today after speaking to experts and studying the Hare checklist that a psychopath can convince you of anything he desires. He can lie comfortably, as if telling the truth. He has this outward, excessive glibness masquerading as charm. Within our relationship, John presented himself with a grandiose sense of self-worth.

John's need for stimulation was extremely high. He craved chaos and conflict. I didn't know then that I was part of it all, feeding his pathology. Nor did I know that John had an enormous lack of guilt and empathy, and zero remorse for anything he'd done. One of the major factors on Dr. Hare's list, a parasitic lifestyle, describes the twenty years of John's life before I met him. How could I have known any of this before our marriage imploded?

"Must have been so hard," I said to him that day. "I cannot imagine what you must have gone through over there—and to have been forced to kill people. My goodness, John."

"I never realized that I had it in me to kill so easily. When someone is in front of you, you know he is the enemy, and it's him or you." He stopped. Grabbed me by the shoulders with force. Stared into my eyes. "Killing in those specific moments, Debbie, is *very* easy to do."

23

"I COULD TAKE LIZ OUT . . ."

I still felt that if only Ben and Scotti, Nicole's husband, got to know John better, they would like him. They would see what I saw in him. One way I could facilitate that relationship was through their common interest in athletics. Ben was in shape and played a lot of sports. Because John was the same, I thought they'd get along—and maybe even start working out together.

"He's an ex-college athlete, Ben," I said when Ben called one night, questioning where John had gone to school. "He attended the University of Arizona."

"You're sure of that, Aunt Debbie? Absolutely certain?"

"I am. I've seen his diploma and other papers from the university."

Ben was a good judge of character. A cautious and smart man. I trusted his instincts. And I felt then that Ben wanted to judge John on his own, without being corrupted by what the girls—or even that investigator, whom Ben had told me about—had been reporting. Initially, after bringing his kids over one night to spend some time with us, Ben considered John a "good, fun guy." He said later that he could understand how I had fallen in love with him. John was excellent with Ben's kids. He'd pull Ben aside and tell him stories about Iraq and discuss his patients and the procedures he performed throughout his workday.

"He wowed me," Ben had said when we discussed John one day. "His intelligence alone and his sense of confidence are insurmountable."

Ben and John were together one afternoon. It was a gorgeous spring Saturday at the beach house. We were all hanging out and relaxing. Ben and John made these delicious margaritas. It was, dare I say, a good time. I felt content. The experience fulfilled my greatest desire, which was to have someone see the John I knew. I looked at the two of them horsing around, laughing, drinking, having fun. It made me feel as though sooner or later my children would come around, too. The day was almost perfect.

That is, until the subject of Liz came up.

"What do you think of Liz?" Ben asked John.

It seemed like casual banter between two guys having a few drinks in the sun. We had this incredible deck on the roof of the beach house. We would sit and watch the yachts pass by, the waves crash against the shore. The atmosphere alone was serene and comforting.

"Liz, huh? Um . . . well, since you asked . . ." John responded.

"She's saying a lot of things about you," Ben mentioned.

John stopped what he was doing and his attitude changed from fun loving to serious. "You know, Ben, I could take Liz out easily from a thousand yards away."

As John said it, I laughed, actually. I thought John was joking around. It was sarcasm, I assumed. Yes, it was a nasty, scary comment. But John could say the most chilling things in a manner that made you question whether he was joking or serious. And let's be honest, none of us wants to jump to a terrifying conclusion when someone says such a thing. We want to believe that when someone utters "I hate him" or "I'll kill him," it's merely a figure of speech.

Ben and I talked several days later about what John had said.

"He's been in Iraq," Ben explained. "At least he says he has. He likely has a lot of emotional, mental issues . . ."

We looked at each other. It was almost as if we both knew—without saying it—that John had never been to Iraq.

"This is strange," Ben said.

We agreed to talk again soon. Believe it or not, part of me still had the mindset of *Even if some of this is true, I love him. I want to help him.*

In late April, Ben called me. He was now actively involved in trying to convince me John was a fraud. Despite what might have seemed like bonding that day at the beach house drinking margaritas, Ben wanted no part of John in a buddy-buddy way. Ben was worried about me. Liz, Nicole, and Scotti were keeping Ben well informed as to what the private investigator had been digging up. Ben's own father had killed his mother and had served fewer than three years in prison, and Ben hadn't been all that interested in a relationship with Billy Vickers after he was released. Ben is a dedicated father himself. He had raised three kids by himself. He had always been protective of me and had viewed me as his mother since Cindi's murder. We were beyond close. I felt his love and respected him immensely. He wanted to warn me about John without scaring—or telling—me too much. He also worried he might be wrong about John. Again, these are the minor details from my story that are often overlooked within the media's coverage and various dramatic productions. As all of this happened, mind you, John was not in a constant state of psychological meltdown, or running around threatening everyone and making me fear him. Throughout this time, John was also showing me love, providing emotional support, and working hard to convince me that everyone was trying to destroy our marriage because they didn't like him and they wanted my money. John had created in me a sense of paranoia—another carefully thought-out tactic of his.

"If John wasn't who he said he was, would you still love him, Aunt Debbie?" Ben asked as we chatted on the phone that afternoon.

"What do you mean? Of course I would love him."

It's crazy to me that people—and I do not mean Ben—think absolute love can be shut off. When you fall in love with someone, you're in love. It takes time to get over love if things go wrong.

"I cannot lose you, too, Aunt Debbie."

That comment hit me hard. He'd been so young when Cindi was murdered, and he'd been forced into a relationship with the man who'd killed her.

"I'm okay, honey. I think maybe everyone has John wrong and might be overreacting here. I'm not so sure all this stuff is true. I am very confused right now."

"But what if he isn't an anesthesiologist? What if I could *prove* to you he was in jail and was never in Iraq?"

My heart ached as all of this unfolded. I loved a guy who was, essentially, lying to me about almost everything in his life—and it was becoming more obvious to me as each day passed. It's just not fair to say I refused to believe it all. What is denial, anyway? A character defect? Lying to yourself? The idea of declaring something in your life to be untrue, when *you* feel it is? None of us knew what John was truly capable of; remember, my kids and Ben were under the impression that John was merely a schemer and con man. It is unreasonable and unfair for anyone who looks at my story with knowledge of John's entire history and the end of our marriage to judge me about the decisions I made in real time.

No matter how confused I felt as April dragged into May, I decided to confront John. What I had read in the papers I had uncovered gnawed at me. I could not let it go. My tolerance for the growing inconsistencies now waning, I asked John to sit down because we needed to talk.

"Look at the names," John suggested. "People have stolen my identity, Debbie. It's not me."

Reviewing some of the paperwork one day while he was gone, I'd seen that his surname was spelled differently sometimes.

Maybe he's telling the truth?

John began using my phone again to text the kids, saying horrible, hurtful things they sometimes thought I was writing to them. He would comment on nearly everything they did. He also dug his heels down deeper into the idea that they were out to take my money. It's the old divide-and-conquer routine, which is partly how coercive control works: it's so subtle, you have difficulty seeing it happen in real time around you. John was a master at convincing me that *his* truth was the only truth. Even when I discovered holes in his stories, he'd convince me to question my own judgment.

And I did.

After placing that GPS tracker on my Tesla, Liz discovered that beyond John hanging out at the house when he said he was at work, he was driving to different doctors' offices throughout the day. He'd park at one office for a while before moving on to the next, almost as if he knew somebody was watching his movements. He would then go to his storage unit *before* driving to a nearby post office. He frequented fast-food restaurants and pulled over on the side of the road afterward. He'd stop at an electric car charging station and then head off to a few more doctors' offices. None of the offices were in Irvine; he would travel to Mission Viejo (a fifteen-minute trip south) or San Diego (about a seventy-five-minute ride from Irvine). He'd take a coastal route on his way back and always stop at a charging portal before arriving home.

Liz believed John was somehow procuring prescriptions for OxyContin and other opioids and then selling the pills on the street or stowing them inside his storage unit. The details of what he was actually doing throughout the day were vague and speculative. The kids could look at the GPS data and ponder what he was doing, but without following him, they couldn't use the GPS to prove anything.

I kept going back to my discovery that John had sent his brother drugs. It scared me. I needed to find the source, his ex-wife. I needed to hear the story from her directly.

"We'll be moving at some point," John said when I questioned him about the storage unit and what he had planned for his belongings stored there. This was a good way for me to ask about the storage unit, which I now knew he was visiting frequently, without tipping him off that I was watching him. "I can just go to the unit and pack up my stuff from there when we do move. I go there because I have some of my things stored in it."

This sounded valid. John had brought very little into the relationship, as far as personal belongings. So it made sense he would frequent the storage unit.

John had committed crimes. I knew this. There was a need in me to rescue and fix him. If my own mother could forgive the man who had murdered her daughter, who was I not to forgive my husband for the sins he'd committed? And John had mentioned to me almost daily that he was in need of forgiveness and repentance. That, too, was a lie. But it hit at the core of my ethical soul.

Around that same time, Ben finally told Liz what John had said about how easy it would be to kill her. This terrified Liz. She took it as a direct threat, whereas I took it as another example of his dark sense of humor. Liz believed emphatically that John meant it *literally*. I wasn't quite in that same space yet. I was still holding on to the fantasy that I could save this marriage and my husband—and he would love my children, and they would accept him.

24

DUPED

A text I wouldn't see until after this whole ordeal had ended told me that in April 2015 John was actively trying to sell my Tesla. He was in contact with a guy he'd met while in prison, someone he was meeting during his days out on the road.

"What u want for it?" said a text from his old cellmate.

"I bought [it for] 135K. I'll bring it by. I can only help you if you want it."

He never sold it, obviously. The fact that my husband was trying to sell my car—and it was there in front of me in a text I saw later—spoke volumes about him. It would become another layer of proof telling me how little I knew about the man I had married. Yet selling my car would have been a minor crime compared with what John was planning.

Ben called me one day in May. "I told you Nicole and Scotti hired a private detective, Aunt Debbie."

"Yes, what about it?"

Ben had mentioned this several weeks before, but without much detail. He knew I didn't want to hear about it then. Apparently, however, the PI had uncovered some things Ben knew I needed to not only hear but believe.

Part of me still wanted to think that the private detective had found a guy with the same surname as John's. This is how your mind works in high-stress situations, when you're not truly thinking logically—not to mention when you're being coercively controlled and have no idea it's happening.

This time I listened. Ben talked about what he knew for certain, confirming John had been in prison and had done hard time—corroborating what I had read previously but didn't want to believe. He also talked about where John went during his days. His prior arrests. Several women he had duped, threatened, and extorted. The truth about Iraq, where he had never served, let alone killed three, four, five, or six people.

It was enough to terrify me. I believed it all now. I could not overlook the obvious any longer. My husband was not who I thought he was—I had been living with a stranger. This became a game changer for me.

After that conversation, I was in shock. I remember walking Fashion Island for forty-five minutes, staring out at the water without seeing it, trying to make sense of what I had learned. I needed to come to terms with the truth. Or at least question John and get him out of my house.

He wasn't in Iraq, he was in prison . . . echoed in my head as I hugged myself, as if cold, and walked. My hair blew in the wind. It's always warm on the beach, with a comforting breeze. But I felt a chill, which came from a place deep within me. I watched families together on the beach, sitting, reading, building sandcastles, and swimming. They seemed so content. I had none of that. My life was a lie. My kids were not talking to—or visiting—me anymore. They were keeping my grandchildren away. I had been standing behind, sleeping with, and defending a man I knew nothing about.

Could everything *be a lie? Why would he lie about so much?*

I was overwhelmed by my thoughts and the confusion of it all.

What am I going to do? Have I married a con man? How could I have been fooled . . . again? I've yearned only for love and companionship. Someone I can trust, laugh with, make love to, grow old with. A best friend. What most everyone else in the world wants. *Why me? How could I be so deceived and blindsided—again and again? I'm so stupid.*

After walking the beach, I had to go back to the house and act like nothing was wrong. I could not just run away from John. That's not who I was. I had to face him, knowing what I knew, put on the happy face he expected, and get to the bottom of it all. Please remember, at this time I believed he was lying to me, but I did not know the full extent of his past, especially when it came to duping women.

I knew it was going to be difficult to face John because he could read me like a profiler. I'm an open book. My emotional state shows on my face. My body language changes with my mood.

I walked in the front door and peered around the corner, looking toward the office John and I used. I saw the light on.

He was home.

I walked upstairs quietly. If he approached me, it was not going to go well. He'd ask what was wrong and then steer the conversation toward my kids. He'd blame them for the way I was feeling and demand to know what they had poisoned me with. Then he'd become angry. He'd defend himself and his "love and devotion." He'd toss the old we're-husband-and-wife-and-we-stick-together nonsense on the table and talk about how we only had—and needed—each other.

He did not hear me come in. I sat upstairs on the edge of the bed, my head in my hands, and I trembled. Everyone had been talking about John for the last several months, but this was the first time I felt the truth sink in. I could no longer push it away. John was not the man he claimed to be. There was nothing I could believe about him now.

Do I go downstairs and greet him like I normally do with hugs and kisses? Maybe tell him I'm not feeling well and climb into bed?

I yelled downstairs, "John, I'm going to bed. I don't feel well."

He didn't say anything.

A week or so after speaking to Ben and realizing I was being lied to and did not truly know the man I had married, I felt I needed to get away from John. I looked into filing a domestic violence action, which is basically a restraining order. Things were real for me. I was growing suspicious of everything John said and did. I wondered constantly what he might do next. With Ben's help, I had managed to pull myself out of the fog of love and believe my family.

Some weeks had passed, and I was acting differently around John. He had a sense I was figuring him out. He looked at me with a quizzical gaze now. Asked probing questions. He left the house more and more.

"Debbie, what the fuck is going on here?"

"I'm not sure what you mean, John."

"You know what I'm talking about. You are different."

"I'm busy with work. I'm dealing with my kids. Things have not been good between us, John. You know this."

One of my girlfriends was going through a similar marital situation. We had both gotten married around the same time. Her husband was proving to be a liar and fraudster. We made plans to meet for dinner to support each other and talk about our options.

"I think I made a huge mistake," I told her as we sat outside at a café. "I don't know what to do. I'm scared and stuck."

She listened and could relate. What most people don't realize, and the television drama series based on my case failed to portray accurately, is that I was terrified and confused. The series, in many ways, made me out to be naïve and ignorant, a repeat offender for choosing the wrong guys; the show implied that it was my fault for making poor choices. I own my part in being married so many times and choosing bad men and maybe even not leaving soon enough. But my life with John Meehan did not unfold over an eight-part miniseries. (I should also point out that major portions of the Bravo series were fictionalized and the entire show was dramatized for maximum effect.) John worked slowly and deliberately, as most psychopaths do, carefully using manipulation and coercive control to augment his crimes.

"I don't even want to go home," I told my girlfriend, crying. I wondered what I was going to find out next and what I should do about it. I said, "How do I face him if I know he's lied to me so much? Should I forgive him and try to help him? I do love him."

My girlfriend consoled me. "It's going to be okay, Debbie. That's number one. Number two, we will figure this out. You *will* be okay."

"I'm so stupid."

As we ate, my phone beeped, indicating a text had come in.

"Sitting out there on Fashion Island must be cold," John texted.

I held up the screen so my girlfriend could see it. "Look."

"How does he know where you are?" she asked. "I thought you said you didn't tell him where you were going."

"I didn't."

We stared at each other.

I looked around the restaurant to see if he was stalking us.

I didn't see him.

John had put a tracking app on my phone. He knew where I was at all times. I did not know this then.

"But I bet there are tons of guys waiting to meet you," John texted next.

I showed my girlfriend.

"You want to compare pics?" John texted a minute later.

What he meant was that he could send me photos of him with other women. Nasty, dirty, graphic photos. That was John at his essence: filled with revenge, waiting to pounce. When he got angry, whenever he felt somebody had wronged him, John went straight for the one place he felt could hurt the person most.

A dangerous, blunt example of this had taken place one month before I met John the previous year. I didn't find out until after my life with John was over. When John was released from prison, he knew detectives had initiated an investigation into several new charges of stalking, threatening, menacing, stealing drugs, car theft, and burglary. He had targeted and stolen from so many women in the twenty years leading up to meeting me that his list of crimes could fill three single-spaced pages. Several women from John's past could tell stories similar to mine, minus the violence and sheer horror my kids and I were about to go through. This was John's chosen way, his psychopathic method, of getting back at those he viewed as enemies. Revenge was John's chosen approach. He grew manic and *needed* to retaliate. A police report I found later explained how John had put a "hit" out on the detectives who were asking questions about him after he was released from prison in 2014.

"[John Meehan] indicated he was willing to pay $10,000 each" to have two police officers killed, one report said. "[He] talked to one of his fellow inmates about paying someone 'to kill Laguna Beach Officers . . . as well as five other people who were to be witnesses at [his] trial.'" John wanted them killed before the next preliminary hearing in his case. "With no witnesses," he told the inmate, "there is no trial."

The police uncovered several threats made against the detectives that John had written and sent to his former cellmate via prison email. After being released on parole, John called and asked to meet with the two detectives to discuss his case. John was clearly more interested in meeting the female investigator. He had emailed her repeatedly that day, each email becoming more hostile. He had called and left voice mails. Sent letters. In one email, John claimed that one of the detectives had stolen $13,000 and several "precious stones" he'd kept in the freezer of an RV he lived in. He said the detective stole the items while executing a search warrant.

"I am not going to rest until the truth . . . is in the light," he wrote.

The detectives were worried enough to file a harassment report, referring to what they'd discovered as a "death threat." They were concerned for the safety of themselves and their families. When a guy has spent some time in prison, he has obviously met a wide swath of criminals. The detectives thought that John had hooked up with a con inside who promised to help him out if he ever needed someone killed. They believed John so seriously that they checked their surroundings wherever they went in order "to avoid personal attack." One of the detectives actually purchased a large-caliber handgun to defend himself. That report, as I read through it, gave me far more insight into John's emotional state at the time I met him than anything else I had seen.

"[John Meehan] is a violent individual with suicidal tendencies . . . not intimidated by authority . . . and is relentless with his continued contact," a detective wrote. John possesses "firearms, ammunition and cyanide while subjected to multiple restraining orders, showing his propensity towards violence, victimization and disregard for the law."

At the end of the report was a comment on perhaps the most sobering aspect, for me, of John's character during this period: "He believes he was falsely arrested [for the crime for which he had been imprisoned] and I feel he is out for revenge and he thinks he has nothing to lose."

A man who feels he has nothing to lose is a man more than willing to die.

That was John's state of mind when I met him. Had I seen this report during March or April, as I began to figure out what was happening in my life, I would have gone into hiding and taken all my children and grandchildren with me (again, this is something the television series leaves out of my story). Instead, however, not only were Liz and Nicole living in town, and without a doubt on John's new hit list, but Terra was still talking about moving back.

John's widening web of reprisal was coming together for him.

Even though I believed what Ben told me about John, I never filed that domestic action. I decided to try to reconcile my worries and concerns about John and attempt to make our marriage work. Why? Part of me still did not want to believe what I was hearing, while another part now feared for the lives of my children and grandchildren. Placating John was not going to work, I knew. And the situation I allowed myself to stay in sounds very volatile and even unstable, I realize. Also, when a woman has been married several times, she faces a plethora of judgment. But at the time, I still did not want to think John was capable of everything I was being told—and I still believed that we could resolve his issues with lying, which was what I thought then to be the main problem, and work on the marriage.

I cannot explain some of what happened. And I have already said that my upbringing, I now know, played a major role in it. What I learned after the Dirty John saga ended and I had time to get help was that coercive control (CC) is a very real, often undetected condition that is rarely talked about.

"I'm not talking about the somewhat controlling boyfriend or husband here," Dr. Evan Stark told WebMD in 2017. "Compliance is fear-based. If there's no fear, there's no coercive control. And that fear is very real."

Think of CC along the lines of what a cult leader employs to maintain power and influence over his or her followers. There's a mind game going on, which you cannot escape, no matter what you do. Mainly because you have no idea you are even being played.

"Coercive control is akin to brainwashing," coercive control expert and victims' advocate Laura Richards later told me. Laura, who has become a good friend and mentor, was the former head of New Scotland Yard's Sexual Offences Section, Homicide Prevention Unit, and Violent Crime and Intelligence Unit. She was violence adviser to the United Kingdom's Association of Chief Police Officers (now renamed the National Police Chiefs' Council), and has worked thousands of cases. "The art of brainwashing is sophisticated. The abuser replaces the victim's inner narrative and thoughts with their own. Gradually, the victim's voice is eroded and replaced with the abuser's narrative—their views, needs, desires, wants, which are placed above all else."

"The abused are usually not outwardly passive," Dr. Stark continued in that same WebMD interview. "Many are successful professionals who've lost personal autonomy even as their careers soar, and who may be too ashamed to seek help."

That quote explains my situation with John perfectly. I was scared to go to a therapist routinely and talk about my life. Terrified, actually. John was poisoning my mind every single day, causing confusion. In this type of situation, you develop a conflict within yourself. You question every decision. You wonder if what you are doing is what your abuser wants you to do. In addition, John was adept at making me feel sorry for him.

"Abusers undermine the abused person's sense of sanity by insisting *their* lies are true," Stark went on to note. "Or by playing mind games such as moving a partner's parked car late at night so she can't find it in the morning."

John made me codependent on him. Several of my marriages turned out the same way. When codependency creeps into a relationship and you have no idea it's happening, it becomes about self-preservation—a survival skill. You don't realize what you are doing. And if CC is part of that codependent relationship, the abuser uses your codependency to his or her advantage.

"These behaviors can include strategies such as pseudo-caring tactics that appear to be attentive and thoughtful, while in reality the perpetrator is actually just micromanaging the victim and limiting their space for action," Laura Richards added. "They may appear super attentive and into the victim in the beginning, but all the while they may be social engineering and data mining and storing up information about the intended victim or creating an atmosphere of codependence."

25

ELEVATOR RIDE

Two weeks after Ben had come completely clean with me about the private investigator's findings, I decided to fully accept the truth about what was happening. I still hadn't confronted John with what Ben had told me. I was building up to it during those two weeks. I also decided that John needed to be out of my beach house and life. I could not reconcile or save a marriage built on lies. I had fooled myself into thinking I could. I had lost ten pounds over that two-week period. My situation needed a change. I needed to be alone and think things through.

During that two-week span, Ben had stood up to John and confronted him over a text exchange about some of what he had been learning. Feeling trapped and backed into a corner, John revealed our secret.

John texted, "Why don't you simply go away? You lost your aunt. You're not invited here. You come near us and I call the cops. Worry about your own miserable life and I'll worry about Debbie, who is a lot closer to me than you can ever imagine. You won't win this."

"You told my grandma and me that you are a doctor, so prove it," Ben texted back, done with being bullied. "You told my grandma and me that you own two properties, so prove it. Once you prove those two, you are good in my book."

"I couldn't give a shit about being in your book."

"I hope she leaves you soon. I have prayed that she opens her eyes," Ben texted.

"Boy, are you in for a big surprise."

"My mom is looking down on me, making sure I don't give up on her sister and making sure I know her sister knows the truth about your lying ass."

"Good thing your mom isn't here. She'd be embarrassed . . . You don't have an aunt anymore—get it?" John was showing how quickly he could become so nasty and threatening. "I am not going nowhere and neither is she. Stay away from the house. Accidents do happen. Again, Debbie wants nothing to do with you . . . If you were on fire, I wouldn't piss on you to help you out."

"If I hear of you threatening my aunt or harming her, you will see me."

"Please show up. And she isn't your aunt anymore. Just ask her. Oh, and your girlfriend, she's not that good. I fucked her," John added before insulting Ben's kids.

"Do not talk about my kids."

"Fuck you and your kids. Come do something about it. It isn't about me or what I've done, it's about you harassing Debbie to the point where she fears for her life."

"LOL," Ben responded.

"She fears you'll hurt either of us. Laugh about that."

"I'm just giving her facts over your lies."

"And, by the way, we're married," John finally disclosed. "That means you're threatening me now, asshole."

"I pray you're not married."

Feeling defeated, depleted, emotionally exhausted, and conflicted about everything going on, I went out to get the mail one morning at the beach house. It was early May. This was just after Ben and John had that nasty text exchange, which Ben had told me about. I was building up the nerve to confront John myself.

The sun in Irvine has the power to heal even the severely brokenhearted. There's something about its energy and warmth that makes me feel alive, even on days when I want to get in my car and drive away from the world. After pulling the mail from the mailbox, I stood for a moment, absorbing the sun's radiance. It gave me a bit of hope.

Going through a pile of bills and your normal waste-of-paper advertisements, I found a letter addressed to John. The return address was from a prison.

I knew John had been in prison. It was easy to push aside, however, within the framework of what was happening in my life. It seemed to be way down on the list of lies I was planning to talk to John about. *So John has lied about being in prison. Okay, I can deal with that.* Everything was moving so fast. My mind was a mixture of fear, mania, and uncertainty.

I stopped before entering the house. I tore the letter open and started reading.

As I worked my way through the letter, I saw proof that John and this guy in prison were friends. This struck me. It made his time in prison seem like a different thing. He was staying in touch with his former cellmate. Why? What reason would he have for this?

John appeared suddenly. He'd come out of the house and came at me.

"What are you doing?"

I looked up, startled by his urgency. Then I remembered that John monitored everything I did in and outside the house through those cameras he'd had installed.

Rushing me, John grabbed the letter out of my hand before I could finish reading.

"What the fuck are you doing reading my mail? That's private."

"What does this letter mean, John? It sounds like you were in prison with this guy." As much as I had wanted to believe that John had merely spent time in a county jail, minimizing it all in my head, this letter confirmed everything I had read and what the investigator had uncovered. He had been in actual prison. I had zero experience with this part of society. It was new to me. I had never known anyone in prison. "What in the world is going on?"

"You don't know anything, Debbie. You have no fucking idea what you are talking about."

"You've been lying to me, John. You're a liar. That is what I am heartbroken by. That my husband, who has repeatedly told me how much he loves me and that I am his world and God put us together, has been telling me lies. It makes me question *everything* about you. Why is the truth so hard for you?"

This was the moment when I truly realized that the man I'd married was a *complete stranger.* I did not know this man or *anything* about his life before we met. As I stood there, listening to him rant and lie even more, I accepted that all that he had told me was nothing more than a narrative he had created. I think back now to how that felt. The weight of it. Here I was, standing in front of a made-up person—and this "character," John Meehan, was my husband. He'd had access to every part of my life, including my grandchildren and children.

"How dare you question me or look at my mail. You are committing a felony, opening my mail. Do you know that?"

"Please, John, give me a break. You've been lying to me. I want the truth. Who are you? What have you done in your life? Why were you in jail?"

My stomach turned and tightened. I thought I was going to be sick. When the truth is so unquestionable, so profoundly sketched out in front of you, you cannot deny any part of it. Your legs go numb, your body aches, and you become physically ill. You feel foolish. Used. Beaten. Add to these universal responses the fact that everyone in my life who loved me had been telling me the truth for months and I had basically shunned them. I had denied the people I love most their truth.

"Look," John said, "my jailhouse friend is just a guy I am helping out, sending him care packages and a little bit of money. Public service."

"John . . . please . . ."

"Debbie, listen to me . . ."

"Were you ever in prison?" I asked. "Simple question, John."

"I'm leaving. I have errands to run."

He walked away. We played the silent treatment game that night.

The following morning, John left the house for his "normal day of business," as he often put it. I decided once and for all that I was going to dig deeper into his belongings and find out what I could. Right after he left, I rifled through his things. What I uncovered was even more devastating than the few scraps of paper and letters I had seen that one other time I snooped. Everything I came across solidified what the kids had been trying so hard to get me to see. But what I found also scared me into surrendering. I was finally at a place where I was not going to ignore the apparent facts any longer. I was determined to accept the reality of my life.

I had asked John once about a large scar he had just below his rib cage. It was a straight line, in the middle of his torso, down past his belly button. The scar was thick, like a night crawler, and raised above his skin. Whatever happened was serious. The cut would have exposed his entire insides: his stomach, intestines, colon, and many of his organs.

"Iraq," he had said. "When we went down in the helicopter. I told you about that. We crashed and, I don't know, a piece of metal sticking out slashed my gut entirely open."

"Dear God, John. I am so sorry," I had said, consoling his anxiety at having to go back and relive the moment.

"I almost died, Debbie. But here I am. I know now I was meant to live so I could be with you and love you."

"I'm here to take care of you, John."

What really happened to cause that scar? Digging through his paperwork, I found out—and, well, it was almost too incredible to believe.

The scar was from a self-inflicted injury, proving how far John was willing to go to get what he wanted. One day during that last stint in prison, in the months just before I met him, John had wanted drugs. He had been stealing drugs from hospitals and clinics all over the country for over twenty years. He had ingested just about every opiate available, in addition to dozens of other drugs. But on this day, confined to prison, John needed to be creative if he wanted to use drugs. So he made a prison shank and sliced his midsection open, exposing his innards.

Bad enough, right?

Not for John.

He then smeared feces inside the wound and all over his abdomen to infect it. Finding this out made me realize that nothing mattered more to John than his own needs. John was able to maim himself forever and risk dying just to get high.

Another report I uncovered much later, detailing the months before John went to prison, involved a judge who had told him to "get his affairs in order" because he was going away for quite a while. This prison sentence was for theft of drugs, a parole violation while out on bail for deception to obtain dangerous drugs. While he was supposedly doing what the judge ordered, John drove to three different hospitals and attempted to steal drugs again. He was successful, in all three places. The cops found him two days later at a Comfort Suites hotel in Saginaw, Michigan, where he was living, with syringes and several empty vials of drugs in his possession. John was out of it when they entered his room. So they called in EMT services and John was whisked away in an ambulance. As the ambulance drove toward the hospital, John jumped up, kicked the doors open, and leaped out the back.

He ran to a nearby mall.

After a long search, law enforcement found him on top of a cargo elevator inside the mall. He was standing, holding on to the cables like a high-flying circus acrobat. The police officers ordered John to come down immediately. There was no way out of the situation for him.

As two police officers yelled for John to come down, he crawled up the elevator shaft, using the steel beams as steps and cables to hoist himself higher and higher. He made it about thirty feet into the elevator shaft system.

"I am not coming down," John yelled.

As the officers put up a ladder to approach him, John made it to a steel beam running across the elevator shaft. He continued to scream he was not coming down.

One slip and it would have been over for John Meehan.

While the officers moved closer, John found a piece of wire and swung it at them, like a whip.

"Stay back," he yelled.

"Come on, John, you have no way out of this, just come down," an officer said.

They cornered him from all sides and John kicked at them.

One cop managed to reach John. As they struggled, both slipped and fell into the cargo elevator, thumping onto the steel floor. Both were rendered unconscious and transported to the hospital. John was taken to the Saginaw County Jail after being treated and released. The cop spent the night in the hospital and was okay.

As I flipped through the papers John had collected—each detailing some of his criminal behavior, case after case, year after year—much of what I read was rooted in drug dependence. Yet there was another element in John's past behavior that rang true in my life: he had met several women and proclaimed his everlasting love, before systematically tearing their lives apart. He stole from each woman. When faced with being outed, John sought revenge for what he believed *they* had done to *him*. These pages revealed a wickedness in John. A dark part of him. This wasn't just a drug addict doing what he needed to survive and get his drugs—there was an obvious undercurrent of evil.

A few days before I read part of the letter John had received from his former cellmate, I had spoken to my therapist over the phone. Therapy scared me so much; it took all the courage I had to call her. But I did. My life was unraveling like a tightly wound spool of wire let loose. What became important about this moment, however, was that for the first time I believed what I was hearing and seeing. I'm talking about honestly believing what Ben, Liz, Scotti, and Nicole were saying.

My therapist encouraged me to be strong and think logically about things before reacting. The session was not much help, however. I was more confused after hanging up with her. I put my phone down and felt my blood pressure spiraling out of control. My breathing became laborious and heavy, and then slowed down. I was in a perpetual state of frayed nerves; the slightest thing made me jump. At sixty years old, I thought I was having a heart attack.

Scared, I drove myself to the local emergency room. I told them I wasn't sleeping. My heart was racing all the time. I had pains in my chest and arms.

They diagnosed me with panic attacks and prescribed Ativan.

Unbeknownst to me, John had checked himself in on the same day.

"I have a bowel obstruction," he wrote to me via an email I received while being treated for anxiety in a different wing of the same hospital.

I didn't respond.

It was a godsend, really, that he had checked himself into the hospital. The idea of lying next to this man in bed after learning the facts that I had seen in those documents—and now believed—was unsettling and made me even more anxious.

That first night John was in the hospital, my phone blew up, one text after another waking me. A small example: between 3:01 a.m. and 3:12 a.m., John sent me nearly a dozen texts.

"Hurry please."

"Hurry."

"Hurry."

"Please."

"Debbie please."

"Now."

"I whereate [*sic*] you."

"Please now."

"Now."

"Get here."

I called my therapist again the following day.

"Look, act as if you know nothing," she advised. "Do not confront him or act like you know any more than he thinks you do. Play his game. You do not want to make him angry. You need to do this for your own psychological well-being and safety."

"I need to confront John about what I know," I pushed back.

"Not right now."

"I need to see his reaction."

"No, Debbie. It's too dangerous."

"I need to do this."

"Debbie, listen to me. *Don't* do this."

I thought about it. This was my moment. The anxiety was far too great.

"I'm going to that hospital to confront him," I told her and hung up.

26

"JOHN IS VERY DANGEROUS, DEBBIE"

I never followed through. My therapist's advice, I realized after I thought about it, was smart. Getting in John's face inside the hospital was a stupid idea. I needed to start thinking about my situation rather than reacting in the moment. I had been running on emotion, triggered by whatever John did next or whatever I found out about him. My logic was skewed, just as it had been with several of my former husbands in similar circumstances. John was in the hospital. As far as I knew, he would be there for at least a few days. That was enough time to weigh my options and begin to plan my next moves.

I began to think clearly for what felt like the first time in a really long while.

When I got home, I went through more of John's belongings and found several handwritten notes.

"Mossberg 500" was one.

I googled it.

A Mossberg is a pump-action shotgun. A tactical weapon designed to kill.

Then I found several references to an "18.5 barrel and a 30-round clip," with the prices written next to it.

"Key-ignition CP mode . . . toy."

I wondered what all of this meant. I looked further and found a note about Epsom salt and acetone. So I googled that.

Epsom salt and acetone are used to purify street drugs.

While I was discovering the real John, Liz and Nicole were getting more information from the private detective.

Later, while being interviewed for the *Los Angeles Times* podcast, Liz explained the totality of what she, Nicole, and Scotti had learned, some of which I was not made aware of until almost a year later. It was this list of crimes John had perpetrated: attempting/threating to extort; first-degree burglary; second-degree burglary; stalking; making anonymous, threatening telephone calls; possession of a firearm by a convicted felon; possession of firearms; and violation of a protective order. He'd pled guilty to stalking and possessing a firearm in the weeks before I met him. John used nine different Social Security numbers. When we met on OurTime, John was homeless. He had just walked out of prison and had nowhere to go. Realizing this, I wondered if that homeless-looking, Ovaltine-drinking woman who had broken into the beach house had been a neighbor of John's on the street or even an associate—a partner in crime, if you will.

All of it was overwhelming. I knew nothing about this guy. Everything I thought I knew was a lie.

As I dug through John's papers, I found copies of records John had received from the Los Angeles County Superior Court. In those documents, which outlined a case against him in California, John was accused of threatening a woman he had been dating. He told her he would send "private pictures" of her to her employer and get her fired. I also learned (for the first time) that John had not one sister—whom he had claimed died—but two.

Both were still alive.

One was a nurse at the hospital where he had just been admitted. His other sister was involved in two court cases with John in Ohio.

God was on my side, however. As I read through this new information, I took a call from the hospital. John was going to be admitted for an extended period of time—weeks—based on a bowel obstruction he'd developed after a rather routine outpatient back procedure he'd had earlier in the year. The obstruction was a complication from the surgery.

I could breathe a bit. The call relieved some of my stress. John wasn't coming back home for a while. Before he was released, I could work on protecting myself, getting him out of my house, and erasing him from my life.

"You need to help me, Debbie. Don't abandon me," John texted. "I'll send our private pictures to all your kids and all your clients. Don't fuck with me. I will do this."

I tried as best as I could to ignore the text.

Ben and Liz came over. We talked.

"It's okay, Mom. We're here to help, not judge."

I cried.

"Let's put all of his stuff in the garage," Ben and Liz suggested.

"Yes. But we can't mess with it."

"We don't want to ruin anything," Liz said. "We don't want to give him *any* reason to become angry."

Could I have called the police at this point? For what? For a man lying about who he was? Could I have filed that domestic action and petitioned the court for a restraining order? Sure. But the chances of a court granting a restraining order under the circumstances were nil. I had spoken to girlfriends over the years who'd tried. It's not as easy as most people believe. This was something I needed to address myself. If John showed any indication of becoming violent or threatening us, I would take legal action and alert the police. But in that moment, at that precise time, I did what I thought was best, as my kids and Ben began helping me.

Ben was going through some of John's belongings as we moved everything into the garage.

"Um, holy shit. Look at this . . ." Ben said.

I looked at him. He'd turned pale white; the blood had drained from his face.

"Oh, my God . . ."

"What is it?" Liz and I asked.

Ben looked terrified.

"Why would he have all of this information about me?"

We looked at one another.

There was an envelope with Ben's name on it and inside was a piece of paper on which John had scribbled Ben's personal information. The question became why.

Was John planning to retaliate for something he believed Ben had done to him?

We dug deeper.

Liz found a little black book in a box. Its pages were filled with bank routing numbers, phone numbers, and, oddly, the names of guns John had been pricing.

"What is all this?" I asked.

John had written "$500 + 475 + 150 + $3,414 . . . a Sig Sauer." Beside that was a list of random gun parts. After reading through the black book, Liz and Ben figured out John was buying gun parts to build a gun himself since he was on parole and couldn't legally buy one. One violation would send him back to prison. Those figures were John's calculation of how much it was going to cost.

I had gone through John's papers a day earlier and found information about guns. There were also several boxes of papers that were all out of order; it would be a cumbersome task to go through and make sense of it all. So when Ben and Liz came over, it was easier to figure out what was what. In that additional paperwork, we found several printouts from websites on which women had posted warnings regarding unfaithful and deranged men they had met online. John's name was included in those printouts. Most of the posts said John was a con man and manipulator. What was clear as I read through them all was how similar each woman's story was and how my John Meehan experience fit in this group. Before this day, it had been easy for me to think, *Well, no one knows the John I do,* and dismiss my misgivings.

The silver lining was John's hospital admission. This was my chance to make plans to have him removed from my life. Or plans to hide from him.

"I need you to return the $160,000 you took out of my safety deposit box," John said over the phone. It was the day after he had been admitted to the hospital.

"What? I took no such money, John," I responded. John was turning the situation around, saying that my money, which he had supposedly put into the safety deposit box, was his.

He hung up.

A few days later, I received the first of many emails from John, sent as he lay recuperating in the hospital.

"Last week I gave you $500 in cash. This was to purchase a BBQ and outdoor furniture. I want the money back since I no longer want or need to be with you. Please send a check . . . Keep in mind that through your supposed Christian [faith], opening another's mail is still a felony. Which is a concept you are soon to learn about firsthand. Let's see if the Christian in you lies or walks hand in hand with a lie. I've obtained counsel . . . I am asking you to return the money you removed from my safety deposit box when you illegally entered it. This is not a game. I am filing a complaint against you."

I sat and stared at the screen. I knew 90 percent of what John had written was false. He was clearly threatening me, spelling out what he wanted: $160,000. This was his way of beginning a conversation—extortion—about what I needed to do in order to make the removal of him from my life go smoothly.

Part of the problem I faced (which I had told no one about) was that due to my own lack of responsibility I had never obtained a postnuptial agreement. I had blown off the idea of a prenup because we had gotten married so hastily in Vegas. The postnup I had promised John I would have ready for him to sign was in the works with a law firm after we returned from Vegas. The lawyers were taking their time and had given me a list of documents and personal and business information to gather and send. While this took place, over a three-month period just after we were married, I became more interested in pursuing an annulment. I had enough evidence to walk away, without the postnup. The problem was time. Things were evolving quickly at this point.

Much later, when I realized I was truly another one of John's victims, I educated myself. The assumption I had worked under was that I was in this fight alone. I had to keep it all under wraps while I played the "John game" with him. What many people who think they are familiar with my story don't understand is that I needed to figure out what I was doing, legally and safely. In addition, legal and psychological counselors were telling me to take my time. "Do it right," my therapist said during another phone session. "You cannot just go on the counterattack with a person of John's psychotic caliber. A man who lives and breathes coercive control is a dangerous man when confronted with the truth and the realization that you will not cower and pay him to go away."

John was not going to get what he wanted this time. Although I might have come across as easily intimidated, I was not going to lie down. If I had learned anything from my previous marriages, it was to keep your cards close and hidden. I needed to fight for myself.

John's next email from his hospital bed said:

> *I would like us to talk before getting attorneys involved. I still love you and simply cannot live without you. I don't want this. I want us without anyone else. You promised me it was forever. I meant it as well. Please don't let the attorneys get involved and all the ugly stuff attorneys bring. Can we at least talk like married adults or do we just let this go and with it a lot of broken hearts for the both of us. I miss you and need you. I am flawed. But it's not so easy to give up on you. When I met you it was simply you. I helped you get back on your feet and stood up for you. You want a divorce, just tell me. It's not what I want. We can move away from all of this and start again without a jury. Without people getting into our life. Please don't do this. I love and need you. Please.*

I read that and felt sorry for him. For us. For the situation. And this is the point in my story where I am most harshly judged, especially when people base their judgments on what was presented in the dramatic television series on Bravo.

How could you fall for John's nonsense time and again?

How could you possibly believe anything he said and even think about taking him back?

Why do you always do this—meet these same types of men and then stay in it too long?

One scary sidenote from my story that many people miss, especially those who judge me by how many times I've been married, is that you can't just walk away from these types of men without a plan. That's when violence—even murder—occurs. If there was one reality in the back of my mind during all my abusive marriages, after I decided the relationship was over, it was what had happened to Cindi, my sister. She ended her marriage. She paid for that decision with her life. Not only was I traumatized by Cindi's murder, but I experienced post-traumatic stress each and every time I was in a similar marital situation. Those who judge me based on how many times I am divorced forget this.

Or fail to see it at all.

For a brief moment, after reading John's first email on that day, I wondered if John was going to come clean, admit all his lies, ask for forgiveness, repent, and turn his life around. All human beings have the opportunity for redemption at any moment of their lives. I believe that and always will. This was the sort of sentiment clawing at the heart of my Christian soul. The base of my moral ground. I wanted to help people. My life's purpose was to forgive and reach out a hand to those who extended one to me in the name of need and remorse.

I was living with John's torment twenty-four hours a day. But did I want to go through another divorce if I could manage to save the marriage? I loved John, even as the lies unraveled one after the other and who he was came to light. This sounds contradictory, and I can understand how it might be perceived. It's important to take into consideration, however, that I felt both as if John could be redeemed and forgiven, and hated him for what I was uncovering. It was all confusing and alarming. It's hard to accept all at once that your husband, a man you thought you knew, a master of charm, is an entirely different person from what you believed.

I had called my attorney the morning of John's emails from the hospital to tell him what was happening. He said, "Debbie, you should see if you can purchase a handgun to protect yourself."

The people in my life were trying to protect me. I was now listening. The biggest threat from a person with John's criminal past is instability and uncertainty. John was unpredictable—a fact I had been unaware of and had not fully grasped until now. No one knew, of course, what John would do next or, more important, how far he could take things in *any* direction. It was clear to me after reading and rereading about his criminal past in those papers we uncovered that his crimes had escalated throughout the years. Each time he was arrested, the charges were more serious. Each time he retaliated against a female who challenged him, his behavior changed and he became more aggressive.

"Tell your attorney to stop contacting me," John emailed next, later that same day. My attorney had been sending John emails requesting that he stop threatening me with lawsuits and making spurious allegations. "I have filed two police reports on him. He isn't a family law attorney and he already fucked you up if this thing goes sideways . . . Be careful here, Debbie. This goes to attorneys and we all lose."

Twelve hours went by. I did not respond to John's emails.

"I guess the no answer is an answer," he wrote. "I still love you but I guess this is going to go south and turn ugly. I wish this wasn't the way it needed to be but there seems to be no alternative. I love you."

Each email had a threatening tone just hovering there, nearly imperceptible. John had this inexorable ability to say, *Okay, if that's the way you want it, you got it . . . watch out*, without actually using those words.

As confusing and threatening as some of John's emails may have sounded, I knew he was not only feeling me out to see where I was, but also sending me a message. I would find out later that John was repeating what he had said in previous emails to other women whom he had victimized. It was clear he was digging his heels in and gearing up for a battle. He was not going away without getting what he wanted.

Surely, John was after money, but also retribution. Payback. And I know that was more important to him than any amount of money he could extort from me.

I gave myself a day to mull over what was happening. I needed to think about every move now, not react impulsively. Then I called my attorney again.

"John is very dangerous, Debbie. Understand this about him. The evidence is clear," he said.

I had explained and showed him some of what we had found.

"He wants your money. We're going to file for an annulment. And one more thing: you need to change your will immediately."

Change my will?

"Why?"

My attorney hesitated.

"Why should I change my will?" I asked again.

"In case something happens to you."

In those days after we discovered John's paperwork and I started listening to my attorney, I heard from Terra in Las Vegas. She was not well. She called and explained that her relationship with Tony had hit a bump and she sensed they weren't going to make it. She was devastated by the thought of a breakup and said she wanted to come home if and when the relationship ended. Like me, however, she was determined to work through the issues to save it.

"Let's figure this out, honey," I told her. "It's going to be okay. I will help you any way you need me to."

Then the topic of conversation turned to John. Terra had long ago stopped giving John the benefit of the doubt.

"He's a scumbag, Mom. He's no good for you. You need to get rid of him."

Liz and I spoke a day after Terra made her feelings clear to me during that phone call. Liz shared a curious theory as to why John would hold on to all of those papers, which proved he was a psychopathic criminal: an extortionist and abuser who preyed on women. We had all asked that question: Why would he keep evidence of his past in a house he lived in with his wife, knowing she could uncover it at any time?

"Mom, he kept it all because he wanted to," Liz explained.

"I don't understand why he would do that."

"So he could go back and look at it. It probably gave him a sense of excitement to relive those moments."

Certain serial killers keep trophies from their victims—hair ties, underwear, a purse, shoes, a necklace, a ring, a driver's license. Psychopaths and serial killers relish going back to the kill and remembering it through items taken from their victims. Liz's argument was convincing. She said John had likely done the same with all his victims by holding on to reminders of his crimes.

"He gets off on it," Liz added.

Each bit of information I learned—and Liz was my beacon at this point, guiding me, helping me see the truth—told me more about the real John Meehan. I began to wonder: *Could a criminal like John ever change? Ever be redeemed? Was it even possible for a psychopath—which we were all beginning to believe John was—to be remorseful?*

I googled this question. The answer—if we're talking psychopath as opposed to sociopath—was an emphatic no.

Liz became my rock over the next several weeks. She was able to cast aside her personal feelings about me, the behaviors I'd exhibited, and the decisions I'd made she did not agree with, and express unconditional, supportive love. I am honored to be her mother. Liz could have easily played the "I told you so" card and thrown it all in my face. But once the shock of my marriage to John sank in, she kept me focused on accepting the facts of John's life we had discovered, divorcing him, and protecting myself, my children, and my grandchildren.

One item in the paperwork we'd found had started to bother me more every day—a nickname my husband had been given long ago: "Dirty John."

27

FILTHY, DIRTY, NASTY JOHN

John Michael Meehan grew up in San Jose, California. What I learned later from talking to people in John's early life was how gifted a student he was—one of those kids who could seemingly pull straight As without much effort. He excelled in sports while in high school and had the pleasure of dating any girl of his choosing. His father was raised in Brooklyn, which was where, I realized after getting to know John better, an Italian accent he sometimes displayed must have originated. John overdid it at times in a politically incorrect and insulting manner—you know, that heavy *Godfather*-like drawl.

John came from a long line of New York City Italians, some of whom, he routinely insisted, had deep bloodlines in organized crime. When John would get playful, as he often did during the early days we lived together, he'd turn on the accent. He'd even add hand gestures, as in those popular Mafia movies we've all seen. He played the part well. I took it for old-fashioned fun. His way of showing off and trying to make me laugh.

According to one of John's sisters, who went to Prospect High School, in Saratoga, California, with him in the late 1970s, John was a popular kid. He was charming and magnetic, attracting people to him. Although he was book smart, John did not seem to have much common sense. He also had a cockiness about him (actually an innate narcissism) he could not contain. He believed he was smarter than anybody around him.

That same sister, later interviewed by *LA Times* reporter Christopher Goffard, said, "[John] wasn't groomed to take [his gifts] and be successful and help other people and be grateful that he was blessed with [them]. Instead, he was taught to manipulate at a very early age and that's the fault of my parents, especially my dad, because that's all my dad knew."

John started his early medical career working as an orderly in hospitals. His sister said that at this time he was "wheeling and dealing, selling cocaine." John was also obsessed with James Bond—that is, Sean Connery's portrayal of Bond. He'd once had a vanity license plate—a great example of his narcissism—in reference to his infatuation with the character: "MEE 007."

That word, *mee*. It explained this was all about one person.

John Meehan.

In the *LA Times* podcast, one of John's sisters said, "[In high school, John was] in trouble all the time. It was just easier for John to just be 007 and to deal with women and money and cars and just hustle. He was a hustler and whatever he had to do to get money, he would do. He went into Taco Bell, picked up a piece of glass, put it in a taco, and bit into it. The company that my dad worked for was the one who paid the claim, so I don't know if they were both in cahoots on that or what, but I know my dad was hurting for money back then."

John once jumped in front of a speeding Corvette and made an accusation against the driver, claiming the man had deliberately tried to hit him. It turned out that John's father was behind the scam and John walked away with a bundle of insurance money.

In the early 1980s, John was living in California. He was arrested for drug dealing. He wound up testifying against his drug-dealing partner, a good friend, and was given a lighter sentence. The judge in that case had, in fact, given John a verbal warning during the sentencing about leaving the state, but he left anyway.

From California, John moved to Arizona and enrolled at the University of Arizona. He earned a BA. Seemingly setting his life on track, he moved to Ohio and managed to get into a Dayton law school.

It was in law school, according to one classmate who appeared on the podcast, that John was given that now infamous "Dirty John" nickname. According to his classmate and peer, the name was based on the way John dressed and a reputation he developed with women (namely, the sexual needs John insisted his women fulfill). Another common name given to him was "Filthy John." At times, that name was revised to a more simplified "Filthy." Another old friend had said the true reason for the Dirty John nickname was too disgusting to repeat and involved sexual demands John had made on other women in his life.

It seems John was *never* concerned or careful about his appearance. In law school, his fingernails, especially, were gross, like a mechanic's. His clothes were sloppy.

During his second year of law school, John disappeared from campus. His departure was so abrupt, many of his peers wondered where he'd gone. One day John was on campus, the next . . . gone. With no warning or indication, he left.

It was his grades. John was scoring far below any possible passing grade. In the 40s and 50s range if we're talking numbers. He'd flunked out. Embarrassed, perhaps, he ran.

John then began his life as a serious criminal. He started simple credit card scams by applying for cards in fictitious names. He also began passing himself off as a builder or roofer. He would accept down payments for jobs he never did. That grew into housing scams. He was also a serial cheater whenever he was married or in a relationship. All of this—and the fact that he preyed upon older women in many cases—contributed to the Dirty John nickname. As he entered his thirties, he continued to move through life by wrecking lives and committing crimes. The name, I gathered from all I could find out, was based not on one particular behavior but a combination of all the dirty tricks and scams—felonies—John was committing.

In 1990, at thirty-one, John married a woman who had just graduated from medical school and went on to become a nurse anesthetist. John had told the woman he was twenty-six years old and his name was Jonathan Meehan, as opposed to his actual name, John.

John invited no one from his family to the wedding.

One friend, who acted as best man, claimed to have given him the Dirty John nickname.

The marriage lasted nine years. His wife had pushed John into nursing school and had been responsible for making sure he made it through. John's wife, who by then had given birth to his two daughters, had never met John's mother or father. But as the marriage dissolved and his wife found out he was having an affair with a woman in Michigan, she searched for and found John's mother.

On the *LA Times* podcast, John's ex-wife read from a journal she'd kept during the dissolution of her marriage to John. She spoke of calling his mother one time and telling her John had asked for a divorce. Then she told his mother that John had "forbidden" her to ever speak to anyone in his family. John's mother opened up. She explained that John's actual birthday was February 3, 1959, and that his birth name was John Michael Meehan, not Jonathan Michael Meehan. John's mother mentioned an arrest in California for selling cocaine in which John gave up his best friend as part of a plea bargain. John's mother, whom his wife had never spoken to until this conversation, asked if he was still using drugs. This was a jaw-on-the-floor moment for his wife, who had no idea John was a drug user.

As I talked to additional family members, one recurring behavior of John's kept popping up: John would tell "women anything to get them to like him."

That was the understatement of my life.

In 1999, after kicking John out of the house, his wife searched their home, looking for anything she could find to explain more about the apparent stranger she had married. She found fentanyl and Versed. She called the police and an investigation began, resulting in John's arrest.

This was when John began threatening those detectives' lives.

During that first marriage, from 1990 to 1999, John managed to earn a degree in nursing anesthesiology, which allowed him to begin working in hospitals. And from there, he began stealing any drug he could get his hands on. He could no longer work in Ohio or Michigan after his wife had initiated the investigation. So John moved to Indiana and started over. One of his wife's friends, however, wouldn't let the case go. She wound up notifying the nursing board in Indiana about him. John was banned from working in Indiana as well.

The Indiana restriction lit a fire in John to take revenge on his wife, who he believed had called the nursing board. As John threatened to retaliate against her, she started recording the phone calls between them. John's intent is clear in a recorded call his then ex-wife turned over to law enforcement.

John called and demanded to know who had called the Indiana State Board of Nursing on him. He assumed it was his ex-wife.

She told him she wasn't going to reveal that person's name because John was "the most vindictive person" she knew.

John claimed all he had done was to protect his two daughters.

John then rambled on about how his ex-wife was the cause of all their troubles. She responded by telling him that she had finally spoken to his mother. She said, "Your mother told me some very horrible things about the person that you really are."

This riled him up. John hated the idea that someone had something on him. It enraged him. He had this internal hatred for women. From talking to him intimately when we were getting along, I got the impression that it was rooted deeply in his upbringing, though he never shared any stories explaining what might have happened. I know he had an abnormal childhood, with a domineering and criminal father who, from what John told me, beat him.

At the time of this conversation between John and his ex-wife, John was living in the homeless shelter at Good Samaritan Hospital in Indiana. For much of his life after college and law school, other than those ten years of marriage, John was basically homeless. Whenever he had money, he chose to live in cheap, weekly-rate motels infested with drug users and prostitutes.

In several additional recordings turned over to law enforcement, John's rage comes through clearly. His tendencies toward trying to control situations and threatening women are evident in each of the calls. In one voice mail, it is clear that not knowing who had called the Indiana State Board on him was eating John up. For John, it wasn't about losing his job, or some inherent need to help people as a nurse; it was about losing the opportunity to be around drugs he could steal. What's more, within the overall psychological scope of who John Meehan truly was, he blamed his ex-wife for his homelessness. Because of her actions, he'd lost his job and could not work. He never saw that his own behavior was the problem. This is typical psychopathic thinking.

Blame everyone else.

At one point during a second call with his ex, John asked, "Do you know why I have this big smile on my face?"

He was cryptic and mysterious, never coming out and saying what he meant, but then took things to another level entirely, adding, "When it happens, remember it was me, okay?"

John was suggesting he had sent someone to kill her. He told her to "enjoy" what time she had left "on this earth."

He again mentioned that he had a "big smile" on his face "because it's going to get done," adding that he was going to be in another country when "it" took place. He continued, "I swear to fucking God . . . it's going to be you."

All of this, mind you, was caused by his ex-wife calling his mother and learning the truth about John.

In the end, John never followed through on his threat. His ex-wife turned over the recordings to the police. John was sentenced to one anger management class. The police could not make a case.

The abuser usually wins. This is a problem women face routinely in these situations; the courts give the benefit of the doubt to the abuser.

John's ex-wife, whose name I have chosen not to use, had lived with him for more than a decade, and he had managed to keep his past secret from her. He also controlled her—until she decided to find out on her own who she had married.

One of the detectives who investigated John's ex-wife's case described John as "just the most devious person I've *ever* met."

This particular detective had been on the job for forty years.

28

THE TORMENTOR

I found a quarter-inch-thick stack of emails one day after we had placed all of John's stuff in the garage. John had printed out each email and saved them together. I found them in a box we had somehow missed. These were more alarming than anything I had seen to date. It was the end of May 2015. I was more aware than I had ever been—and planning my stealthy exit from the marriage. How to do this safely was going to become the challenge. I understood John Meehan was not someone whom I should confront or make angry. I was still trying to decide how to free myself. Restraining order? Divorce? Annulment? Maybe I could go into hiding somewhere and deal with him from a distance? He was still in the hospital. It looked like he'd be there for another two weeks. Time was on my side. And as much as I hate to say this, as an added bonus in my situation, John was not doing well. He was extremely ill. He was losing weight, and his back and knees were swollen and arthritic. It was possible he had an internal infection.

Reading his printed email exchanges was beyond sobering. John told one woman he had become involved with that he was going to tell the school where she worked she was a prostitute. He warned her that he was going to show pictures of her in various sexual poses to school officials, post the pictures online, print them out, and hang them inside the school where she worked.

One email said:

You will leave town and do so by end of the month . . . Go home to mom and dad, if they will have you . . . You understand what I am capable [of] . . . You don't want this . . . If you so much as think about sex with another, I bury you both and I will video[tape] it. The last guy you fucked, you will tell me who it is. You will take care of me the entire year. You will find a girlfriend and the both of you will do me. You will do this within a month.

Those were John's demands, if she wanted to avoid embarrassment and being fired.

I could not believe what I was reading. Turning the pages, I understood that John was a vile human being, capable of anything. He had a hunger for revenge I had never thought existed in people.

"You will do my laundry," he continued in another email to the same woman. "You will swallow my sperm. And you will gladly accept wherever I want to fuck you. [For] one year."

He continued to threaten the woman's job, saying he was ready to send pictures to the school board and her colleagues.

"This is going up on Facebook, you hooker," he emailed, along with a link to some rather risqué photographs of her.

"When your herpes clear up," he continued, trying to scare her into believing he had herpes and had given it to her, "you can start dating under another name."

If that weren't bad enough, he wrote, "Keep in mind suicide works with the garage door down. Your mom might even come out to see you then."

The woman wrote him back, asking what the heck he was talking about. He responded:

I have all your contacts, you stupid shit. Makes me even more pissed . . . Suffer [her name]. Suffer alone . . . Tomorrow . . . your life goes into the shit can.

She asked how much. What was the amount John wanted to make all of this madness go away?

"$845,000," he demanded. "I despise the day I ever met you. As you will despise the day you met me. This should make us even, though. A ruined life for a ruined life."

Pure blackmail—but he never received the money.

This was my husband, in front of me, in black and white, with documents he himself had printed and saved. The same man who had access to my computers, my personal life, and my business and banking accounts, as well as my children. The same man who had tossed my grandchildren in the air and caught them in a playful way. The same man I had slept next to for the past six months.

Finding all of this shook me to the core. Was it even possible to leave him? To tell John it was over and I was filing for divorce? What would he do? How would he react when I abandoned him?

In April 2015, I finally went to the Irvine police. I was scared of what John would do once he was out of the hospital. Was he going to start emailing my clients? Was he coming after me? Was he going to clean me out of all my money? Was he going to harm my children?

To say it was humiliating when I spoke to the police the first time would be to understate the seriousness of the situation; it was far worse. The Irvine police had me sit for hours waiting for someone to talk to. I was amazed by their lack of response and empathy. When officers finally sat down to hear me out, I felt as if they were annoyed that they had to deal with a troubled marriage. It was as if this was some sort of wife-versus-husband quarrel they didn't want to get involved in.

I went to the Laguna Beach police and they responded in the same way.

The Newport police treated me like I was the aggressor, the victimizer.

Law enforcement officers concluded there was nothing they could do. I had no bruises, no proof I had been abused, and no confirmation John was planning anything. There was no direct threat. I felt the police had judged me to be a hysterical female overreacting to a domestic squabble. The message was clear: go home and settle your marital differences between the two of you. Was it the 1970s? I could not accept that I was being victimized by a man who had a history of harassment and nothing was being done to protect me or my family.

"I'll be back," I told them.

I walked away from those meetings, which occurred over a two-day period, thinking something had to change.

As I drove back to the beach house to figure out my next moves, I realized I had always been John's target from the moment he saw my profile on OurTime. A seasoned grifter, John had carefully and deliberately chosen his next mark—me.

I needed to protect myself and my family. I knew I had to focus on when John would be released from the hospital and what I would do. At the same time, I struggled with feelings of empathy and of wanting to forgive him. I had thought a lot about John being alone in the hospital. Upon hearing of my sympathy for John, some who read this will go straight to disbelief. Yet another way to describe what was happening is Stockholm syndrome, which is most famously known from the Patty Hearst case. The victim begins to develop affection, a bond, for the hostage-taker/kidnapper, and even trusts them. Patty Hearst was a California newspaper heiress who, in 1974, was kidnapped by revolutionary militants and, over a period of time, appeared to develop sympathy for her captors, before actually joining them as a willing criminal in an armed robbery. You experience Stockholm syndrome when your captor alienates all your feelings of loyalty to those you love and makes you believe he or she is the only answer. This takes time. It doesn't happen over the course of a miniseries on television.

John had not kidnapped me. But he had hijacked my mind and soul. He had a hold over me. Even as he lay in a hospital bed, incredibly ill, he knew what he was doing. He'd been honing his skills for twenty-plus years.

I felt reconciliation was out of the question. In a way, I blamed myself for part of what was happening; perhaps I wasn't being compassionate enough. John needed compassion, maybe someone to love him unconditionally. As I have said, my response resulted from living in constant conflict and fear.

One thing was clear: I couldn't just come out and tell John it was over. The information I now had told me John *never* walked away.

After thinking about it and talking to close friends, I decided to start playing against John at his own game. I needed to become the aggressor, without him knowing it.

It was time to con the con man.

29

RAP SHEET

Kept from me when I first met John was the fact that he had not just come back from Iraq after a stint helping the wounded and innocent victims of a war-torn country. In stark contrast, John had stepped out of prison just two months before we shared that delightful first date at Houston's. Once released, he was picked up on a parole violation and then spent another month in jail; just two days before our date, he was released again. John had been arrested for theft of drugs and possession of drugs, on top of a weapons offense—just a few of the felonies in a shopping list of charges, a rap sheet two pages long. Also included in that list were multiple charges of harassment. A half-dozen more charges of breach of contract. Professional negligence. Slander. Libel. Auto theft. Another half-dozen charges of medical malpractice. Civil harassment. The list went on and on.

Among the dozens of crimes John had committed were printing the business cards he gave out indicating he was a doctor; telling people he worked for the Department of Justice and the Drug Enforcement Agency; scamming people out of money for remodeling homes in Ohio; obtaining personal information about people (family, associates, and friends) and using it against them whenever he was scrutinized; and providing a false date of birth on all his records since college.

In one instance, between 1999 and 2000, John had dated a woman for eighteen months. She was a doctor. They met at a hospital where John was a nurse. John was still married. The woman wound up having one of John's children. He'd never paid her child support of any kind. The doctor ended the relationship when she found out John was married. John then threatened to ruin her career by disclosing her personal and intimate emails if she didn't stay in the relationship—that is, before threatening her with violence.

On a website designed to warn women about impostors lurking on dating sites, which I was shown in the months after John was out of my life, one woman who had dated John reported him as "a fraud," noting that John wasn't an anesthesiologist or a doctor—he wasn't even a licensed nurse. "Not qualified to change bed pans," a second woman had written on the site. A third woman claimed John "will travel far to come to meet you . . . and knows every trick in the book to make you fall for him." A fourth woman he had dated said, "[John] tried to tell me he was a doctor, a nurse anesthetist and physician assistant," but she discovered he was a "drug addict."

I then discovered on my own that the state of Tennessee had reported John was stealing hard-core drugs—OxyContin, fentanyl, Demerol, codeine—from emergency rooms and had no medical license.

Another woman on that same website mentioned that she was forced to claim bankruptcy because of what John had done to her, adding, "Emotionally needy, not very good in bed, and doesn't even own a car."

Then there was a list of restraining orders against John.

In one restraining order I obtained, he had admitted (in a handwritten response by him to the accusations), "On or about April 8, 2013, and June 30, 2013 [merely sixteen to nineteen months before I met him], I did willfully, maliciously, repeatedly and unlawfully make a credible threat with one intent to place her in reasonable fear for her safety, and on July 1, 2013, I did unlawfully possess and have custody and control of a firearm, after having been previously convicted of a felony."

One Laguna Beach police report I later obtained—dated 2013, the same year as the restraining order just quoted—charged John with felony burglary, felony extortion, and felony stalking. The accompanying list of evidence found in a storage locker John rented spoke for itself: binoculars,

GPS units, heavy-duty cable ties, a .38 Special revolver, an "Official Police .38 revolver," boxes and boxes of ammunition, gold watches, pocketknives, several gold rings and diamonds, a sodium chloride injection bag, several single-dose syringes, sterile dressing kits, a timer, a sportsman's saw, a bottle of cyanide, hospital scrubs, and a host of miscellaneous items he had likely stolen.

I've seen enough true-crime television to know that what John had in his possession was akin to a serial killer's kill kit. The guy was far more dangerous than any other man I had ever met, dated, or married.

John's lies about being in prison and everything else at the time would turn out to be but a fraction of the pathological untruths that were out there. The revelations were mind-boggling, and I wondered if it had been naïveté, post-traumatic stress, ignorance, or just plain denial that had kept me from seeing the truth.

30

LIES AND MORE LIES

At first, during John's hospital stay, I was in shock as I came to grips with everything I had read; the paralyzing anxiety and the concern for my family's safety were almost too much to deal with. I could not focus on anything, and my stomach was constantly twisted and tight. However, after a week of numbness, I pulled myself together and made a decision not to lie down this time and take whatever came my way. I was not going to allow my past to dictate the future. I did not have to accept any of it and cower. I had choices. I was determined to be proactive this time.

In April 2015, I made my first move on John in an inconspicuous way. I was working from home one day and my cell phone rang.

"John?"

"Debbie, listen to me. I'm being released and have no one to pick me up. You are still my wife. I need your help."

He sounded desperate, needy. Unlike the aggressive and demanding John I knew.

After a long pause, I said, "John, all you've done is lie to me. Look, I know everything. I found your papers and have compiled other information about you."

There was risk in showing a few of my cards. Telling John I knew things about his past would either turn him into a revenge-driven maniac or calm him down. He might think, *She's not just going to accept whatever I say anymore.* The idea was to throw him off the game plan that had worked for him in the past.

"Debbie, I will share everything with you—the truth. I'm sorry."

"John, I've read through some of your police reports. How do you explain those?"

"All those police reports you read, well, I saved them because they are not about me. I was set up. My name and information were used. If you read them and recall, there are seventeen other names in those reports similar to John Meehan." He rattled off several: "Michael Meecan. Mike Merchan. John Meeham. John Michael."

"John, are you serious?" I asked with feigned compassion and naïveté.

He went on. "Debbie, please, look at the descriptions of me in those reports and you'll see red hair and six feet tall. Large and small build. Blond hair. Different people, Debbie. Those guys either stole my identity or just pulled out a name."

"John, why should I believe you now?"

"Debbie, Debbie, Debbie, listen to me. Please. My first wife set me up with those drugs in the house because we had a child custody case going on. I can prove it all if you *just* give me the chance."

I stayed quiet—by design—for a few moments. He sounded desperate. He needed to regain my trust. I was in a position to make him *think* I might trust him again, which would work to my advantage.

"Debbie, please, I am your husband. Please help me. I have nowhere to go. I'll be on the street."

"You are not coming here, John. I don't want you near this house."

"Debbie, please . . ."

A feeling of empowerment washed over me. I was in charge of my life. It's difficult to get people who have not experienced the stealthy torment of coercive control to understand how powerless you feel when someone infiltrates your life and gains access to every part of it for nefarious reasons. You think you know someone, you are married to this person, and suddenly everything you find out about him is a lie. Trust is not even part of your reality any longer. You question everything about not only him but also others who walk in and out of your life. Remember, coercive control works without you realizing you are being controlled. Your mind is slowly poisoned by your abuser. You believe the lies. You feel a loyalty to this person.

I was out of that space, however. It was my turn to wield some control.

"I'll tell you what," I said.

"What, Debbie—tell me. Please."

"I will pick you up. And I will put you up in a hotel room."

I wasn't offering alternatives. John knew this was his one choice.

So he agreed.

Once inside the hospital, I found John. I was disgusted with him, and upset with myself. Looking at me, he could tell a shift in our relationship had occurred. I was no longer scared of him. If there was one talent John had besides his criminal behavior, he could read people—especially me. I was now aware of this.

"Start explaining, John. Because I will just walk out of here and leave you on your own if what I hear is not the truth."

He didn't speak, but instead began to cry and then sob uncontrollably.

"Please don't do this to me," I said. "I can't handle watching you cry like this. I will get you out of here and then you can share everything with me. No more lying. I want the truth."

John nodded in agreement. The tears, I believed then, were genuine. Now I know John could turn them on and off and this was part of a playbook he had utilized with all his victims for the past two decades.

I wasn't one of those people anymore—only he didn't know it.

After wheeling him out of the hospital and helping him into the car, I dropped him off at a run-down hotel outside Irvine. I gave him some food, his prescriptions, and a bit of cash. Then I turned and headed toward the door to leave.

"I'll be back after work tomorrow. We can talk then. Prepare what you need to say, because I am giving you *one* chance to come clean with me."

"I understand," he said.

The man I saw that day in the hospital was physically ill. He had lost forty pounds. He appeared helpless. He was in pain. Beaten down by whatever ailments he'd been in the hospital for. I was never sure what was wrong with him. His back, I thought, was the cause of this particular hospital stay. He'd mentioned a bowel obstruction as well. I knew John had a history of getting injections in his back. I had brought him to several procedures and sat and watched. But who knows why he was hospitalized for as long as he was—almost thirty days.

The next morning, I pressed John for the truth. I wasn't going to accept that he had been set up and none of what I had read was true. That was the old Debbie. The woman who had appeased him and never put up a fight.

"No, John, I don't believe you were set up all those times. It's impossible, actually."

"Debbie, just hear me out, please."

"Go ahead."

You need to understand that John was a convincing, pathological liar. I don't think most people realize how powerful the manipulation can be when you're dealing with a psychopath who is an expert fraudster. It's easy to write this off by saying, *Oh, you must have had a feeling he was lying.* No, actually, I didn't. A lot of what John had told me before this point was not hard to believe. He could convince me of almost anything. He believed his own lies—just as most psychopaths and narcissists do—which made him that much more convincing. I did not understand this entirely then, but John was a professional con man. A grifter who had decades of experience lying to people. Remember, he was married for over a decade to a woman who never knew anything about his past or his family. That kind of manipulation takes an expert to pull off.

"I want to take you to my lawyer's office and sit down with him," John said. "My lawyer has all the same paperwork you read, and he can tell you that I was set up, that I am the victim in those cases, and that my ex-wife is responsible for it all. Please, Debbie."

"You know, John, I will give you only this one last chance. One meeting in your lawyer's office. If I don't believe either of you, I am out of there and you will never contact or see me again. Can you agree to that?"

"Okay, I understand."

I knew darn well that was impossible.

"I'm going back to work and then home. Don't call or text."

"Okay, Debbie. But please come back and do this. You'll see. My lawyer will explain."

I left the hotel, worked all day, and drove home. Along the way, I decided annulment was the way to go. But I needed to plan it out carefully. John was not going to accept it without a fight. He'd make demands and threats, no matter how he was currently acting. The police were obviously not going to help. I needed advice. More than just a lawyer scaring me and telling me to arm myself and prepare for the worst. I thought about who could help me.

Should I get security? Hire a bodyguard?

A friend recommended I look into meeting with a forensic psychologist and, at the least, get a professional opinion and profile of John Meehan. Find out the exact type of human being I was going up against.

I made a few calls.

31

GAME CHANGE

It was a Monday. I recall this day in late April 2015 with an amount of clarity reserved for those traumatic moments in our lives. Trauma works that way. Neuroscience has proved time and again that intense emotional memories imprint in our brains. Routine, mundane, day-to-day events do not cause much of an emotional reaction. Our brains tag (file) important events. Fear is such an intense emotion that it causes us to recall traumatic events clearly even when they happened decades ago. There were so many of these memories during my life and during my relationship with John. This is one reason why my story comes to me with ease and detail. I also took a lot of notes while I was with John. His presence will always be in my life.

John was ready when I arrived at the hotel. He came toward me for a hug and kiss, as though nothing had happened and we were that married couple again, living in the beach house.

"No, John. I am not anywhere near that yet. Give me time." I paused to see how he would react, then added, "I'll get there, honey. I just need some time."

Yeah, right.

It was my turn to lie to him and make him think we were going to work things out. Otherwise, there was no predicting what he would do. On top of that, I did not know how strong John was. He'd had this sluggish, slow-moving way about him since being released from the hospital.

I couldn't tell whether or not it was part of his act. Was he lying about his recovery? Weight loss aside, when would John be back to his old self? I had to be careful.

We drove to his lawyer's office. I went alone because bringing my lawyer would have just incensed him and worked against me. As I pulled into the parking lot, I had a thought and made a mental note: *Hire yourself a private investigator to watch John and see what he is doing during the day.*

A feeble man, in what looked to be a suit a size too big, John's lawyer approached me as we walked into his filthy office. He said hello, introduced himself, and mentioned a few things about our imminent chat.

I knew immediately that he and John had discussed what was going to be said.

"Have a seat, Debbie," John's mousy lawyer said.

John stood for a moment, then limped his way over to the leather chair next to me and sat down with a painful thud.

"Darn back is hurting me today," John said.

I did not respond.

"Okay, so, John here . . . tells me you do not believe he has been set up for those charges he once faced when a custody battle for his children ensued."

"I do not," I said.

"John is innocent, Mrs. Meehan. I can prove this."

"I am all ears," I said.

John cringed in his seat, complaining of back pain.

The lawyer began to lay out John's case from his perspective. I listened and, perhaps recklessly, thought, *Well, if a lawyer believed that it wasn't as bad as I thought it was, who am I to question him?* Would a lawyer lie for his client—and actually contradict the police reports and witness statements?

Sure he would.

John's lawyer was convincing, however.

I could almost feel myself being pulled back into John's world. It was as if I had no control over it. I would say I was 90 percent out and 10 percent in at this point. I was nowhere near giving John another chance. And, honestly, I knew that he was never going live in the same house with me again. That was not an option.

Another factor I was considering at this time was my relationship with Liz, Nicole, Brandon, and Terra. We were mending difficulties, figuring out issues, and moving forward as a family. They were helping me understand what was going on. Giving me sage advice. And for the first time, I was taking it.

There was no way I could tell John I had reconciled with the kids. He despised my children in every way. I had sensed my pre-John life was slowly returning, and this invigorated me.

After meeting with his lawyer, I dropped John off at the hotel. He seemed to think he'd convinced me of everything the attorney had confirmed. Some of it I believed. Yet the overall takeaway was that I did not trust John anymore, and his lawyer was most likely lying for him. I was still his wife. I could help him—to a point. But I was still planning my escape.

"Well," I said before John got out of the car. "Thank you for clarifying all of that. I understand better now."

"You see what I mean, Debbie? I was set up. You believe me now, right?"

"I do, John."

It felt good to placate John. Turning this around on him was one of the best decisions I'd made since we were married.

A girlfriend of mine lived in Santa Barbara, a two-hour drive northwest. It was close enough to home, but also far enough away from John. He had no idea where she lived. I could effectively hide out there and begin to put an end to the marriage. I also started changing my passwords at least once a week. It scares me to think back now and realize that a small part of me was still in because I loved him, had married him, and had always lived according to the principle that everyone deserves a second chance, a behavior I had vowed to steer away from but that still lingered. The one clear fact about myself I focused on, however, was that I had rushed quickly into my marriages. I had not given relationships the chance to blossom and had not allowed time for my partners' true personalities to emerge. I own that part of my life. Because of where I stood with John, I was not going to divorce him or annul our marriage—I was going to get out of it without being wrung through the lawyer-court-divorce wringer. I was determined to escape without having to deal with John and his payback method of revenge.

John knew where some of my money was locked away in a safety deposit box in the desert and had access to it. If he had found out at this point that I was leaving him, I figured my money, my life, and my children's lives would be at risk. He knew too much about my work, my finances, my every move. I had to change up my day-to-day behavior to throw him off.

In a few weeks, I thought, *I'll make him think I am* totally *back in.*

Searching through John's paperwork one afternoon, I came across a police report. There was no question it was my John Meehan. The date of birth, weight, eye and hair color, height, full name, and Social Security number lined up. The report was dated July 1, 2013, about a year before we met. It essentially outlined for me what I would be in for when I dropped the hammer and dismissed John, letting him know I was filing for divorce or annulment.

He had harassed the woman who'd filed the complaint in the most extreme, abusive ways. He emailed her, telling her he knew where she slept, how she slept, and where and how she was spending her time. He stalked her endlessly. John broke into her vehicle one day and used a piece of paper from inside the vehicle to leave a disparaging note about getting even. Law enforcement contacted John on three different occasions to tell him about the complaint and the pending charges, warning him not to contact the woman. The day the police spoke to him, he emailed her "over 80 times and called and texted . . . more than 20 times." She attempted to get a second, temporary restraining order in addition to one she'd filed, but no one could find John to serve the order. The woman wound up moving out of California "for fear of her safety," the police report stated, "and . . . has been hiding out . . . in order to keep Meehan from finding her."

He had actually scared her enough to leave the state.

Part of my plan, I decided after reading that, had to include travel. I needed to make sure I had a "busy" work schedule. I put my assistant, who was absolutely incredible during this stressful period, on it. She booked me stays in Washington State, Oregon, Colorado, Arizona, Nevada, Texas, and several additional states. I even spent some time in Lake Tahoe. Some of the travel included work, but a lot of it was designed to keep me away from John as much as possible.

John was doing everything he could to show me he was innocent of the charges I'd uncovered in his papers. I made him think I bought into his lies and believed him. He had no idea I had seen *all* his papers. So he believed then that we were talking about a single incident in which another man supposedly stole his identification and threatened his ex-wife and two detectives. I felt the coercively controlled part of me dissolving a bit more each day. Faking who I was became part of freeing myself from the control. You cannot tell anyone else what you're doing until you have a solid plan activated. For that reason alone, I waited to tell the kids my plan—and when I did, I explained only what they needed to know, when they needed to know it.

Because John was getting anxious, having trouble acclimating to the hotel room I was paying for, and questioning me about my feelings and actions, I decided to allow him to move into an apartment with me, which I had found and rented. Sounds dangerous, right? Perhaps this was not something I should have done. But making John believe we were eventually getting back together took courage. I was changing my MO by stepping into his world of control.

Before I allowed him to move in, I changed all of my bank accounts, and started collecting my paychecks in cash. Meanwhile, I discovered John had forged about $10,000 worth of checks, which he had made out to himself from my personal account. He had signed my name. In fact, John had been stealing from me from almost the moment he entered my life. I never let on to him that I had found out.

I felt a persistent sense of urgency brought on by being on the verge of getting caught. At the same time, however, patience was going to benefit my plan. Also, putting John close to me, as much as the thought made my skin crawl, was by design.

Then, as another part of my multipronged approach, I made an appointment with the forensic psychologist I had found to learn all I could about people who suffer from personality disorders, like John Meehan. This would heighten my anxiety and create conflict for me, but it was essential that I know the type of person I was dealing with.

Learning about psychpaths, narcissists, and coercive-controlling predators, I developed a better sense of how horrible a human being John Meehan was, but I also gained valuable insight into how I could deal with him. You survive an enemy by learning as much as you can about him. The most important, if not most terrifying, information I would learn later was the fact that men like John were highly capable of killing their wives.

"A psychpath, like John, who has an antisocial personality disorder, is a very dangerous human being," the forensic psychologist explained during our session. "He will deceive in ways we do not realize."

We have no idea we're being manipulated.

"What about my children? I am scared for them and my grandchildren."

"It's unlikely a man like John would make your kids the target of his rage—it's you, unfortunately, he would go after."

The psychologist explained that John had set a precedent. Those police reports and papers I had found, copies of which I shared with her, proved that, in every instance, John had targeted the source, not those connected to the source. He might threaten family and friends, but John's radar, according to this psychologist, was set on the person he viewed most responsible for the refusal of his demands. This felt positive. In the world I had created for John and me, we were still teammates, not enemies, as far as he knew. Getting rid of John was risky and dangerous. But I was willing to take the chance.

A takeaway from the meeting was that many psychopaths play the victim role to their advantage. They tell stories about people from their past taking advantage of them. They work overtime trying to make people feel sorry for them. Later, I did some of my own research. I found that psychopaths view people from their past who they believe have wronged them as "high-conflict people." Unstable people like John often engage in extreme behaviors, become preoccupied with blaming others, and harbor an all-or-nothing thought process. Their emotions go unchecked and unmanaged. They are intent on punishing others in vicious and fatal ways.

I asked the forensic psychologist to talk about anger.

"Their rage, especially, is directed mostly at those who stand in their way."

This scared me. John saw Liz as an obstacle to controlling me.

My other thought was that as long as I kept the facade going, John would feel as if our marriage was not in jeopardy. This was important to my survival and exit strategy. He might not seek to destroy me if he believed I was still on his side.

"I don't want to scare you, but I want to educate you," she advised. "You should continue to play the game with Mr. Meehan. Try not to let on to him that you're on to him, if that makes sense."

"It does. I have been doing that and will continue."

The session was sobering. John was far more dangerous than I had thought. On my own, I learned that a married psychopath's worst behaviors—in both men and women—were exacerbated by the marriage itself. Psychotic spouses who feel wronged by a partner can be the most deadly. There's an overflow of revenge and payback reserved for the moment a marriage implodes. A failed marriage brings out the worst.

Thinking about this, I considered something. Those five, or at one time six, people John had said he killed while serving with Doctors Without Borders (both lies disproved by private investigation) could have been killed here in the States—by John. I wrestled with the idea of John being a serial killer responsible for cold-case murders. Yet as I considered allowing him to live with me, I realized doing so was my only ploy at this point; learning about him became a strategy that would help me protect myself—a new part of the plan I was putting into play immediately.

32

"I KNOW YOU ARE GOING TO LEAVE ME"

I had found an available apartment at the Irvine Spectrum and moved some of my belongings in. One of the reasons I invited John to stay at the apartment was to convince him I still had one foot in the door of our marriage. The other reason was that I was not going to be home much anymore. If I hadn't done this, and had left him to fend for himself in cheap motel rooms, he would have suspected that I was up to something. Meanwhile, John had returned to being the charming, doting, pampering husband. He washed my cars. Ran errands. Grabbed my mail from the post office. He even picked up my dry cleaning and did the grocery shopping. He was trying to show me he was back to his old self. He claimed his injuries were healing and he was on the road to becoming more productive.

I saw right through it.

One everyday action most people take for granted, which produced overwhelming anxiety for me, is walking through the door of their own home. Would I find John booting drugs with some strange woman he'd met during his days out?

Arriving home at the Spectrum during the summer of 2015 was always tense. Would John realize I was on to him? There wasn't anything in that apartment I cared much about. So, if I walked in one night and he'd cleaned me out, big deal. I didn't think he was able to get into my accounts or find out where I was on most days and felt a sense of safety.

Then something odd happened about the first week of June. John and I had gotten a golden retriever together, and I decided to take him for a walk to a nearby park one afternoon. John insisted on coming. It was almost as if he was worried about me going to this particular park by myself. When we arrived, there was a woman strolling about. She kept staring at the two of us, smiling at John. He acted like he didn't know her, but I had this instinctive feeling he did.

On most days, when he wasn't running errands, John took off in the Tesla.

"I'm going to the gym."

There were days he spent on his computer.

"I'm looking for work."

I'd walk in. He'd flip the screen down quickly so I couldn't see what he was doing. I'd tell myself, *I need to get rid of him and end this marriage . . . put my plan into action.* I know now that John was working on his next mark, meeting women online. Grooming, it's called. He sensed our life together was coming to an end. He needed a backup plan.

Fundamentally, I was playing the role of wife, telling John what he wanted to hear. But this could not go on much longer.

I had given up the beach house and moved everything out of there. The Spectrum was perfect for me, but I needed to find a place for John to live. I wanted to get him out of the Spectrum, while making him think I still lived there. Then I could slip into hiding. When I pulled the trigger on that part of my plan, my world was going to change. Timing was everything. I had managed to keep John at a distance throughout most of the summer. I even stayed with him at the apartment on some nights. This was hard for me. Walking in and acting as if I didn't know he was a dangerous predator and criminal. Forever worrying he would catch on and, in the middle of the night, do something to me. But I had no choice. Taking control of my life, I needed to ignore the idea that he would hurt me or the kids and focus on executing my plan. If I cut ties completely, he would know. Slowly, John was getting stronger, though

I am not certain to this day there was actually anything seriously wrong with him physically, other than a dependence on hard drugs.

June 2015 turned into a standoff. My plan was still in the development stage. The annulment, I was told, would take ages. When dealing with John, I listened more than spoke. He recognized a difference in me, which put him on constant guard. Within that context, I believe, John dug deeper into his well of con games and tricks.

"I found out I have MS," he told me one night. In the weeks before this, he had started to walk strangely and act as if he were exhausted.

"You have what?"

"Multiple sclerosis, Debbie," John said through tears.

I did not believe him.

"I am so sorry, John. How can I help you?"

"Just be there for me."

As awkward as it felt, I hugged him.

By the end of July, I had purchased a house south of Las Vegas, in Henderson, Nevada. It needed interior work. I hired a contractor to get some of the work started, while planning to put John up in the house until I could start my plan to end the marriage.

"I'll move into the house in Henderson with you soon," I told John. "I'd like to get you set up there as soon as we can, though."

"Okay. But you're coming, right?"

"Yes, John. I just have business here to tend to and the house needs to be fixed up. I'll put $10,000 in an account for you to use while you're there."

Money was one of John's love languages; it serenaded him with a symphony of comfort. Think about that: a drug addict with $10,000 to spend as he wished. At this point, even though I still felt love for John alongside the hate, it didn't matter to me if he bought drugs with the money. I was going to survive and protect my family.

At any cost.

As the renovation began on the Henderson home, I put John up in a hotel not far from the Nevada property, about a four-and-a-half-hour drive from Irvine. There were cameras inside and outside the hotel, which had a casino attached to it, as well as on-site physical security. I planned this. I needed any interaction with John to be visible and, if possible, recorded.

There came a point when the contractors working on the house had finished one room completely, which I had told them to do. John could move in and they could finish their work around him. John claimed that he was not able to move much again—that his back and legs were not functioning properly.

"The MS is beginning to cripple me, Debbie."

"You poor thing, honey. You'll have whatever you need out there."

He limped and winced in agony whenever I saw him.

"You can stay in the house now, John," I told him after we moved his meager belongings from the Spectrum in Irvine, along with some of my own clothes and shoes, to give the appearance that I was eventually going to move in with him. By now it was the beginning of October. "I'll be coming soon, a few weeks from now at most," I continued. "I need to be in Irvine for just a bit longer in order to travel for work. But I'll be out there as soon as I can."

"Thank you, Debbie. I love you. I don't know how I would survive without you."

I left an SUV and the Tesla at the Henderson house. I drove a Jaguar I had bought one year earlier. I loved this vehicle. But I chose that car specifically because I knew John could not have put a tracking device on it. It had been in storage and he had no idea where the car was parked. John had rigged the other two vehicles to track my every move. In addition, I was using burner cell phones to make work calls and contact my children.

Another plus was John's abuse of painkillers. He was on everything, from OxyContin to Percocet to fentanyl and other narcotics. I played naïve about it and didn't let on I knew he was falling deeper into the abyss of drug addiction every day that passed.

One step at a time, I was moving him farther out of my life.

There were days, obviously, when I worried about my plan. Sometimes I'd let my guard down and John would pick up on it immediately.

I vividly remember one night in the new house with John.

"You know, Debbie, you don't look at me the same way anymore. I know you are going to leave me."

"That's all in your head, John. I am super stressed from work, you know that."

"I do not know what I would do without you. My plan is to die in your arms someday. I want to be with you forever."

"Oh, John. I do love you. Stop worrying."

I cooked him his favorite meal that night: pork roast and roasted vegetables. We sat together and watched television. As hard as it was for me to play a role, I must be honest and say I still cared for John. I wanted to forgive. I could not just turn off caring for the guy; my feelings were mixed.

I met Liz one afternoon in October. John did not know where I was going—or so I thought.

"Where were you?" John asked when I got home.

"Out with a friend. We had lunch and talked."

"Look, I know where you went. And if you decide to see Liz again, I need you to know that I will toss her into the ocean and make damn fucking sure she doesn't come out alive."

I believed him.

"Stop being so dramatic, John. I didn't go see her."

Then it occurred to me: I had driven the Tesla.

"Do not see your kids again, Debbie. They are poisoning our marriage. I won't allow it."

There was my sign: it was time to hide.

33

HAPPY ANNIVERSARY—I HATE YOU!

Over the next few months, I kept things quite balanced. John saw me enough so he wouldn't worry about me doing things behind his back, while at the same time, I was working hard to get that annulment or serve him with divorce papers. After thinking it through, I did not think I needed to hide out yet. I had decided that at some point I was going to disappear from John's life completely and he was not going to be able to find me. I traveled a lot from August through November for work (and made separate trips to appear as though I were always working), which gave me an excuse for not being out to see him much at the Vegas house.

In December, John penned a letter to celebrate our anniversary. We had been married a year. He started out by saying, "Happy anniversary. One year . . . and forever means forever."

"Forever means forever" was one of John's sayings.

Continuing, he added:

> *We've been through some hard times, complicated times, but at the end of the day, I have you to myself. No family. No issues that we can't work out. I love you. You have the kindest, most forgiving heart of any person I've ever known. I want to grow old with you. I want to hear your breath in the middle of the night, feel you reach for me when there is nothing else between us. I can't imagine living without you and you're* [sic] *absolutely*

nutty family . . . I hope to get over what they did. I wish I could now, because I see the pain you have being away from them. I wish I could just fix this. I wish I could make all those problems and issues go away, but sometimes life is so complicated that there is no turning around. Sometimes the issue is bigger than us. Sometimes letting go is better than holding on . . . We have each other . . . forever. I will never cheat or disrespect you in any way. I have no desire for anything other than you. You are simply the best person I've ever known, with the biggest heart imaginable. I wish I was more like you. I wish I could see the world like you do.

It's clear John still believed he had control over my relationship with my children. He thought he decided if, when, and where I saw my kids. That was John Meehan applying his coercive control stealthily, thinking I was still the robot he dominated. I had educated myself, however. I had people advising me. I knew he was desperate and hoping that I had reverted to the brainwashed victim I had been during most of the marriage.

John's letter went on:

I love the way you smell and the way you drift off to la-la land while I'm talking to you. I love the feel of you and, needless to say, making love to you is about as close to a religious experience as I have EVER had. What's in the past is gone. What we have is each day now. That's really the only thing we can count on. I want to spend it with you . . . There are no more marriages in our future. Just us . . . I hope I die in your arms because this world would be a dark place without you. I hope you love me and we grow old together.

He said bizarre things about his parents next, all of which he'd fabricated in an attempt to draw empathy from me. Everything John said, I now assumed, was a lie. He could tell me the sky was purple, and six months before this, I might have said okay, without stepping outside to check. But now I was informed. I was in a state of heightened awareness. My eyes were open, and I had placed a shield around my heart. He was not poisoning my thinking anymore.

Interesting to me was how much I *had* changed. How I was now this new person who could understand I had jumped into this marriage too soon, without truly getting to know John. But also, I had let go of unhealthy thinking, like blaming myself.

I hadn't done anything wrong. I had fallen in love.

My superpower then was not giving up on myself. I realized my mistakes. John had been a gift, I kept repeating to myself. He was showing me who I was and where I needed to grow. I saw gratefulness and healing on the horizon for that reason. I wasn't quite there. What I needed to do was get far away from John, keep him away from my kids, forget about an annulment, and initiate a divorce.

34

MONEY—THE ROOT OF JOHN'S EVIL

By February 2016, I was ready to initiate all my plans. I'd given Liz the tuition money she needed to enroll in real estate school. It was something I wanted to do. Liz is one of my heroes. Her gut had told her to check John out and she had followed it, despite how negative and naïve I had been. She had gotten together with her older sister, Nicole, and her brother-in-law, and they had decided to hire that private investigator. That's family. That's love. Each of them had cared enough about me not to give up. Even when I'd stared them in the eye and denied John was evil.

John had now been living in the Henderson, Nevada, house for months. The paperwork for our divorce was in the works. I had not yet come out and told him, keeping to my policy of playing his game. But sooner, rather than later, he was going to find out—and everything I had learned by then about John's pathology told me that a volcano of rage would erupt soon after.

John found out I had given Liz the money for school. He must have checked my phone or hacked my email. He exploded. Giving her the money told him I had not severed contact—that I had been in touch not only with Liz but also the other kids and had been visiting them behind his back. I had betrayed John in the most egregious way. He realized that the control he *thought* he'd had was slipping away.

In Irvine one afternoon in late February, when I had just returned from a business trip, John found me coming out of a grocery store. He was living in Henderson then, so he must have been driving back into Irvine and stalking the kids and me.

"How long, Debbie? How long have you not been listening to me? How long have you been seeing your kids?"

"Get over it, John. I am trying to reforge my relationship with them."

"I will not have you seeing those kids, who have done nothing but try to destroy our marriage since the day I met you. They want your money—how many *fucking* times do I have to tell you this?"

I managed to get away from him, make it to my car, and take off. This was my life now: constantly looking in my rearview mirror, wondering if my husband was following me.

John had this hatred for Liz that went beyond his loathing for my other kids. Liz had been pushing me to leave John from almost the day I started dating him. She had proved time and again he was a liar. John knew she was a direct threat to his plan.

Based on John's previous behavior, the forensic psychologist I had consulted thought John wouldn't go after my family. He was wrong. John started sending incredibly crude and appalling text messages to Liz. Then he called the real estate school she attended and told the administration department patently false stories about her. Liz was so embarrassed that she dropped out of school.

I was heartbroken.

Then John emailed Liz a photograph of her birth certificate, which he had stolen while at the penthouse and kept inside his storage unit. He had spit on it.

Liz responded by googling a "pile of shit" photograph—I told you my daughter was tough!—which she emailed to John with a message: "If you had a life, you wouldn't be wasting your energy emailing me. Let's just stop wasting each other's time. Nobody cares about you."

"You do not have a mom anymore," he wrote back. "She's right next to me, here, and we're reading your emails together."

That was a lie.

Liz responded by telling John to leave her alone.

At the beginning of 2016, I had hired a private investigator of my own to watch John. Now the PI would park down the block from the Henderson house and observe John lifting heavy items in the yard and walking without any issue. John would hurl heavy, bulky items over his back and clean up the construction materials as if he was a healthy, middle-aged man.

The situation had reached an impasse. John and I knew where the marriage was headed. And I understood he was not going to walk away without fighting or lashing out. But now I worried more about my kids than myself. I needed to pull the trigger and serve John divorce papers, before disappearing from his life completely, but I was worried about what he would do.

"Mommy wants nothing to do with you," he emailed Liz one day. "That will kill you. [You] jumping off a tall building would make me and your mom smile. Headfirst will work."

"Leave me alone, you sick pervert," Liz shot back.

I had $30,000 hidden in the bottom of my bedroom dresser drawer at the Irvine Spectrum apartment. I had put it there after John moved to the Henderson house. This was on top of $120,000 I had withdrawn from my bank, crossing my fingers John wouldn't find out. I spread the $120,000 among a friend and my children to hold on to until I needed it.

In March, I walked into the apartment one night. My plan was to grab the $30,000 and a bag of personal items and head back to my girlfriend's house, where I was staying from time to time.

John was standing in the kitchen when I walked in. He had this coy, smug look on his face. I said nothing and walked into my bedroom. I grabbed a few outfits from the closet and one shoe (I'm not sure what I was thinking).

While I was tossing my things into a bag, John walked into the bedroom. He was holding the $30,000 in cash. Stacks of banded hundred-dollar bills.

"What is this?" he asked.

"Money, John. What does it look like? And listen to me, you cannot keep me from my kids. That is *never* going to happen. My children are more important to me than anything."

The tone of the communication between us had shifted. I was no longer the cowering wife, agreeing with everything her husband said. John understood his control over me was gone.

"And why are you withdrawing all that money from your bank accounts?"

He was referring to the $120,000. He had obviously figured out a way to track my accounts, even though I was changing my passwords as often as I could.

I took a minute and collected my thoughts. When you push back at a coercive-controlling psychopath like John, you need to realize the unexpected could happen. If I was going to challenge John, I had better have a backup plan.

I made the decision at that moment that this would be the last time I saw him. I was going into hiding after I left the apartment.

"It's mine," I said, pointing to the banded cash. "It was mine before I met you. You have no rights to it. I don't want you to have it—and you are *not* taking it."

John laughed in a villainous way, cocky and confident. Then, "No, Debbie, *everything* that is yours is *mine.* That includes this money right here." He poked his index finger into one of the bands of hundred-dollar bills. "Right here! You fucking understand me? I am not playing with you—get that through your head—or your fucking spoiled kids. I'm not messing around anymore."

"No, John, you have that wrong. Anything that was mine before I met you is *still* mine."

A spasm of anger rose inside me. John understood I was getting more irritated with him as we talked. I breathed heavily, a direct, somatic response to his comments. Those who know me can tell you I rarely ever raise my voice. It's just not who I am. But there I was, getting louder as I explained to John that the money in his hand was mine and he was not getting it.

I sensed John's rage festering. I could tell when he was about to explode. And sure enough, that switch inside him flipped and he kicked holes in the walls of the apartment, while tossing furniture and clothes around. Fear struck me like a blow. As I watched him unravel, I felt the need to grab my possessions and get out of that apartment. Or I might never be able to leave.

I need to go straight to the Henderson house, I told myself. *I need to clear out my belongings there and disappear.*

John calmed down and pulled out his phone. He scrolled though a few pictures and came to the one he wanted me to see. "Come here," he said. "I want you to look at this."

It was a screenshot of my computer. My bank accounts—the same accounts for which I had been changing the passwords.

"You think you can keep me out of this?" he said, laughing.

"John, what—"

Before I could finish, he said, "You are *never* going to leave me—because if you do, I will *destroy* you, your fucking family, and your shitty fucking business."

"This is scaring me, John."

"Good! I hope the fuck it is. Get this straight, Debbie," he said, drawing closer to my face, nearly touching me. "I will kill you if you leave me and I will bury you in the backyard of that shitty Vegas house, six feet under."

To put my life with John into the appropriate context (which was never truly clarified in the podcast and Bravo series), I must explain that once I knew who this man truly was, I stayed as long as I did because I feared for my life. At the expense of repeating myself, you cannot leave a coercive-controlling situation without a fully thought-out plan. There is no clean break. It is always dirty. The key to survival is making sure you minimize the level of uncertainty. Effectively, the abused needs to take control *back* from the abuser.

"I will kill you," John said again.

These types of threats twist your sense of reality. They put you in a state of questioning the validity of the threat, while understanding you're dealing with someone who has no remorse, no conscience. Did I want to find out if John was being hyperbolic? I had heard Cindi, my sister, mention some of these same fears, and it had been easy to think an actual attack would never happen.

I knew better.

Steering the conversation away from the bank accounts and John's threats to kill me, I refocused him back on a subject I knew was dear to his cold, black heart.

"Keep the money, John," I said, pointing to the banded $30,000.

He looked at it. Then at me.

"Chump change right there," he said. "You are going to give me a *hell* of a lot more. That is a fact."

Allowing him to keep the money was my way out of the apartment. I was incensed. He could tell by looking at me. He got back in my face.

"Go ahead, hit me, Debbie. I know you want to." His voice had a sarcastic, taunting tone. He spoke slow and methodically. John towered over me. He was sixty pounds heavier than me. He could pick me up with one arm and throw me across the room. He drew strength from rage. "Go ahead, Debbie, *hit* me," he said again, in a near whisper. "Because if you hit me, I will make *damn* sure you never, *ever* get up again."

"I'm not going to hit you, John."

I needed to get out of there. No more game playing. It was time to disappear.

"I'm filing for divorce," I said before walking out of the bedroom toward the front door. I stood with one hand on the knob, the other holding my bag.

Before he could respond, or attack me, I ran out of the building.

What many don't comprehend fully—and this is a warning to anyone in a similar situation—is that you don't cut and run from someone like John Meehan. That is when violence usually occurs. I was lucky to escape with my life that night inside the apartment. I don't think John had been ready for me to push back. I had thrown him off his game. It was just enough to allow me to get away.

I wouldn't get another chance.

35

A SHARK AND HIS PREY

I needed to act fast. After leaving the apartment, I drove to Liz's place.

"I need your help."

"Okay, Mom. What's up?"

I explained the situation.

At about midnight, we drove toward the Henderson, Nevada, house. The plan was to get a room in a hotel nearby. Then I'd head over to the house at some point that day and grab everything I could and conduct a quick search to see if I could find anything explaining what John had been up to and planning. He had installed cameras throughout the house. I knew that once we arrived, with John likely still in Irvine (and monitoring the Henderson house), we would have four hours at most to go through each room and get out of there before he showed up.

On the way to Henderson, I called my professional movers to meet us out there. I told them to grab what they could, get it into the truck, and get out of there.

They were there when we arrived.

"I'm putting tape over the lenses," I told Liz as we walked in.

"Good idea, Mom."

It felt as if we were burglarizing my own home. And this proves a point: that John manipulated my feelings and nearly every situation to his vantage point. I would have bought into his perspective months before. But not any longer. He was good at making me believe I was doing something wrong, yet I had severed those emotional arteries of the past and was finally on my own path.

While we were at the Henderson house, my phone buzzed.

We must have missed a camera.

I looked at the screen.

It was the Irvine police.

"Hello?" I said, frazzled.

"I heard you had an altercation this morning," the officer said.

"With whom?"

"Well, we heard you had an altercation with your husband, Mrs. Meehan, at your apartment—and that you hit him."

"Um, no, that is not what happened. I ran for my life last night. I did not touch that man. I asked him to get out of my way. It took place in my apartment."

"He's saying you hit him and the altercation took place at 8:00 a.m. this morning."

"Not possible. I am in Vegas. Please call the M Resort, where I stayed, and look at the security surveillance footage—and you'll see where I was at that time. But please do not tell John."

"Okay, ma'am. But we need to sort this out."

"I understand. But I want you to look at John's record and look at my record and then tell me who you think is lying!"

"We will, ma'am."

The police called me back a few hours later. "We get it," the officer said.

As the movers packed and loaded my belongings, I grabbed clothes and other personal possessions. Liz recorded it all on video with her iPhone so John could not come back and say we damaged anything or took any of his belongings.

"I think we've got everything," Liz said.

I took one last look around.

"Yeah. Let's get out of here."

Liz followed me with her iPhone as we walked out. I stood by my vehicle, looking back at the house; the movers were in the background of the video. Then we took off.

"It's going to get ugly really fast now, Liz," I said as we sped down the 215, heading back to Irvine. "He's already been threatening my life . . . he's entered a new stage of this."

I didn't hear from John for the rest of that day. He must have been planning his next move. Meanwhile, I contacted a new attorney, a guy I was told specialized in family law.

"I'll call John," the attorney said after our meeting. He thought perhaps he could talk some sense into John and negotiate the divorce.

A day later, the attorney called me back.

"Listen, Debbie . . . I . . . I have a family. I am going to pass on taking your case. I heard something chilling in your husband's voice when we spoke and I need to think about my family."

What could I do? I thanked him. Then I found another attorney who was unafraid to go to war with John Meehan.

"I keep a shotgun in my office," family attorney Michael O'Neil told me. He'd been practicing law for forty years. Michael is an old-school westerner. John was not going to intimidate him.

This was the kind of support I needed.

Michael once explained that, just like a shark, people like John have to eat. So they choose vulnerable prey. They know *exactly* the type of victim to focus on. He went on to call John a chameleon, a psychopath who changed according to the situation.

That is a dangerous human being.

In John, Michael knew exactly whom he was dealing with. Michael made me feel like I had not only a voice but an advocate willing to back me up and fight. He saw clearly how John had inserted himself into women's lives under the pretense of love and promises of being together forever. John's true purpose, however, was to marry the woman and take everything she had, destroying her in the process.

In early April 2016, Michael filed for divorce on my behalf, which sent John off into a new dimension of crazy. We knew it would. We just didn't realize how far he would go.

The first indication that things had taken a potentially violent turn was an email John sent me shortly after learning I had filed:

> *You get your family, I got the dog. I got the better deal . . . For once in your holier than thou life, listen to me: you are going to have to pay both sides, which could easily take a year. We had a good run except for your family. There is no trust, but the last thing I want to do is break you.*

Blatant threats. John made it clear he wanted a lot of money. He then promised to bankrupt me through the divorce courts if I fought back.

Give me what I want, in other words, *and I will go away . . . or else.*

He didn't stop there. The daily routine of emailing and texting ad nauseum began once again. He had used the same tactic in the past with other women. I now understood what all those other women I had read about in John's paperwork had experienced. Only now I was the focus of his madness.

Upping his game, John sent me photographs of himself and another woman. Not wearing much clothing, she'd posed in a provocative manner. He thought this would somehow wrestle me back into submission.

It didn't.

When John realized he couldn't stir up a reaction, he showed me racy photographs the two of us had once exchanged. He was planning to disseminate the photographs to everyone I knew, including my clients. He had downloaded the entire contents of my computer and phone address books. He had access to everyone I had ever been in contact with.

There was nothing I could do. I had learned by then to focus on what I had control over.

John complained about my lack of communication with him regarding the divorce. My lawyer had advised me to have zero contact. This infuriated him.

I enacted my plan to go into hiding. I moved from hotel to hotel each night. I wore a disguise: wigs and sunglasses. The getup made me feel as though I were in some sort of spy film, running from the CIA or a hit man. I was literally afraid John was going to be around every corner. I was now terrified he would find—and hurt—me.

The emails and texts continued—and got much worse.

Make yourself available or I ruin a family. There are children involved, Debbie. This is bigger than you. No more being nice. This will turn an entire family inside out. You're selfish to allow this. You'll never forgive yourself, but I am doing it . . . You don't know how to live. Sex is not love. Get help.

I heard from the Irvine police again. The officers had investigated and told me they were pressing charges against John for filing a false police report.

He then logged on to Yelp, the most popular app and website for publishing crowd-sourced reviews of businesses. In a full-page posted review of my business, he wrote, "Debbie Newell is a liar, a cheat, crook, not to be trusted . . ."

I am not proud of sharing risqué photographs with John early in our marriage, but it is something I did thinking they would remain private. He was my husband.

John sent them to my family members.

"I know where you are all the time," he texted so many times I cannot recall how often. "I know where and when you pick up your grandchildren. I've watched you."

It was a direct threat to my grandchildren. Because of my choices, my children and grandchildren had been thrust into a risky game with a dangerous criminal.

"I will kill you, Debbie—*and* your fucking children," he texted several times as the days passed. He became frustrated because he couldn't keep track of me or find out where I was hiding. John was unafraid of law enforcement. Just as that one police report I had read insisted, John Meehan had no sense of responsibility or remorse. He welcomed conflict and chaos. He had a purpose and nothing was going to stop him.

The threat against my grandchildren was too much. I stopped picking them up and visiting family. I basically stopped working. I was a prisoner of John's threats—held in bondage by a maniac. I was living inside a box built by an abusive man, every moment of every day. The difference between this period and the earlier days of the marriage was my awareness of what was going on.

"Debbie, you did everything right," coercive control expert and victims' advocate Laura Richards later told me. "You are a victim—don't *ever* forget that."

John then did something he knew would cut my nephew Ben and I to our cores. In a text to Ben, John said, "Your dad should have put one in the back of your useless head, as well as your brother, just after he blew your fucking mom's brains out all over the wall."

Gloating, John focused on me. "Debbie, I saw all of this coming." He meant the divorce and the fact that I was not going to give in to his demands. "It's pathetic it has come to this point. But you leave me with no options after your storm of lies."

I could not help myself after that text, so I responded in kind: "Storm of lies? Wow, John. You are the expert in that area."

In the weeks after my lawyer, Michael, filed the paperwork, John announced to my attorney his demands for the divorce. In other words, what would be required for him to disappear and leave us alone.

Michael called me into his office. He explained John wanted $7,000 a month in spousal support, on top of $75,000 in attorney's fees.

"He's claiming you stole $90,000 in cash from him and $30,000 in gold coins."

"That's utterly ridiculous."

"He has to prove it, Debbie. I do not know how he ever could."

John complained about having to live on a $558 monthly disability check with his bad back. This was absolute rubbish. I had videos of him using that same bad back to pick up heavy items on the Henderson, Nevada, property.

After leaving Michael's office, I received a phone call from John. The entire situation felt like an inferno that was about to flare up. John was not someone who could let anything go. He held on to grudges and thrived on revenge. This was his job: to manufacture a marriage to a wealthy woman and then destroy her emotionally—and when it came time for the divorce, bury her financially and embarrass her personally.

He'd threaten and intimidate women until they caved. Yet, as the spring and summer passed, while I was still hiding out and wearing disguises, I sensed another shift had taken place. John had ascended to a new plateau of cruelty. I educated myself by reading John's history—or at least what I could get my hands on. I contacted several of his previous victims and began to find out more about what he had done to other women. This time I was getting information not from police reports or secondhand sources, but from the mouths and minds of the people he had victimized. In each case, I realized, his unpredictable behavior had escalated. He became angrier and more disparaging, and his threats included violence. John was going to get his way or he was going to make your life hell.

"For John, it's always been about the money," one former victim told me. I was surprised to hear that she had been in touch with John during our marriage. A month into our marriage, John had told her I'd left him. "He sounded desperate," she said. After I filed for divorce, he started emailing this same woman "ten-plus times a day." She suspected he wanted her help finding (and paying for) an attorney. She never did. But, she added, "I thought he might kill himself."

This told me I was getting to him. He wasn't the big, bad wolf he once was.

I sent John a text and told him he was not a "real man," but more of a disgrace to masculinity. My aim was to hit John's ego with as much intensity as I could. Go toe-to-toe with him. He had pushed me to the point of engagement. I needed to step up.

"It doesn't matter that paying support isn't what a 'real' man demands," he shot back. "It's what the court feels is equitable. That's all that matters. Think, Debbie. There is no alternative to this unless you start thinking. That, or, let me say, you will eventually get bled dry. Be smart, Debbie. You have no idea of the mistakes you've made. Be smart and you'll save a fortune."

"I don't trust anything you say," I wrote back. "You are evil."

This was typical coercive-controlling behavior, straight out of the CC playbook. John was turning the situation around on me. Coercive-controlling men will try to make the victim feel as if she is the persecutor. I had felt that way for a long time.

No more.

"It's my life's work, being a voice for the voiceless and creating change to better protect women and girls," Laura Richards said during one of our conversations. "John Meehan was a serial stalker who used coercive and controlling behaviors. By undertaking an indirect personality assessment of Meehan, I can say with certainty that he was a psychopath. Many of them hide in plain sight and, unfortunately, professionals ask the wrong questions of the wrong people."

What Laura was saying is that nobody took John to be a psychopath—over and over again, John was arrested and charged. All of those charges, however, were for parole violations, weapons, and drugs. He'd never been prosecuted for violence against women. In the eyes of the courts, it appeared John Meehan was just a bad guy who did bad things.

"Serial murder, serial rape, . . . and domestic violence murders would be prevented if abusive men's violent histories were proactively joined up and if the women who reported them were listened to and taken seriously," Laura told me.

I was determined to see this through with John. Whatever it took.

"You are a pathological liar," he wrote next. "Face it, Debbie. Please. I'm smarter than you."

"Please don't contact me again. I will go to the police."

I had already filed for a restraining order and submitted an eleven-page addendum/affidavit outlining everything John had done up to that point. That document made it clear that John had the potential to be violent and maybe deadly. The evidence in the filing was clear. I had signed it under penalty of perjury.

"Domestic and stalking murders are both preventable and predictable," Laura said. "They do not have to happen in a vacuum. These are murders in slow motion—the drip-drip-drip happens over time on an escalating continuum."

Laura had a way of explaining my situation as if she had been there.

The restraining order court date kept getting pushed back because law enforcement could not locate John to serve him. No one knew where he was at any given moment. This put us all on guard; we were on the lookout for him wherever we went. Especially Liz. Terra never came up in the email and text exchanges, almost as if John had forgotten about her.

One less thing to worry about.

"Fuck your family," John texted me next. "I'm coming for you."

36

I AM THE VICTIM

It's important for me to say a few things at this point about domestic abuse and violence. What happens next in the John Meehan saga is a warning to anyone reading this book, along with those who might have someone like John in their life. If you are in a similar situation or are experiencing even one-tenth of what my family and I went through, please do not overlook or deny the fact that this type of domestic violence rarely de-escalates.

"Abused women generally finally leave after the sixth attempt," Laura Richards explained to me. "That is, if they don't end up being murdered first."

Incredibly, a woman goes back to the man who has been abusing her, on average, five times before finally leaving for good. If she doesn't wind up dead before she can escape.

Domestic violence in this country—men abusing women mostly—has reached epidemic proportions. When we think about domestic violence, however, we often go straight to physical violence. Men beating—or killing—their partners, girlfriends, or spouses. But domestic violence is, at its essence, about power and control. The abuse we suffer as victims is not always easy to see, feel, or even understand. Mostly, we have no idea we're trapped—and that the abuse is actually happening. John Meehan was extraordinary at abusing me emotionally, without my knowledge—that is, until I educated myself about what was happening. Half the victims of domestic violence do not even know they are being abused. That is how prevalent and silent coercive control, which falls under the domestic violence umbrella, becomes in a relationship. When I think about my sister's life with Billy Vickers, I now see clearly that Cindi was being abused and coercively controlled for many, many years before she, and all of us close to her, understood what was happening. In addition, I wanted to be the one and only in my parents' eyes, and of course later on in my marriages. I craved the attention I never got as a child, when I was deathly ill while foster kids came in and out of our lives. I need to be clear that I don't blame my parents. I am not using my upbringing as an excuse for the mistakes I've made or for allowing a man like John Meehan into my life. I am simply stating how my life evolved and what I have come to terms with regarding the decisions I've made.

"Debbie, like all abused women, you cannot ever forget you are a victim—that *important* fact gets lost in your story as it is portrayed on television and even in the *Dirty John* podcast," Laura said. "John used mirroring techniques, matching [copying and pasting information you've written about yourself in your online profile onto his online profile], falsifying everything about himself to manipulate you. He was always keen to please you in every possible way, whether in the bedroom or daily life. You were victimized. None of this is your fault—I cannot say that enough times. You did nothing more than fall in love. Your past marriages have *nothing* whatsoever to do with your nightmare with John."

Compared to the next several months of my life, living in a nightmare would have been welcome. The horror John was planning would be like nothing I could have ever imagined any human being doing to another.

In the spring of 2016, John must have felt as though he was losing the battle to destroy my life and get out of the marriage with what he wanted. His latest round of threats, demeaning messages, and emails became deeply personal.

"Everyone is a better Christian than you," John wrote with his characteristic, overstated sarcasm. "Paybacks are costly and a bitch."

John had always told me how beautiful I was. He had adored me that way and had never been shy about letting me know. He had often promised I would never have to be lonely again. It had been another tactic, seizing on my lack of confidence and fear of growing old without connecting with a soul mate. The consummate aggressor now, he changed the narrative: "You lying old bag, you *will* grow old alone."

With that particular email, he included a list of my top clients. "I will call them twice a day and ruin your business."

My lawyer, Michael O'Neil, had copies of the legal papers documenting John's criminal history. All those emails, police reports, and affidavits outlining the harassment he had been charged with before we met. I went to see Michael.

"I need that restraining order," I said.

Michael had originally filed for the order back on April 11, 2016. We needed to file again. Part of me thought, *What can a restraining order do, anyway, when I'm dealing with a psychopath as open and honest as John is about his plans to retaliate and seek revenge?* John was going to do whatever he wanted and nobody was going to stop him. Certainly not a piece of paper the court had issued against him.

That stack of legal documents sitting in front of my lawyer told an ugly side of the story, with sobering accuracy. After I thought about it more, I realized that having a restraining order in place, one that made it unlawful for John to keep threatening me via phone, email, and text, would serve to show how he had violated the law without conscience. It would be a record, in other words. Primarily, I wanted protection for Ben, Nicole, Liz, and Brandon. Michael rolled up his sleeves and worked day and night for three days on getting the order, finally submitting an inch-thick stack of documentation supporting my case. I did not list Terra on the petition because John did not seem interested in her and did not appear to pose any threat to her. In addition, Terra was still living in Vegas. John had not even mentioned Terra in any of his messages.

Several problems arose with the restraining order. The request for an order must show that an immediate emergency exists and the applicant is in fear for his or her life. In addition, we had to prove John had the ability and the means to carry out what we were outlining in the request—that he was planning on ruining my life and could become violent, perhaps even deadly. (The laws that constrained us, I might add, need to be challenged and changed.)

In May, to my alarm, the court came back and said it could not provide a restraining order, based on the idiotic premise that John had not yet laid hands on, or hurt, me. John would have to actually hurt me first before the court would restrict him from contact with me? It made no sense. But that was where the law stood with domestic violence in California.

Furthermore, John's address was listed as Henderson, Nevada. So the logistics of the order, on top of jurisdiction, became tricky for Michael to figure out.

Meanwhile, John continued. He seemed to be spinning his wheels with threats. I wasn't responding to them. And he wasn't getting anywhere.

This concerned me.

I went to Michael in those days after the order was denied. "John is going to do something. I can feel it. He's not getting anywhere with his emails and texts."

"Debbie, I understand your fears are real. We are dealing with one sick . . . son of a bitch."

Michael felt that since John had never actually hit me in the past, his latest round of threats was likely idle. He would continue to threaten until we settled with him. He was after my money, trying to get as much as he could out of me.

This was a mistake. Not on Michael's part. My attorney could never have guessed or even considered what was going to happen over the next several weeks. My mistake was simply not having enough information available, beyond not knowing how domestic violence and coercive control worked at that time. Remember, I was living this in real time, in the moment. While a traumatic situation is going on around you, it's all-consuming and ubiquitous. There doesn't seem to be time for anything else but protecting yourself and your family, while dealing with what comes your way.

"In two weeks," Michael told me, "we can reapply for a permanent restraining order." We had to keep trying. The idea was to gather any additional incriminating evidence, aside from the stack of paperwork Michael already had, that could prove John was an immediate, direct threat—which wouldn't be difficult. With the right judge, showing a precedent would hopefully convince the court that John was not playing. He had shown a pattern throughout his life of threatening and intimidating women; he was going to follow through on his threats sooner or later.

After our first application for a restraining order was denied, I went to see a lawyer in Nevada, seeking advice on my options in that state. I also needed guidance about what I could do beyond a restraining order. Something had to give. You cannot bend a stick for too long without it snapping. I could not live in different hotels, wear wigs and disguises, and keep running from John on a daily basis for much longer. As it was, I was hemorrhaging money from traveling so much and paying for hotels all over the country to keep as far away from John as possible.

"Look, Debbie," the lawyer in Nevada told me, "if you can get John to settle with you, you will save on legal fees and a host of other expenses. See if he'll accept a dollar amount."

"Pay him off?"

"Maybe. See if he'll accept a certain dollar amount to annul the marriage."

I thought, *Buy him off. Give into his demands. Negotiate with him to see what he wants in order to disappear from our lives.*

I believed this new attorney had suggested I meet with John in person to talk about what he wanted. The impression I left the lawyer's office with was that sending a lawyer to conduct the negotiation for me would not appeal to John. He'd respond better to me personally. I think my decision to follow this lawyer's advice was partially justified. A lawyer, in John's face, would only amplify the situation and his anxiety and force him to go on the offensive. By talking to him face-to-face, I might be able to calm him down and negotiate under the notion that there could be a settlement. It was a risky move. But I was desperate. I should have asked Michael O'Neil about it.

I didn't.

"I'll be out to the house to talk to you soon," I texted John.

"You will?"

"Yes. We need to resolve all of this conflict."

"I agree," John said. "I still love you, Debbie. We can work this out."

His response was a good sign.

When I arrived, John was inside, standing in the living room. He looked worse than I had ever seen him. He was emaciated, frail as an elderly man. The drugs he was addicted to had taken a noticeable toll. He'd lost even more weight than when I had last seen him.

"What is it you want to talk about, Debbie?" John asked. He didn't come across as confrontational. I had the choice to face off with him and dredge up all he'd done—threatening us, denigrating Ben and my kids, destroying Liz's opportunity to continue real estate school, threatening and insulting her, and all he had said to me—or to not go anywhere near all of that.

Diplomacy was the best way to a resolution.

"John, listen. We need to stop all this madness of name-calling and threatening . . ."

"I . . . I . . ."

"Allow me to finish, please. We should consider a divorce." As I said this, a thought occurred to me: *Negotiate on his level.* "But, the more I think about it, maybe we should consider starting fresh *after* the annulment—no more lying or deceiving. You come completely clean. We see if we can make the marriage work."

John had this habit of wiping the back of his hand across his lips from time to time. I thought it was just something he did. I now understood—staring at this shell of a man, obviously high—that it was an indication he was on drugs.

I had no intention of saving the marriage; it was a calculated, direct lie.

He sat down with a heavy thud. The guy looked tired. Of running. Of keeping track of all his lies. Of being in a constant state of chaos and conflict.

"No, Debbie. Not a chance. You promised me 'till death do us part,' and I am willing to live up to that. That does not mean divorce."

"John, please . . ."

"You listen to *me* now."

"Okay, John, I'm sorry for interrupting."

He began to cry. "I need you now more than I ever have. Look at me. Look at how sick I am."

For a brief moment, I considered he might fess up. Admit to being dependent on drugs. Explain to me that he was a pathological liar and couldn't help himself. Reach out for help.

"Debbie . . . I . . . I have cancer. I'm dying. I do not want to die alone. How the *hell* could you ever consider leaving your husband to die alone of cancer? I would do anything to make this right."

The cancer card. John actually went there.

I reached in my purse and wrote him a check for $10,000.

His language.

"This is to fix up the house any way you want to. I will allow you to stay here while we figure things out." My goal, in handing John this check, was to buy some time to devise a plan and keep him busy while I figured out my next move. I did not care about the money or whatever he did with it. He'd already stolen $30,000 in cash from me—back when I had narrowly escaped him in the Irvine apartment. I considered that he was likely to use this $10,000 I was handing over to buy more drugs. In some way, perhaps, I was hoping he would.

John took the check and held it in front of his face, staring at it.

"Will you do me one favor and just stay here tonight?" he asked.

The test.

I thought about it.

"I will sleep on the blow-up mattress in the living room—not with you, John."

He accepted that. I slept the night with an open eye and ear on him. I had now gone from wearing disguises and running from this man to sleeping in a room next to his. It sounds scary and maybe even irresponsible. But what I saw that day was a man on his deathbed, incapable of doing anything to harm me.

In thinking that way, I'd made a terrible mistake.

37

"YOU WILL LOSE"

When I returned to Irvine the following day, I continued my habit of staying on the move. I stayed at my daughter Nicole's house and began to roam from hotel to hotel, wearing my garish black wig and tortoiseshell sunglasses, as if I were Jackie O. ducking the paparazzi. I needed this standoff to end. I had been hiding out for months. I could not live like this much longer.

"I am dying. Can't you see that? Slowly dying every day," John texted me a day after I returned. "I am doing even worse without you. I need you."

I did not respond. He had called the police once already and lied about the incident inside my apartment. His tactic with women had been to turn things around on them. This situation was no different. My decision to approach him with an annulment buyout had been wrong. Moreover, I had to view anything John said or did as a con or a lie. I could not trust anything coming out of his mouth.

Michael O'Neil called me in for a chat. I told him that under the advice of a second attorney I had hired in Nevada, I had gone out to see John at the Henderson house.

Michael's eyes widened. "And you stayed the night?"

"Yes."

He shook his head. "Debbie, what were you thinking? The danger factor aside, do you think a judge will *ever* grant us a restraining order now?

How scared are you, in the eyes of the court, if you're spending the night with John?"

"I didn't sleep with him. I slept on an air mattress in the living room."

"It doesn't matter. You have now taken away every muscle, every hammer, every degree of strength that we had to even consider getting that restraining order signed. You have completely vitiated the situation . . . and we have no chance now."

I walked away defeated and destroyed. I'd made a terrible mistake. There is no playbook for this type of madness when it pervades your life, however. No, John didn't have cancer; he *was* the cancer. When you are in an abusive relationship, you learn how to deal with each situation as it comes. One moment at a time. You learn to survive. It would have been nice if I could have made all the right decisions in every circumstance. But high levels of fear, stress, and anxiety, coupled with pressure from my kids and self-blame for allowing this psychopath into our lives, led me to make hasty, emotional choices that, in the moment, felt like the right thing to do.

For the next twenty-four hours, John went quiet. I wanted a divorce and I was going to fight him. I texted him that he should take the offer of an annulment and give me a figure we could both live with.

"You are not going to want to do that [threaten me with an annulment]," John texted back.

I recall this date with certainty: June 10, 2016.

"Debbie, you *will* lose."

John had apparently gotten some of his strength back. I could tell by his tone. He'd called and sounded like the old John: shaming me, threatening, promising to destroy me. He was back to his fighting ways. Or that act he'd put on in Henderson was gone. Clearly, he was not going to back down.

"I will destroy you and your kids," he texted.

I called Michael.

"Okay, I'll speak to the Irvine Police Department."

The police could not help. John hadn't done anything other than threaten. While they took the threats seriously, the fact that John lived in

Henderson, Nevada, made it difficult for the police in Irvine to get involved unless he committed a crime in town.

I was back to square one.

Meanwhile, in June, Terra decided to move back to Irvine. Just before their lease was up, her boyfriend broke up with her. I don't know exactly what happened, nor was it any of my business. All I knew was that my daughter was distraught and heartbroken. She needed her mother.

I drove out to Nevada to get her. We decided she'd live with Liz until we could find her an apartment. This did not take long. The Coronado, a seemingly secure complex between downtown and Newport Beach, was perfect. Terra needed to feel safe. She was depressed. Fortunately, after the breakup she was able to keep Cash, her Australian shepherd. A lover of animals, she was hoping to find work at a kennel, grooming and taking care of dogs. This would help her recover from the breakup.

With Terra now back in town, preparing to move into the Coronado, the stakes were higher. She was now part of the circle of victims John could terrorize. We all lived within a few miles of one another.

Liz and I had a chat around this time, in early June. We decided she would start looking for a new apartment. One with tighter security. I could move in with her and stop this exhausting madness of moving around from place to place every day.

"I'll find one, Mom," she promised.

On June 11, 2016, I decided to go into my office. I needed to sort out a few business affairs I could not finish without being there. After working a few hours, I got up from my desk and looked out the window because I could almost feel John within striking distance. I'd had this unease creeping up on me all morning, as if something was about to happen. I became anxious. Paced. Unable to focus on my work, I stared out the window.

It was a Saturday, so the office was quiet and mostly empty. The parking lot was just outside the window on the street. I had parked my Jaguar there so I could check on it periodically. Because I was in hiding, I was used to taking Ubers and taxis and having the kids drive me around. I believed that if I changed vehicles and routines, John could not find me or figure out where I was at any given time.

While staring out the window, I noticed the empty parking space where my Jag had been.

"It's gone," I said after Liz picked up.

"What?"

"The Jag—it's not here."

"John," she said.

"He's going to kill me," I said. "I can feel it. If I don't get away from him, I will be dead."

We knew he had stolen the Jag. There was no other answer. This was the start of something. Liz and I knew it. John was advancing, planning some kind of final chess move.

Around this time, I learned John had opened email accounts under my name and started emailing people I worked with. He did this mainly to learn my schedule. He bought burner phones and texted my assistant under the guise of being a coworker or client. He called the office, claiming to be a client or friend, and was able to find out where I was or where I was off to.

Monitoring my bank accounts in the days leading up to June 11, I discovered several checks had been cashed recently. John had forged one for $10,000 and another for $4,000. He'd done it in the past, but he was at it again.

Then, during several phone calls, he demanded $17,000 a month in alimony, claiming he was 100 percent disabled.

"I'm going to need a full-time nurse to take care of me."

"You're full of crap," I said.

"I'm dying of kidney cancer and this is the way you treat me? I have five months left to live. You won't have to pay alimony for long."

Unbeknownst to me then, John had been able to get his hands on a Smith & Wesson revolver.

He now had a gun.

My lawyer and I went ahead and filed once again for a restraining order, and my lawyer showed up in court to argue my case.

John never appeared. He claimed to be too disabled.

The judge, because of John's no-show, would not grant the order.

I could not win.

Liz and I contacted the Irvine police about the car. We explained the situation and told them we were certain John had stolen it. There was no chance the theft was random.

They told me they'd get right on it.

Two days passed before a detective called with the news that they had found it.

38

WHERE THERE'S SMOKE . . .

By July, Terra was settled in Newport; her new job working with dogs was fulfilling and was keeping her busy. At her housing complex, the Coronado, to get into the parking garage, you had to enter a passcode to open the gate. To get into the building, you needed a key fob. Security cameras recorded most of the movement outside the building, in the parking garage, and near the entrance. She kept mostly to herself and seemed indifferent about what was going on with John. Liz was calling and updating her, but Terra had so much of her own pain to deal with that the John situation didn't seem to faze her much. The breakup had affected her in ways I had not seen before. My baby girl was hurting badly.

"I was just trying to forget about everything that was going on, with my life and yours," Terra told me later. "But John was so evil, it was hard. I did my best. He seemed to be leaving me alone. I heard what was going on—you in fear for your life, hiding out—it was horrible. I thought John was a scumbag and his intentions were always impure and full of spite."

As much as we thought John wasn't interested in going after Terra, I realize now that nothing should have been off the table. No sooner had Terra begun living her new life in Newport than John zeroed in. The problem for John—perhaps a lesson I should have learned—was that Terra chose not to engage, which seemed to throw John off his game slightly. Via Facebook Messenger, for example, John sent Terra messages replete with rumors about Liz, several of which John had posted on a popular website exposing people for their "dirty deeds." The site offered no proof or corroboration—it was just a gossipy, rumor-driven mishmash of venom spewed by exes and angry people. John tried blackmailing Terra, demanding money to take the posts down.

The problem was, Terra rarely checked her Facebook account. So she didn't read the blackmail note until long after he'd sent it.

Terra leaned into her enthusiasm for *The Walking Dead* television series. As the insanity of my running from John stirred around her, Terra lost herself in watching the show when not working.

The Walking Dead is a megahit television series that depicts the months and years after a zombie apocalypse, as a group of survivors travels in search of safety and security. There's constant fear that the zombies will show up and kill those who have survived the unexplained Armageddon. In perhaps an overdramatic, even cartoonish way, the series captures the spirit of survival and displays skills survivors must master if they want to have the slightest chance against the zombies. Think knives, guns, swords, machetes, hammers, blood, guts, and lots of gore. In 1978, *Dawn of the Dead*, a film based on the same premise, initially received an X rating for the same amount of shocking gore. I think that the similarity between what was assigned an X rating forty or so years ago and what is shown on mainstream television today reflects how desensitized we have become to violence and the sight of blood and guts on television. Doesn't sound like that big of a deal? When you consider how the true-crime genre has evolved on television and in pop culture, it becomes extremely important.

The Walking Dead was Terra's favorite television show. She was obsessed with it. Terra is a visual person; she needs to see things in order to interpret them best. And as she consumed the series, Terra paid attention to how the main characters managed to survive day to day by fighting off the zombies in a variety of ways.

Terra once told me, "My boyfriend and I would watch that show, then we would watch it again. We would watch *The Talking Dead*, a discussion series airing after *The Walking Dead*, where guests come on and discuss the most recent episode. I just thought while we watched, if there's ever a zombie apocalypse, then maybe I might know what to do."

I mention *The Walking Dead* because, honestly, that television series would soon save Terra's life—and maybe all our lives.

While Terra went about her life, unable to take in the enormity of what was going on with John, Liz, by contrast, fought back. She wasn't going to be bullied by John without responding. Liz kept a protective shield around herself and knew how to endure and overcome struggle. She was also people smart: she had proved she could read people better than anyone I know.

Liz was also protective of me. She was nurturing and focused on what was going on daily, sharing her advice and perceptive wisdom.

I believed both Liz and Terra were safe where they lived. The new apartment in Newport had tight security. We believed there was no way John could get in.

Although I was worried about them and what John could do, since he'd included both in his recent attacks, I focused on hiding.

I constantly reminded myself, *Do not allow him to find me or know where I am at any given moment.*

This was the best way to protect myself. Something *I* had control over.

The truth was, however, that John was stalking all of us.

He knew our every move.

The black-and-white surveillance footage was grainy. At times, it was hard to make out. Yet there was no mistaking John Meehan in the video. Clad in jeans, hiding in a crouched position behind some bushes near my Jag, John can be seen stalking my vehicle, seemingly waiting for the right opportunity.

After a time, he suddenly walks out of the shot.

About sixty minutes into the video, John reappears. Now, however, he is wearing gloves and white painter's overalls. He looks like some sort of crime-scene technician on a cop show, minus the silver briefcase.

As I watched this, I thought, *What the heck is he up to?*

In keeping with his need to seek revenge, John hadn't stolen the car to chop up and sell for parts. Nor had he set up a buyer, as he'd tried in the past with my Tesla.

On this day, John had other plans.

"It's just a block from your office," the Irvine police officer said, calling to tell me the police had located my Jag.

"What . . . really?"

The investigator explained that the car smelled of gasoline. And there was some fire damage. The doors and seats had been burned. Inside the vehicle, the police had found a gasoline can.

"Whoever did this, well, they did a terrible job. If they were planning on torching the entire vehicle, they failed."

"John Meehan," I said. It wasn't *they*; it was John.

John had failed to roll the windows down and had left the doors closed, so the fire had had no oxygen to feed off and had extinguished itself quickly.

The officers told me the investigation was continuing and they would contact John.

"Yeah," John said while being questioned by police a day or so later. "I took the car. But my wife gave me permission, as she always has."

They asked him what he did after taking the vehicle.

"I drove it around and put it back in front of the building where it was parked. There was nothing wrong when I returned it."

He never explained why he decided to stalk the car, leave, and then return dressed in white overalls and gloves. He never admitted setting it on fire.

The question remained: Why was John in Irvine when he lived in Henderson, Nevada?

"Doing some business," John said when the policed asked him about this.

Michael O'Neil contacted the Irvine police several times. He applied pressure for them to do something. "We've shown you the video . . ."

I mean, what else did they need?

They repeatedly told us they were still investigating.

It felt as if law enforcement didn't care—the police seemed to believe that sooner or later John would throw up his hands in defeat and go away. As it was, John had reached out to Michael with his settlement demands. This told us he knew he'd made a mistake by being caught on video.

"You see," victims' advocate Laura Richards told me, "this is typical. Law enforcement routinely gives the abuser the benefit of the doubt. They almost make the victim feel as though she is in the wrong. You did *nothing* wrong, Debbie. I cannot repeat this enough. *None* of this is *your* fault. Your past marriages, any mistakes you've *ever* made, none of it is relevant."

This attitude of law enforcement (which, I must add, not all Irvine police officers share) sends the abuser a direct message to continue without repercussions.

"Look, Debbie, if I can convince the police it's John in that video," Michael told me, "I will get you that restraining order, and it then becomes a crime for John to come anywhere near you."

Convince them? What more *convincing* did they need?

39

LAURA

I met Laura Richards by chance on the anniversary of Cindi's murder. We were both speakers at a crime convention, and we hit it off right away. I knew then—two years after my ordeal with John was over—that my life's work would consist of educating women about CC and pushing for new domestic violence laws to be enacted. Laura had been a crusader, initiating new laws concerning CC, and had gotten many through Parliament in her native country, the United Kingdom. She has a bachelor's degree in psychology and sociology and a master's in forensic and legal psychology, along with a background in intelligence-led policing. She has single-handedly engineered law reforms to better protect victims. She founded Paladin, the world's first national stalking advocacy service. In 2012, Laura actually spearheaded the Domestic Violence Law Reform Campaign to criminalize CC in the UK. There is so much work left to be done. But Laura's dedication to victims and her fight to criminalize CC around the world have made a huge impact.

"It was incredibly moving," Laura recalled, referring to the first time we met. "You, like many, had not heard of the term *coercive control* until we met. It was not a popular way to interpret domestic violence. Professor Evan Stark, in his book *Coercive Control: How Men Entrap Women in Personal Life*, seems to have been credited with coining the term. But it was actually coined by three feminist psychologists . . . and Stark references them in the book as having called what was happening to their clients coercive control. But he never names the psychologists."

CC has been described as a liberty crime—meaning it is a domestic issue.

"Those three women talked about a *coercive* aspect of control for the first time," Laura explained to me. "Professor Stark's book was seminal at the time [2009] in explaining how CC entrapped women, but it's much more about the qualities that keep women entrapped. Stalking, an element of CC, same as domestic violence in general, is a *pattern* of behavior. The elephant in the room we never talked about was the coercive-controlling nature of domestic violence."

Laura educated me. She explained that CC is more sophisticated than brainwashing, which is what cult leaders rely on to contain and control their followers. And if we point our radar in the cult leader direction, we're missing the target.

"There are several layers to it—the brainwashing and the grooming, the love bombing, and of course all those other things that get someone under control in the beginning. But then there is an intimacy aspect to it—the sexual coercion that happens as well."

It started during my first date with John, Laura explained. That was the moment CC entered my life and John went to work on his next victim.

"When women say, 'He is too good to be true' and present this perfect image of a man, I am always very curious," Laura said. "Because, truthfully, perfect doesn't normally exist. On this first date, John did very little talking. He asked a few questions and you did all the talking. He was drilling you for information. He was constantly pushing boundaries to see how far he could take it early on. In one sense, he seems like a great date. A great listener. But actually, it's very one-sided in terms of the exchange of information. After that first date, and the red flag when John hopped on your bed and you kicked him out of your penthouse, he returns, becoming everything you need him to be."

John planned all of it. I was devastated to learn I was being controlled the moment he set eyes on me. But this fact also answered questions I had regarding how this could have happened. And realizing, after getting to know Laura, that the situation was not my fault was a huge step in my recovery process.

"This is matching. Mirroring. In every way, John becomes the perfect man in your eyes and heart—rubbing your feet, making smoothies and going out for them any time you want, showering you with gifts and flowers. Running all your errands. All of these things play into image management. He is forcing you to fall in love with him by falsifying who he is."

Charm is a choice. It's not an innate characteristic we are born with, Laura believes. We choose to be charming. Yet we can also use it in manipulating ways.

"Anyone who is overly charming is on my radar because it is a sign of manipulation," Laura told me.

Even inside my bedroom, in those intimate moments I believed were an expression of love between us, John was controlling me.

"John was very keen to please you sexually, even at the expense of his own enjoyment. That is another huge red flag for me. He went the other way in the bedroom to overcompensate. Sexual coercion can come under many different guises, but he was *very* good at matching and being exactly who you needed him to be. And remember, what's very important is that you know none of this. You believe this guy is perfect. You believe he loves you and you are falling in love with him."

For over twenty years, Laura investigated and studied serial killers and domestic abusers. She sees the same patterns in serial killers as she sees in John Meehan. The only difference is that John was not as "criminally sophisticated" as a serial killer.

"John wasn't a good criminal, but in terms of his ability to dupe and charm . . . he was quite skilled at spinning a yarn, pathological lying. He also had a solid veneer."

Laura further clarified that when someone like me finally starts to dig into a psychopath like John, peeling back that veneer and uncovering secrets about his life, he begins to spiral.

The fact that John and all his previous crimes were known by law enforcement during this tenuous time, when my family and I could feel something major brewing, Laura pointed out, "is a cultural issue—it says that domestic violence is *not* taken seriously."

I was screaming out to law enforcement. Providing evidence. We all knew John was about to strike. Where and when was anybody's guess. He was planning to fulfill his need for revenge. The torching of my Jag was a direct warning.

And he got away with it.

The Irvine police had corroboration. John was on tape stealing the car. They had all the emails and texts I had provided, in addition to an eleven-page affidavit I signed under the penalty of perjury.

"His escalation is over time," Laura concluded. "He's pushing boundaries over time. Nine times out of ten, he gets away with it . . . John's biggest mistake in all of this was not getting Terra and [Liz] on board. He couldn't charm them. That was his downfall."

For what was about to happen next, the scope of it all would prove undoubtedly that Laura Richards's assessment is infallible. Why no one in law enforcement heard me will continue to baffle and haunt me for a long time to come.

40

LOCKED AND LOADED

As July passed, John continued to send nasty texts and threaten all of us. The Irvine police would only say that they were in the midst of investigating.

"Getting closer" was a common statement I heard.

Closer? You have the guy on video stealing my car.

"We're building a case against him; he has been inconsistent with his statements and we're closer than ever" was another frequent statement Michael O'Neil would share with me after talking to Irvine detectives. Michael was as frustrated as me. And he had firsthand knowledge of how these types of situations played out. Two of Michael's friends, both of whom worked in family law, had been murdered by people connected to a case they had been working on.

One day, shortly after those murders, I walked into Michael's Santa Ana office and noticed he'd installed additional locks.

Meanwhile, I was scared—no, *terrified*—that John was plotting his next move, which could be bigger than unsuccessfully torching my Jag. In fact, I began to wonder if he was actually sending a message by *not* incinerating the vehicle—and knowing what I now know about John and his psychopathy, there is no doubt he could have turned my car to a charred steel carcass if he had chosen to. He was simply showing me what he could get away with and how far he could take things when he wanted to.

Either way, John was being fueled by one source—internal, volcanic rage—as August began. He was still living in the Henderson house. I was mainly staying at the Spectrum with Liz, who had moved into the apartment after the lease at the penthouse was up. But I was still moving around, scared of John being around every corner. Fortunately, my business had not suffered because of his behavior; I had explained to clients I was dealing with a psychopath. My reputation spoke for itself. The people in my circle trusted me.

But by lighting my Jag on fire, John had shown me he was being driven by one emotion.

Rage.

I truly felt that at some point he was going to try to kill me.

In August, I contacted an ex-girlfriend of John's. We exchanged emails and texts. A lot of what I learned reinforced what I knew. We shared the same chaos with John, although my story proved John had intensified and heightened his abnormal, antisocial behaviors and taken things to a new level.

One story his former girlfriend shared spoke to an aspect of John that would actually work to my advantage—and that of my two daughters—as mid-August approached and the situation became volatile, intense, and nerve-wracking.

John had once taken a work-related business trip to Mexico with a group of people. He went along as a companion of one of the women working for a law firm. She explained that, when they arrived, the plan was to meet everyone for dinner. John, instead, "holed himself up in the hotel room." After John failed to show up for the dinner, the woman went to check on him.

A woman answered and opened John's hotel room door and let her in.

John was sitting on the sofa inside the room with a needle sticking out of his arm, nodding in and out.

"Hydration," he said after she asked what was going on. "I am terribly dehydrated."

This was John Meehan—a junkie. It doesn't excuse his psychotic behavior, answer the ubiquitous question of his true psychosis, or give me any satisfaction. But it says a lot. John went through his days in search of dope. Whatever he could get his hands on. Working in hospitals for a good part of his life, he managed to steal enough hard-core drugs to stock a small pharmacy. Add that addiction to his psychopathy and what you have is "a ticking time bomb—capable of unpredictable violence," one detective who had investigated John later told me.

Another ex-girlfriend I spoke to told me John had been arrested for stalking her. As detectives searched his car, they found documents indicating he owned an RV, which he kept in Cathedral City, California. So they checked it out.

One of the detectives later said the RV looked "like it was out of *Breaking Bad*," the hit AMC network series in which Walter White, the main character, cooks meth in a recreational vehicle. John's was filthy beyond anything they'd seen; he had been living in squalor. Empty prescription drug bottles, used needles, and garbage were everywhere.

They came across a brand-new computer. Turning it on, they saw "hundreds of JPEG photos of women," which John used as his home screen wallpaper. All the images were of women he had previously conned or the woman he was currently stalking. Then they opened the refrigerator. Inside was a backpack containing a gun and hundreds of rounds of ammunition—along with a bottle of cyanide capsules.

"Pretty much a very complete killing and kidnapping kit," the detective concluded.

I was on a collision course with this man—and the crash was going to be akin to being inside an exploding bomb. I lived under the assumption that the confrontation would involve Liz, me, or both of us. The problem I didn't see was that psychopaths like John are unpredictable. You think you know what they're planning, and that's the exact moment they change their game.

Liz had a feeling John was following her. She'd pull up to the Spectrum and think he was somewhere near the entrance, lurking, waiting for one of us.

"He was the boogeyman," Michael O'Neil explained to Christopher Goffard on the *Dirty John* podcast. "I don't mean to say that I was intimidated or I was scared. [I had] a big old shotgun . . . underneath my cabinet. But still, it doesn't do any good over there under the cabinet if somebody barges into your office and you're sitting at your desk."

Up until John burned the Jag, Michael didn't think he was capable of taking the situation to such a dangerous level.

"Whether or not he would take it to the extreme that he ultimately took it to," Michael added, "I would have never thought that until [he torched her car]. It was *then* that he became hands-on."

I blocked John on my phone. He knew I wasn't seeing his texts or getting his calls. I shut him down financially. He wasn't getting any more money from me. I moved all my bank accounts so he couldn't steal from me. Although I still allowed him to live in the Henderson, Nevada, house, I took the Buick Enclave he had been driving after he smashed it up and it was impounded.

John Meehan had no car (I had also taken the Tesla back). No money. No way to get ahold of me, unless he tracked me down in person. We'd even taken in his golden retriever, who had been roaming around for days in 115-degree heat until she was finally found and I picked her up at the shelter.

What did John have left to live for?

As the third week of August came, an uneasy quiet settled over my life. I should have reminded myself that before a hurricane and even in the midst of it, there *is* a gentle calm, before the force of Mother Nature inflicts total destruction.

"He's watching me, Mom," Liz would tell me when we spoke. "I know he is."

Thus far, two months had gone by since the Jag torching.

No charges.

No arrest.

Not even a restraining order.

On Friday, August 19, 2016, somewhere near 11:30 p.m., Liz and a male friend were on their way home from dinner. They were talking about the tense situation we were living through.

As Liz and her friend pulled up in front of the Spectrum, they passed a row of cars parked on the street. Liz recognized John right away. He was sitting in a car, crouched down in the driver's seat, waiting.

John's cell phone had given him away. Liz saw his face because of the light coming from the screen.

As they drove up, Liz looked right at him and John looked back at her. When they locked eyes, John tried to hide by ducking farther down.

"That's him . . . that's him," she said to her friend. "Holy shit. There he is."

"What . . . what are you talking about?" her friend said.

John took off as soon as he knew Liz had recognized him. He'd smashed the taillights out on the back of his rental car and removed all the other lights so he could move around stealthily. With the lights off, he headed toward the traffic light up ahead, at the corner of the street.

"Follow him!" Liz shouted to her friend, pointing.

When John realized Liz and her friend were behind him, he ran the red light and floored the gas pedal, speeding off.

"Go, go, go," Liz said. "Catch up to him."

Not far ahead, near the entrance to the freeway, John took a hard right onto the ramp.

Liz and her friend drove past, losing him.

John was gone.

"The more I thought about it," Liz told me that night, "he was there to kill you, Mom."

The fact is, John Meehan was hoping to catch one of us alone, heading into the building. Because Liz had a male friend with her, it threw John off. He got spooked and ran.

After that event, Liz walked into the apartment and sat down.

Terra, she told herself. *He's going after Terra.*

Terra lived just a few miles away at the Coronado.

"I knew that it was game time," Liz said. "It was on."

John was making his move. Terra was now his target.

I kept picturing John calling me: *I just killed your daughter—and now I'm coming after you.*

41

DIRTY JOHN MAKES HIS MOVE

After pacing inside the Spectrum apartment for a time, Liz and her friend drove to the Coronado to check on Terra.

By now it was after midnight.

"I would have preferred to have John come back to my apartment," Liz told me later. "Then, whatever he was going to do, we'd have had some sort of chance of catching this psycho ass on camera."

Liz is smart. She gets these guys. She believed that because John's attempt at killing me had been thwarted (I wasn't home), he was even more dangerous. And now we had no idea where he was headed. Should we even bother calling the Irvine police? What good would it do? They'd proved that they didn't take any of what was going on seriously. They'd had months to do something. They wanted me to believe it was a marital squabble the courts would resolve. Or that John and I would figure it out between ourselves.

"Mom, we are hopeless in that regard," Liz told me at the time. "We've contacted the police every time something happened and they've done absolutely nothing. They've *never* helped us." I respect the police and the job they do, but when it came to John, Liz was right.

Part of me, in those moments leading up to the next day, when our lives changed forever, was skeptical of what Liz had seen that night. She could have an overactive imagination. Yet, as I thought it through, I felt John was now unhinged, unstable, and unpredictable. Liz had never sounded so serious and concerned. Ultimately, I believed her.

Liz and her friend drove around the Coronado several times, looking for John. He would not be hard to spot. The car he was driving had no lights. He looked beaten, weak, and emaciated, Liz said. And so it would not be difficult to recognize him.

For an hour or more, they circled the Coronado but never saw him.

"Stop by the entrance," Liz directed her friend.

He pulled up. She got out and ran into the building.

Liz was worried John might have gone inside and hovered near Terra's door, waiting for her to emerge.

When she got to Terra's door, everything appeared to be okay. John was nowhere in sight. She thought about knocking but didn't want to wake her sister up. What comforted Liz was Terra's cat, whom Liz heard inside the apartment walking around. Terra had put a bell on his collar. Then Liz heard Cash, Terra's Australian shepherd, growling softly as he sniffed someone—Liz—outside the door.

"I was really tripping, totally tripping out," Liz said later. "But I was like, at the same time, *Okay, cool. She's inside with Cash and she's safe.*"

As Liz walked out of the building, it occurred to her how surreal the situation had become. She kept asking herself if she was going crazy. If what she had seen back at the Spectrum was actually John Meehan stalking the front entrance.

"I actually *wasn't* crazy," Liz remembered. "I thought, *This is really happening.*"

Liz went to bed at 4:30 that morning and got up ninety minutes later at six. The first thing she did was call Terra.

"John's in the area! Please be careful. I saw him last night in front of our apartment building. The lights were off on his car. We followed him. And then lost him. Be on the lookout for a white Camry."

"Oh, my God," Terra said. "Okay . . . I see. A white Toyota Camry."

Most people meeting Terra for the first time say she is sweet—someone who doesn't bother anybody. She is very petite and speaks softly, almost in a whisper sometimes. "She wouldn't hurt a fly" is a cliché I have heard people use to describe Terra. Trauma has been a part of Terra's life since she was six years old. One night, Terra claimed, she was awoken by an intruder. The guy who'd climbed through her window picked her up and started carrying her out the window. Terra screamed. He dropped her on the floor, jumped out the window, and took off, never to be seen again.

This could have been a dream. The only evidence of a possible break-in was an open window that had originally been closed. There was a lot going on inside our home at the time. I was fighting a lot with her father. Terra was having vivid, scary nightmares quite often. She had been reporting "dark shapes . . . that were ghosts or aliens" in her room. So I do not know if the attempted kidnapping was a dream or real. Over the years, however, I've realized that it doesn't matter whether the event really occurred. My daughter was traumatized. Whatever she was experiencing was real for her.

Leading up to the night when Liz chased John away from the Spectrum, Terra had been having different friends sleep at her apartment. She was under the impression that John didn't know her address. I would have thought the same five months prior. But I took nothing for granted where John was concerned anymore. He knew where we all lived. There was no doubt. I also believed he was routinely stalking us.

What I didn't know was that the gated entrance to the Coronado was constantly broken. This gave John access to the parking areas for the building. John undoubtedly went online to Google Maps or a similar site and studied the layout using the image capture function, as anyone with a smartphone could have done. So he knew every way in and out of the Coronado. If John had been unable to get through the gate, finding where Terra parked would have been a crapshoot.

"I kind of felt," Terra told me later, "that John had been watching me ever since I'd been back in OC [Orange County]. Not every day, but certainly on and off. I was always looking in my rearview mirror and checking out my surroundings, looking out for him."

John had created an atmosphere of constant fear. He was all we thought about.

There was one night when Terra sat down inside her apartment, pen and paper in front of her, and wrote a note to her ex-boyfriend. The note was brief and direct: if something were to happen to her, she wanted her boyfriend to take Cash. That dog was Terra's world. Unconditional love aside, Cash provided Terra with comfort and protection. Cash went everywhere with Terra, and he was devotedly protective of her. An "Aussie," as Australian shepherds are known, weighs an average of forty to sixty-five pounds, depending on gender. Aussies are lean, muscular animals. Commonly known as "ranch dogs," Aussies are associated with the cowboy way of life and were bred to protect herds of farm animals. They are extraordinarily loyal, smarter than your average breed, and rugged and agile. Aussies also have unparalleled stamina and can work all day and not tire.

Beyond the note she'd written and left in her clothes drawer, Terra had developed "premonitions of death" leading up to this day—specifically, dreams of John Meehan attacking her. In each dream, she had a knife.

"And I had to stab him to save myself," she told me later, when describing her dreams.

She'd picked up defensive techniques while watching *The Walking Dead*. For example, when a character was surrounded by a group of men looking to do him harm, the character walked up to one of the men and bit his jugular vein. This convinced Terra her teeth were a weapon.

Where to target someone was also a tactic she'd picked up on the series, along with *CSI* and *Dexter*.

"You can't kill a zombie unless you stab or shoot it in the head," Terra said.

From watching these shows, Terra learned that the bottom line was simple: *You get into a situation and it's kill or be killed.*

John had stopped at his storage facility outside Irvine during the third week of August. He parked the Dodge Dart he was driving near the storage unit door and proceeded to load the vehicle with several items—a "kill kit," one detective later called it: thirteen plastic cable ties, six various-sized knives from a Belgique cookware set, an Oakley backpack, camouflage-colored duct tape, a passport, several syringes, a vial of injectable testosterone, and several additional vials of various drugs.

The Dodge Dart rental was important because Terra had been told, mistakenly, to be on the lookout for a white Toyota Camry. John had also removed the license plates.

Between July and August, John had changed remarkably. When I met him in 2014, John weighed 230 pounds and was six feet, two inches tall. I did not know it, but he was on steroids then, jacked up and muscular. By August 2016, he had lost close to 70 pounds and was down to 163 pounds. Even so, my husband was still 40 pounds heavier than Terra, not to mention a foot taller. I believed that if he was going to confront Terra, he would have had no trouble, sick and weak as he was, handling her with one arm tied behind his back.

On Friday, August 19, 2016, Terra was working at Rebel Run Canine Suites, in Newport Beach. The Coronado apartments where she lived were a ten-minute drive northeast.

As she went about her day, her phone rang.

"Hi," a man in a French accent said. "I think we've met before. I think I've brought my dogs there." He made it appear as though he'd appreciated Terra's overall demeanor around the dogs and was wondering if she was going to be working the following day, Saturday, August 20. He wanted to bring his dogs in for the day. "I have two Rhodesian ridgebacks I'd like groomed."

Terra did not recognize his voice and did not recall caring for two Rhodesian ridgebacks, a breed of dog, it should be noted, that is not easy to forget. She also felt it was an odd request because at least 90 percent of the grooming requests Rebel Run received came from women.

"I'll be here until 5:00 p.m. tomorrow," Terra told the stranger with the French accent.

The next day, just after hearing from Liz that John might be in the area, Terra went to work and began her day. Liz called a second time to make sure Terra had made it to work safely.

"Keep your pocketknife handy," Liz suggested.

Terra thought about it. The little pocketknife she kept in her purse was at home, on the kitchen counter. During the course of what had turned into a hectic morning, with Liz warning her about John, she had forgotten to put it in her purse.

As she cleaned the kennels, fed the dogs, and let them out for playtime, Terra didn't think much about the guy with the French accent who'd called the previous afternoon and failed to show up on that day. Her mind was on a concert she had tickets to that night. Jason Aldean, one of her favorite country artists, was playing at Irvine Meadows. Terra had lawn seats.

My daughter would never make it to that concert.

Before leaving Rebel Run at 5:00 p.m., Terra slipped on her knee-high, leopard-print rubber rain boots. She let the dogs out for one more run while she hosed down the cages.

"Come on, Cash," she said to her Aussie after putting the dogs back in their cages.

Cash ran toward the car and jumped in.

Preoccupied with all that was going on, Terra forgot to change into her sneakers and drove away, still wearing those rubber rain boots.

The three-mile journey home was uneventful, save for Jason Aldean blaring through the speakers of her Toyota Prius.

In her pocketbook, Terra carried a can of bear mace, which shoots farther than the more common pepper spray. The bear mace had been a gift from Liz several weeks earlier, when things had become scary.

The gate at the Coronado was open when Terra pulled into the parking lot. The keypad system to open it was not working—which meant anyone could get in.

Terra made her way toward the parking area, pulled up the gradual incline until she was one level aboveground, and headed for the same parking space she used every day. It was bright out. Irvine at that time of day in August (5:15 p.m.) was in full sunlight.

Terra pulled forward into her space, Jason Aldean banging out his "Big Green Tractor"–inspired country music from the Prius's speakers. As she inched up to the curb-high concrete barrier to stop, Terra noticed a dark-colored Dodge Dart backed into the space next to her. The trunk was open.

A tall man was leaning over the open trunk, rummaging through a backpack. Cash actually noticed him first and started growling, before barking loudly.

Terra came to a stop and shut the Prius off. The front of her vehicle was now adjacent to the back of the Dodge Dart and the man standing over his trunk. He had a tire iron in one hand and the backpack in the other. Terra didn't recognize him. In fact, as she got her stuff together to get out of her vehicle and head up to her apartment, she assumed he was homeless. She'd sometimes see homeless people living out of their cars parked in the Coronado lot. Nothing troubling stood out to her. Although she couldn't make out his face, the man did not seem familiar.

"Come on, boy," Terra said as Cash jumped out of the vehicle.

Terra slammed the door shut and walked toward the back of her Prius.

As soon as she reached the tail end of the Prius, John lunged at my daughter, reached around Terra's waist, and pulled her close to him.

Holding Terra tightly, John said, "Do you remember me?"

Terra did not respond; she knew it was John immediately.

Instinctively, she began trying to wriggle herself out of his grasp.

John put his hand over Terra's mouth.

So she bit him. As hard as she could. Just as she'd seen on *The Walking Dead.*

As they struggled, Terra felt her upper body thumped by several hard blows, which she believed were from John punching her.

My daughter was wrong. Those heavy blows weren't from John's fist. John held a Del Taco bag with a steel boning knife hidden inside, and he was now thrusting the bag-encased knife into my daughter.

Terra crossed her arms over her chest and used her handbag to protect vital areas of her torso once she realized what was happening. At one point, the knife plunged over an inch into her right arm, near her shoulder, opening up a long gash down to the bone, exposing muscle tissue.

Terra and John wrestled for about fifteen seconds as she did whatever she could to get away from him.

Nothing worked.

John kept grabbing and pulling at her, trying to keep Terra as close as he could, while propelling that knife into her repeatedly.

My husband was killing my daughter. Our biggest fear was playing out. We had believed John was going to attack Liz or me, but he'd changed his focus and was now stabbing Terra in broad daylight, atop the parking garage of her building.

At some point during the struggle, Terra fell to the ground.

John fell on top of her.

By now, Cash was biting John's ankles and calves.

On the ground, Terra ended up on her back. John positioned himself in front of her, kneeling and stabbing wherever he could land a strike. Cash continued to bite him, tearing at his pants and legs.

Screaming, Terra kicked her short legs as hard and fast as she could.

The Coronado parking lot is elevated, with a waist-high concrete barrier wall surrounding it. With the sky bright blue and the sun still high, Terra and John were on full display. Anyone paying even the slightest bit of attention and looking toward the parking lot from an apartment window would have seen them, not to mention heard Terra's piercing screams.

On the north side of the area where they fought, overlooking the lot, were several rows of apartment windows. These particular apartments also had balconies. Thinking back now about what happened next, I cannot help but feel God played a role on this day. The courage my daughter displayed, along with the fact that she did not panic and went directly to her self-defense knowledge, was beyond humbling. Even while being stabbed repeatedly by a knife-wielding psychopath, my precious and petite daughter had given herself a chance to survive.

42

FEARLESS HERO

Skylar Sepulveda pedaled as hard as she could. Close to 5:30 p.m., on August 20, 2016, the fourteen-year-old junior-lifeguard-in-training was on her way home to the Coronado, cruising along on her pink beach bicycle, taking in the warm Pacific breeze after a tiring class.

Rushing into her apartment, Skylar found her mother and gave her a big hug.

"Hi, honey," her mother said. "How was training?"

Before Skylar could answer, she heard screaming coming from outside their third-floor apartment window.

Skylar had a clear view of parking space SR 423, the spot Terra parked in every day. She looked out and saw a man kneeling over my daughter, plunging that boning knife into her. The parking space was directly in front of Skylar's apartment, across the elevated lot.

Skylar and Terra had never met. But the fearless, heroic teen with ash blonde hair knew the ear-piercing shrieks coming from outside meant the woman on the ground was in trouble.

Which was when Skylar's lifeguard-training instinct kicked in.

The teenager backed away from the window and ran toward the door of her apartment.

"Call 911," Skylar yelled to her mother, fleeing the apartment. "I gotta go right now . . ."

Skylar didn't even put her sandals on.

After grabbing the wet beach towel she'd put down while walking in the door, Skylar bolted down three flights of stairs in bare feet, her swimsuit still damp from training. When she reached the ground level, she pushed the door open and ran up the parking garage ramp, directly toward Terra. This child never thought, *He has a knife; he could come after me.* The only thing on Skylar's mind was helping my daughter.

The fearless teen had put another person's life before her own, the definition of courage.

"She's bleeding," Skylar heard someone yell as she ran up the parking garage ramp. A crowd was gathering, summoned by Terra's screams.

Back upstairs, Skylar's mom was on the phone with a 911 dispatcher: "There's a man up here with a knife and a girl screaming . . . My daughter is taking a towel to her right now, because somebody yelled, 'She's bleeding,' so we're running over there right now with a towel."

"Okay—and she's bleeding?" the dispatcher asked.

"It's really bad."

"All right, I understand. We have officers on the way."

"It was like, 'Mom, somebody's screaming, somebody's screaming,'" Skylar's mother told the dispatcher, conveying what had just occurred. "And then she saw this guy just raising his hand up and down, up and down."

"Okay, all right . . ."

Skylar ran as fast as she could toward Terra. Several cowardly bystanders, literally watching John plunge a knife into my daughter, did nothing. Skylar acted on the unselfish, humble belief that another human being was in trouble and needed help.

"I thought it was incredible that people could . . . witness other people being abused, or even their life being possibly taken away, and [they were] just watching it happen, and not stepping in to try and help," Skylar told Christopher Goffard on the *Dirty John* podcast.

Terra was on her back, kicking at John as hard and fast as she could, as if pedaling an invisible bicycle. What helped her—tremendously—was the fact that she had forgotten to change out of those rain boots back at the kennel. Not only did the boots give her an edge on gripping the concrete, thus helping her push away from John, but the thick rubber protected her calves and feet from the knife as she landed kicks to John's upper body and head.

Cash barked and bit at John.

John kept flailing the boning knife above his head, plunging it up and down, determined to kill my daughter. By this point, the Del Taco bag in which he'd concealed the weapon had torn and fallen away.

Unbeknownst to Terra, John was succeeding, striking her a half-dozen times in her arms and body.

As Terra continued to kick, one foot struck John's wrist and sent the knife flying.

As God's grace would have it on this day, the knife flew out of John's hand and landed a few inches from Terra's right hand.

With the handle just within her reach, facing her, Terra seized the opportunity—and she grabbed the knife without thinking about it.

Instinctively, she turned the knife on John, carefully choosing the best targets.

My daughter then began stabbing my husband.

The first strike Terra landed was to John's right shoulder. This sent John wincing in pain as he grabbed at the wound. The blow was enough to stun him, giving Terra a chance to use those rubber boots to position herself firmly, so she could mount a proper defense.

In rapid motions, one after the other, she struck John in the shoulders, shoulder blades, upper back, forearms, biceps, triceps, and chest.

John was hurt—badly. Each blow weakened him.

Then came the final blow. Something Terra thought about deliberately. With as much strength as she could muster, Terra strategically plunged the knife into John's left eye.

The tip of the knife reached the back of his brain.

John fell on top of Terra with a heavy thud and a loud, airy gasp.

"I guess, like, that was my zombie kill," Terra said later. "The eyeball shot. I wanted to kill his brain, essentially."

John convulsed as Terra pushed him to her left side on the ground. Then she crawled away. Her upper body was covered in blood. Her injuries were life-threatening.

In shock, she had no idea how badly she had been injured.

Crawling, bleeding, exhausted, Terra used what little energy she had left to cry out, "Please . . . please help me . . ."

As she uttered these words, heroic teenager Skylar Sepulveda came running up to her.

43

TORTURED

When Skylar reached Terra, she could tell my daughter was dazed, hurt, and in shock.

The first thing Skylar noticed was John, facedown on the concrete, twisting and jerking in an epileptic-like seizure, bleeding profusely from his face and upper torso.

As more bystanders arrived on the scene, Skylar knelt by Terra. My daughter was shaking and babbling, bloodied all over, and in tears, like the heroine from a horror film after the final showdown with the boogeyman.

Sirens interrupted the eerie silence.

"Please help me," Terra said. "He's been stalking me and torturing my family. He's going to get back up . . . and hurt me."

Skylar looked at John and knew he was *not* getting up.

The teen helped my daughter sit up and, seeing how badly she was hurt and bleeding, wrapped the beach towel she'd brought with her around the deep gash in Terra's forearm. Skylar had been trained to stop the bleeding by manufacturing a tourniquet from a beach towel—her preparation was surely a gift from God.

"You're safe," Skylar reassured Terra. "He cannot get up. He's not going to be hurting you anymore. You're safe now. It's going to be okay."

This fourteen-year-old girl responded with the love and empathy that several spineless adults on the scene did not provide.

Skylar comforted Terra. Leaning again on her training, Skylar asked Terra random questions to keep her focused on staying alert and conscious.

"Where were you going tonight?"

No response.

"When is your birthday?"

Terra answered and seemed to be emerging from the shock. She was losing blood fast, however. John, bleeding out on the ground, had stopped convulsing.

Skylar believed he was dead.

No one knew John Meehan like I did. John was Freddy Krueger, Jason, and Michael Myers all in one. Can you actually kill evil?

After a few moments, Terra stood and, without speaking, stumbled down the garage ramp toward the sound of sirens, arriving law enforcement, and paramedics. She was desperate to get away from John. *Zombies keep coming back to life*, Terra thought, *no matter what you've done to defeat them*. She believed John was going to wake up at any moment and kill her.

The PTSD my daughter suffers from to this day began in that instant.

"Cash . . . Cash, come on, boy . . . come on," Terra said to her shepherd as she ran as far away from John as possible.

Cash followed.

By this time, scores of people stood around John near parking space SR 423 as paramedic vans and police cruisers arrived.

"I'm really, really sorry, Mom . . . I think I just killed your husband."

Those were the first words my sweet daughter said to me over the phone on the early evening of August 20, 2016. It is a memory forever seared into my mind. When I think about that night, I can still hear the hopelessness, humility, and fear in Terra's voice. I was on the way to my Spectrum apartment after dropping a girlfriend off at work. Along the way, my girlfriend and I discussed my estranged husband.

"I will always live in fear," I had told her just before we hugged and she stepped out of my car. "I will always be in fear of him, *even* if he ends up in prison."

"Debbie, for the rest of your life he will consume every bit of your serenity," she said, "*if* you allow him to. But always remember this: I will be here for you."

It was not a minute after that conversation when Terra called.

Clicking the speakerphone icon on my phone, I knew something was wrong. Before Terra said anything, I *knew* John had surfaced and done something.

"Terra, what are you talking about? How . . . *what* do you mean?"

"He's dead, Mom. *Dead.* I killed him. I'm *so* sorry."

She was crying.

"There's nothing to be sorry about, honey. But what do you mean, you 'killed him'? Do you mean John?"

"Yes . . . yes . . . he attacked me . . . and I . . ." Her voice trailed off.

"Terra, where are you? Are you hurt?"

A vortex of emotion stirred in me as my twenty-five-year-old daughter relayed what few details she could dredge up. Her voice was depleted of all energy, weak and cracking. As she faded in and out, I felt I was losing her.

"Terra, honey . . . talk to me. Are you hurt? What's happening? Are you okay? What do you mean, you killed John? Where are you? It's okay. It's okay. Just tell me where you are. I am coming to you right now."

"I'm home. Come, Mom, please."

All you want to do is get to your child, hug her, kiss her on the forehead, smell her hair, wipe her tears. Tell her it's going to be okay and you love her.

As it happened, I was about three miles away from the Coronado. Earlier that same day, while at work, I had left a voice mail for my private investigator: "Is John ever going to be arrested for theft and arson, among many other potential charges? What in the name of God is going on?"

My private investigator never returned my call.

Questions swirled as I drove toward my baby girl.

Why had he attacked Terra and not me?

Is he coming for all of us?

Was Liz safe?

Is Terra going to live?

"Terra? Terra, baby, stay with me . . ."

"Hurry, Mom. Please."

I drove as fast as I could, and when I hit Irvine Boulevard, where the Coronado is located, I heard the sirens and saw the fire trucks, ambulances, and paramedic vans near the building. As I pulled up to the parking garage, I could see additional fire trucks and EMT vans, along with what seemed to be a dozen police vehicles.

People were everywhere.

Why my *child?* I kept wondering. *Why Terra?*

I just wanted to hold her.

I don't even remember the drive. One moment I was on the phone, trying to gauge how badly my sweet girl had been injured and if she was going to make it, and the next, I was staring at the parking garage in front of me.

There were dozens of onlookers and first responders milling about. A haze of blue and red, flashing and spinning lights cut through the Irvine, California, sunset. The sky, I can recall, was pink and purple—surreal. Men and women in yellow reflector coats stood, walkie-talkies in hand, directing traffic and keeping people back.

My God . . .

Seeing the yellow crime-scene tape flanking the parking garage near Terra's car was chilling and sobering. As I put my vehicle in park and flew out the door, the scene took my breath away, stunning me into complete surrender. I realized that our worst fear had come true. After all John's veiled threats, along with his taunting emails, texts, and calls and his stalking of Liz the previous night, John had made his move.

As I turned toward the garage and ran, an ambulance hit its lights and siren and burned out of the parking lot.

"Terra!" I screamed, watching the vehicle speed away.

An independent and driven woman with a passion for animals, Terra Newell is the easygoing, carefree, and shy child of my four. As she grew, Terra's attitude about her childhood became different from that of Brandon, Nicole, and Liz. Without hesitation, Terra's three siblings would say they had "great childhoods." But Terra feels differently. Because I worked so much and she was the youngest, Terra spent a lot of time with nannies and grew up feeling neglected. I didn't get much financial help from her father, and I was forced to take on both roles, mother and father.

All I could think about as that ambulance sped out of sight was that my daughter was alone, bleeding, suffering, and dying. I needed information. I had to find out what had happened, how badly she'd been hurt, and which hospital the ambulance had taken her to.

The police pulled me back as I tried slipping under the yellow police tape.

"Ma'am, you cannot go up there."

"I'm her mother, I'm her mother . . . I need to get to her. Where is she going?"

As the police held me back, I looked toward Terra's vehicle and saw what seemed to be a throng of first responders and law enforcement officers crowded around someone sitting on the ground.

"Stand back, please."

"My daughter, where's my daughter? She called me . . . she said she killed my husband."

I had no idea what I was saying, who was around me, or who was sitting on the ground.

Had Terra called me before help arrived, just after the altercation? Why hadn't law enforcement called me? Or Liz? Why wasn't someone explaining the situation to me?

Then a second, alarming thought: *Liz? Oh, my God . . . Liz . . . was she okay?*

A psychopath had taken control of every part of my life. Terra had been back in town only a few months. "The Coronado is secure," I had insisted. "You'll be safe and close by."

Now she was fighting for her life?

It didn't matter to me if John was dead. Honestly, we had all wished this, anyway. He had hurt—maybe killed—my child. What difference did it make now if he was gone? My only concern was Terra. I was actually hoping John *was* dead so that we wouldn't have to live in fear any longer.

He didn't deserve to live another day to torment another woman. Even if he went to jail, I knew fear would dictate the rest of our lives. What a waste of life. John could have had it all. He was blessed with intelligence, opportunity, looks, and children, and he threw it all away.

Why?

As I paced back and forth, outside the yellow police tape, I walked to an area where I could get a better angle of Terra's vehicle. The first thing I made out was a woman sitting on the curb, surrounded by people. Then I saw her blonde hair, tangled and bloodied.

"Terra . . ."

She was sitting up. They had placed one of those tinfoil-like blankets over her, just like you see on the news after a mass shooting. Terra's arms were bandaged up. There was blood all over the front of her shirt. She looked tired, pale, and scared.

But alive.

Oh, my God—she's alive.

John must have been inside the ambulance that sped away. In fact, I found out later, he had no pulse when the paramedics reached him. He was not breathing. A few moments after the medics administered CPR, however, John's pulse returned and he was breathing on his own.

John was taken to the hospital.

"Will I be able to make it to the Jason Aldean concert?" Terra asked one of the medics after they got her into the back of an ambulance.

Cash was allowed to join her and stay by her side.

"I don't think so," the medic told her. "But we can put on some country music for you."

Terra had stabbed John a total of thirteen times. He might have been breathing, but John Meehan was brain dead after that strike Terra had plunged into his head.

44

NO ONE DIES ALONE

We dream in black and white for a reason, experts claim: your unconscious mind is sending your conscious mind a message that a problem needs to be resolved. My entire life over the past several years seemed to be black and white. Now, however, as my daughter was being whisked to the hospital, after being stabbed over a dozen times by my husband, I was seeing things in color.

Clearly.

Terra was alive. She would be okay.

The first few days after the attack were, for lack of a better way to explain this period of time, inconceivable. Making sure Terra was going to be okay and she hadn't sustained internal, life-threatening injuries consumed all of us.

After her initial admittance, Terra was moved to a different hospital so doctors could perform surgery on a stab wound in her chest. It was one of the injuries doctors were concerned about. We were all very worried. My daughter might never be the same.

As his wife, I was responsible for John. But my first priority was to make sure Terra was going to be okay. Screw John Meehan. I would make that call once I knew my daughter was safe and healthy.

Word came on day three that Terra's body was going to heal. She was out of surgery and recovering. There was no internal damage. It was the emotional trauma of the attack I worried about more than anything after that. My daughter had been through so much; she would have a long road to recovery from the emotional injuries as well as the physical ones.

When Ben heard what had happened, he commented to the media, "Impossible! The last person on earth I'd even think would send John to hell would be Terra."

Everyone who knew us could have echoed that statement. It just didn't seem fathomable that Terra, all of a hundred pounds and a foot shorter than John Meehan, had fought him off, turned the knife he'd brought to kill her on him, and survived.

Leaving Terra's bedside for the first time in a few days, I called one of John's sisters.

"Could we meet, please?"

She agreed, asking, "Is it okay if the three of us visit Terra when she comes home?" She was referring to John's other sister and niece.

"Yes, that would be okay."

"We just want her to know that what she did is okay. That we are glad she is alive and, well, we don't hold anything against her. We need her to know that."

John's sisters are nothing like him. They are honest, good human beings. They brought flowers and a teddy bear to my apartment for Terra a day after John had attacked her. They did not think visiting her in the hospital was the right thing to do.

We sat and talked for over an hour.

"I was always trying to help John," his older sister said. "He turned on us—and I actually had to get a restraining order against him."

What I heard that day was a woman with an empathetic heart.

"I walked away from John many, many years ago," his younger sister told me. "He tried to destroy me. He beat me so badly on my sixteenth birthday. After that, I wanted nothing to do with him."

John's younger sister agreed to meet me at the hospital where John was in the ICU. We met inside John's room. The doctor explained that even if John survived—and they weren't sure he would live another day—he would never come out of his vegetative state. I recall standing at John's bedside, staring at his face. I was disgusted. Here was a man hooked up to life support, an empty shell of a human being. He didn't even look like himself. He had lost so much weight that he appeared skeletal. I wondered if he had kidney cancer or MS, as he'd said. Could drugs alone strip a man of his humanity and physical self? What had happened to this man?

I didn't know.

Nor did I care at that point.

As I stood there, tuning out the conversation between the doctor and John's sister, I wondered, *Why would John attack my daughter? What was he thinking? Was it a kidnapping gone wrong, in which his rage took over because I had been hiding so well? Was he planning to take Terra for ransom in order to flush me out of hiding?*

I'll never know—and what did it matter anymore, anyway?

As I looked at the bite marks on John's legs, I thought, *Thank God for Cash.* As my gaze moved up to his eye, where Terra had stabbed him fatally, I told myself, *Terra is my hero. She saved not only my life and her sister's life, but so many future victims.*

"I'm signing over the rights to her," I told John's doctor, pointing at John's sister. I wasn't going to be responsible for pulling the plug on this man. With a potential case pending against Terra for stabbing him, I did not want to create a conflict. She had defended herself. But the law and prosecutors can sometimes see things differently and I was not interested in taking *any* chances. John's sister was, after all, a nurse. It felt like the right thing to do.

His sister asked what I thought they should do. We sat down later that day and decided it was best to pull the plug and allow John to die. We would donate his organs. Hopefully, some light could shine from the decades of darkness this one man had created.

"Not his heart, though," I demanded. "I cannot live with having his heart in another human being."

They agreed.

The doctors came back and told us it was a noble gesture, but they had found "suspicious material" in John's kidneys (they never elaborated) and none of his organs could be donated.

So be it.

That night—four days after John Meehan attacked and nearly killed my daughter—his two sisters, his niece, and I walked into his room to say goodbye.

As evil as he was, I thought as we stood around John's bed, *no one should die alone.*

The doctors unplugged all the machines keeping him alive.

I held his hand.

"John," I said, "it's okay to go."

Death took longer than expected. I don't recall how long exactly, but it seemed like forever—as if John wouldn't let go.

Then the machines monitoring John's life flatlined.

I continued talking to him. And every time I said something, the doctors pointed out, there was a bump in John's heartbeat.

"I have never seen that happen," John's doctor said. "It's quite shocking, actually."

I don't care to know why John hung on as I spoke. After I knew he was dead for certain, I walked out of that room, prepared to close this chapter of my life and move on.

45

LIFE GOES ON

Terra went back to work in the weeks after the attack, but she just couldn't do it. Hearing the dogs barking all day triggered a memory of Cash attacking John. In addition, when she was out and saw a man even remotely resembling John, she had a panic attack and couldn't breathe.

We found Terra a therapist who helped change her way of thinking. Now, when a thought or circumstance brings her back to John, Terra forces herself to mentally go to a lake in Montana her father used to take her to. The grandeur of the scene (of course, Cash is there with her), the images of wildlife, and the bucolic serenity of being out in the middle of nowhere help Terra cope with a moment of her life she will never forget entirely.

I struggle with being the one who let John into our lives. That ugly monster guilt wants me to believe it was all my fault. And yet, what many fail to understand about the entire Dirty John experience is that the love I had for John Meehan was genuine. I loved the man I thought John was, the man he perceived himself to be. Even if he lied to me about every part of his life, including being in love with me, it doesn't change this.

I once loved him.

And I'm never going to apologize for falling in love.

EPILOGUE
UPDATES AND IMPORTANT CONTACT INFORMATION FOR VICTIMS

I need to say a few things about judgment. You've heard me mention this word many times throughout the narrative. Now I want to address the topic directly.

I fell in love and married a psychopath. I am no longer his victim. None of this is my fault. I have been judged for falling in love, as well as for how many times I've been married. Of course, a comment or opinion is one thing. I have been in design for over thirty years. I can take criticism, even rejection. But vulgar emails, phone calls, and abhorrent, hurtful social media messages attacking me personally and my life choices are quite another. I have been revictimized for telling my story of abuse. In this culture of instant (anonymous) judgment, I get that some people cannot resist. Yet what message does this sort of revictimization send to abused, coercively controlled women who are in serious danger of being murdered, are living in secrecy, and are terrified to leave a violent relationship and step out of the shadow of abuse?

Whenever a woman comes forward and talks about abuse and is judged, the tacit message she hears is: *If you tell your story, your behavior and your past will be the lens through which your present circumstances are viewed—you will be judged harshly and humiliated.*

That type of secondary abuse sends a terrified victim deeper into her shell, increasing the chances of her becoming a statistic.

Thousands have responded to my story. Personal #MeToo-type messages from around the world have come in. The Dirty John experience has changed my family's lives forever, obviously. There's not a day that passes when I am not reminded of what happened or triggered in some way. My daughter bears the physical and emotional scars left behind by a man who embodied evil, yet people make fun of Terra in unspeakable ways and blame me for what happened to her, making the erroneous accusation that it was my fault.

It's sickening.

Abusive.

Unfair.

Beyond painful.

And gives the abuser more power.

Something coercive control expert Laura Richards told my coauthor, M. William Phelps, when he interviewed her has stuck with me. Laura was speaking about an interview she'd done with Christopher Goffard while he was promoting his *LA Times* podcast. Christopher told Laura that had he known about coercive control before the release of the *Dirty John* podcast, the narrative he told would have been different.

Christopher's comment gives me hope that readers of this book will understand the *entire* story and see past its salacious and dramatic moments to conclude that my family and I were John Meehan's final victims.

During the years after my Dirty John ordeal, I educated myself about coercive control.* That research led to a new calling in my life: to reach as many men and women as I could to help explain what they might be going through and offer empathy and a way out. What happened as I began

* *Please visit Laura Richards's website, www.laurarichards.co.uk, which is the authority, in my opinion, on coercive control. Laura and I became friends in 2018. Since then, I have educated myself on all aspects of this dreaded, often silent, worldwide epidemic.*

running from John during those terrifying months leading up to his confrontation with Terra changed my outlook entirely. The urge to blame myself is always there. The type of judgment and abusive, denigrating criticism I endured after I went public with my story was unrelenting and extreme.

More than at any other moment in history, too many people judge victims of crime based on their response to the situation; they are no longer simply victims. Society has created a rating scale in which the score victims receive reflects their response and reaction to being victimized. Every time someone judges and condemns the decisions I have made in my life and proceeds to blame me for what happened, it not only tears at my soul and scars me deeper but also gives victimizers and abusers more of that power and control they so desperately crave.

These days, Terra has been using her platform to help others struggling with PTSD. She hosts a podcast called *Time Out with Terra*, on which she offers practical, nonprofessional advice on PTSD, dealing with an abuser, and the red flags to look out for. She interviews self-care and domestic violence experts, as well as those dealing with PTSD. She shares her ongoing fight and story on the podcast and her Instagram. In 2020, Terra created her own yoga and charity event to benefit Dr. Phil and Robin McGraw's foundation, When Georgia Smiled.

I recently opened a new showroom in Irvine called Ambrosia Home at Town Square, and my business—the true love of my life—is picking up. I speak about coercive control on panels and continue to appear on television shows, such as *Tamron Hall* and *Watch What Happens Live with Andy Cohen*.

In October 2019, I met with Los Angeles mayor Eric Garcetti to endorse and advise on proposed legislation aimed at exposing and ending coercive control, which is on the rise in California and worldwide. Following that meeting, I sat on a panel of psychology and domestic abuse experts at the Family Justice Center in Los Angeles, which was followed by an open forum and panel discussion with residents and local media.

On September 29, 2020, California governor Gavin Newsom passed a bill introduced by state senator Susan Rubio expanding protections for domestic violence survivors by allowing them to use descriptions of psychologically damaging and abusive behavior, referred to as coercive control, as supporting evidence in California family court hearings and criminal trials—a major victory for abuse victims and survivors.

Senate Bill 1141 added "coercive control" to the Family Code. The behavior described in the bill includes isolating the victim from friends, relatives, or other support; depriving the victim of necessities; controlling the victim's communications, daily behavior, finances, and economic resources; and many other behaviors causing severe emotional distress.

If you are an abuse victim in California, you are more protected today than at any other time in history.

"I'm grateful to be at the forefront of such groundbreaking domestic violence policy, and I look forward to working with my partners and allies to spread coercive control legislation across the nation," Senator Rubio said. "I thank Governor Newsom for signing this bill. My hope is that it empowers victims to come forward, and it becomes something that our society understands and recognizes as domestic violence."

"SB 1141 advances the rights of domestic violence victims under state law. My office was proud to sponsor the legislation, and I thank the governor for signing the bill," Los Angeles city attorney Mike Feuer added.

The bill was sponsored by the Los Angeles City Attorney's Office. Supporters included Crime Victims United of California, Elizabeth House, FreeFrom, Pathways for Victims of Domestic Violence, Peace Over Violence, Strength United, and the YWCA of San Gabriel Valley.

My passion now is to expose and help bring about awareness of what I and others view as a worldwide epidemic affecting millions of people, many of whom do not even realize what is occurring in their lives until it's far too late. This is my fight. Getting people to understand coercive control and providing a safe way out for women trapped in abusive—even deadly—situations and relationships. Reaching these women is the silver lining within the horror my family and I endured and, thank God, lived through. Educating women about the warning signs of being controlled, as well as the dangers of online dating and what they should be looking out for, is my life's work.

Please, if you've read this book and find that even 1 percent of what I went through reflects your own experience, reach out to Laura Richards or me and allow us to help you. You don't have to identify yourself. You can remain completely anonymous. But please speak up and hold out your hand.

We will be there to take it.

And remember Laura's definition: "Coercive control is a strategic pattern of behavior designed to exploit, control, create dependency, and dominate. The victim's everyday existence is micromanaged and her space for action, as well as potential as a human being, is limited and controlled by the abuser."

We *can* help.

We *want* to help.

We *will* help.

Reach Laura Richards at:
Website: https://www.laurarichards.co.uk/
Email: laura@laurarichards.co.uk

Reach me personally at:
Email: debran@ambrosiainteriors.com

ABOUT THE AUTHORS

Photo by Fiona Corrigan

Debra Newell is the founder and president of Ambrosia Home, Inc., as well as the founder and former president of the multimillion-dollar company Ambrosia Interior Design, Inc.

Newell is known for creating beautiful interior spaces and relies on her ability to clearly understand each client's vision, aspirations, and lifestyle. Newell's goal is to create a harmonious environment that not only is functional but reflects each client's individual personality and taste.

Newell launched Ambrosia Interior Design in 1984, creating a national and international, full-service, award-winning interior design firm that specializes in customized model homes, residential homes, country clubs, clubhouses, and office spaces. Additionally, Newell's niche is critiquing architecture for architects and those homes designed for first-time home buyers all the way up to the luxury market.

Newell's work has taken her all over the world. Her projects include a development called Orange County outside Beijing, China; two textile ventures in Egypt; and a hotel in Sharm el-Sheikh, Egypt.

Currently, Newell has expanded her career ventures with a design center in Las Vegas, Nevada, called Ambrosia Home, Inc. Newell's oldest daughter took over Ambrosia Interior Design in Irvine, California, freeing up Newell to focus on one of her passions, residential interior design. Recently, Newell did staging work for the HGTV series *Property*

Brothers and has teamed up with Madison Hildebrand from Bravo's *Million Dollar Listing Los Angeles*. On October 1, 2017, the *Los Angeles Times* launched a six-part article series and an accompanying podcast created by Wondery, both titled *Dirty John*. *Dirty John* is a story of love, deceit, denial, revenge, ruin, and, ultimately, survival; it chronicles Newell's life between October 2014 and August 2016. The story was adapted into a miniseries that premiered on Bravo on November 25, 2018, and on Netflix on February 14, 2019.

Moving on to the next chapter of her life, Newell devotes much of her time to advocating for change and awareness and helping women caught up in coercive-controlling relationships. Newell has been featured in publications such as *People*, *Us Weekly*, *Harper's Bazaar*, *Forbes*, the *New Yorker*, *Vulture*, Refinery29, and *Bustle*, to name a few. Additionally, Newell has made appearances on *Dateline NBC*, *Dr. Phil*, *The Dr. Oz Show*, *Megyn Kelly Today*, *Inside Evil with Chris Cuomo*, Fox News, and Oxygen's *Dirty John: The Dirty Truth*, among many other media outlets. Newell, alongside Laura Richards, was a speaker at CrimeCon 2019, discussing coercive control and her relationship with John Meehan.

Photo by Collette "Coco" Sandstedt

True-crime analyst, serial crime expert, creator, executive producer, and host of Investigation Discovery's *Dark Minds* (2011–2014), and award-winning investigative journalist **M. William Phelps** is the *New York Times* bestselling author of forty-four nonfiction books and winner of the Excellence in (Investigative) Journalism Award from the Society of Professional Journalists. Phelps has written for numerous publications, including the *Providence Journal*, *Connecticut Magazine*, and the *Hartford Courant*. Diversifying his talents, Phelps consulted on the first season of the hit Showtime cable television series *Dexter* and is a constant presence on crime film sets.

In July 2017, Phelps published his definitive seven-year project with Happy Face Killer, *Dangerous Ground: My Friendship with a Serial Killer*.

A two-hour documentary special under Oxygen Network's "Notorious" brand is set to air in 2021.

In August 2020, Phelps released season one of his investigative narrative nonfiction podcast from iHeartRadio focused on four missing Connecticut girls, *Paper Ghosts.* A major project eleven years in the making, it shot to number one on all the podcasting charts. The second season of *Paper Ghosts,* along with his hit weekly podcast, both with iHeartRadio, were released during the summer of 2021.

Phelps grew up in East Hartford, Connecticut, and now lives just north of Hartford, in Tolland County. Reach him at his website, www.mwilliamphelps.com.